Interest Rates and Inflation in India

Issues and Concerns

Interest Rates and Inflation in India

Issues and Concerns

K.R. Gupta

ATLANTIC

PUBLISHERS & DISTRIBUTORS (P) LTD

Published by

ATLANTIC

PUBLISHERS & DISTRIBUTORS (P) LTD

7/22, Ansari Road, Darya Ganj, New Delhi-110002
Phones : +91-11-40775252, 23273880, 23275880, 23280451
Fax : +91-11-23285873
Web : www.atlanticbooks.com
E-mail : orders@atlanticbooks.com

Branch Office
5, Nallathambi Street, Wallajah Road, Chennai-600002
Phones : +91-44-64611085, 32413319
E-mail : chennai@atlanticbooks.com

ISBN 978-81-269-1735-8

Printed in India at Glorious Printers, A-13, D.S.I.D.C., Jhilmil Industrial Area, Delhi-110095

Preface

India is under the grip of persistent high inflation for the last two years or so. The Reserve Bank of India (RBI) increased interest rates 13 times during the period March 2010 to October 2011 in pursuit of tight money policy to control inflation. The repo rate, the rate at which banks borrow from the RBI, which was 4.75 in February 2010, stood at 8.25 in March 2012. The reverse repo rate, the rate at which RBI absorbs cash from the system, went up from 3.25 to 7.50 during that period. The banks raised their interest rates following the increase in their costs due to RBI policy rate hikes.

The primary purpose of keeping interest rates high is to decrease liquidity, curb demand and control inflation. But economists have called it a flawed approach as monetary measures alone cannot attend to all the causes that stoke inflation. India's economic history bears testimony that the policy of keeping interest rates high to control inflation has not succeeded in the last 50 years, and the interest rates in our country have been one of the highest in the world.

Large money supply is not the only cause of high inflation. There are supply side constraints with various types of goods produced, including food articles failing to meet the demand, pushing the prices up. The upward movement of international commodity prices, particularly crude oil, also leads to high inflation. The weakening of rupee against the dollar November 2011 onwards has hardened the prices further in India. A weak rupee directly cranks up the government's expenses of goods imported. The value of goods imported by India in dollar terms has been declining, but increasing in rupee terms due to domestic currency's depreciation.

Some social development programmes like Mahatma Gandhi National Rural Employment Guarantee Scheme (MGNREGS), etc. having a potential expense of ₹ 1,00,000 crore per year, tend to increase demand and contribute to high inflation as also put a heavy burden on the exchequer and worsen the fiscal position. Food and oil subsidies and other populist measures like free electricity to farmers and waiver of loans also have similar effects. But monetary measures provide no solution to these problems.

Interest rates have short-term as well as long-term impacts on inflation. In the short-term, increase in interest rate makes money supply costly and more money flows towards bank fixed deposits and treasury bonds. This reduces supply of money for buying goods and services. This is the logic behind monetary measures to tame inflation. However, this impact is only for a short period. Demand for major items of consumption in India is less elastic than in developed countries. Soon people start buying and the impact fizzles out.

The long-term impact is that higher interest rates increase the cost of production due to the burden of high interest rates. High interest rates also make the investment in modernisation of plants expensive and unviable. They also make creation of new capacity difficult to justify. These three factors put together contribute to higher cost of production. This results in the supply not increasing as planned or envisaged, not able to meet the ever-increasing demand and thus higher prices.

While RBI's high interest rate policy has failed to tame inflation, it has on the contrary, adversely impacted India's economic growth, which is evident from the fact that the expected GDP growth for 2011-12 was lowered from 8 per cent to 7.6 per cent and then to below 7 per cent, i.e. 6.69 per cent, which is much below the pre-slowdown period. Although the RBI stated in its January 2012 policy review that growth risks have increased on account of 'global headwinds'—a reference to the prospects of recession in the US and a sovereign debt crisis in Europe—it cannot be denied that what is afflicting India's industry at present is RBI's high interest rate policy. In acute shortage of funds to run their businesses, many companies including those in the real estate business and airlines have pledged bulk of their holdings to raise capital. Besides, loan defaults in banks are increasing, resulting in more non-performing assets (NPAs) and consequent higher provisions by banks, further reducing their lendable resources.

The Index of Industrial Production (IIP) data for different months of the year 2011-12 points to a dismal growth story. The December 2011 data was much below expectations with several industrial segments including textile, wood products, rubber, machinery and equipment and electricals showing a decline. The data released by the Central Statistics Office (CSO) on 11 May 2012 revealed that while the overall industrial output fell 3.5 per cent in March 2012, the manufacturing sector was down 4.4 per cent in March 2012 compared to 11 per cent growth in March 2011. The mining sector fell 1.3 per cent against an expansion of 0.4 per cent in the same year-ago period. The industrial sector rose 4.1 per cent in February 2012, but poor performance of the crucial infrastructure sector hurt overall growth.

Industrial growth in 2011-12 stood at 2.8 per cent compared to 8.2 per cent in the previous year and almost near similar levels in the aftermath of the global financial crisis in 2008-09. CSO data also suggested that some sectors such as garments, where production is estimated to have declined 57 per cent, are under stress. Some other consumer demand driven segments such as inverters (78 per cent decline) and air conditioners (49 per cent drop) too felt the heat. Data glitches have dogged official statistics prompting the government to scale down industrial growth in the current financial year, 2012-13.

A slowing economy in India is squeezing government's finances, and the analysts have questioned its inability to restrict fiscal deficit at budgeted level of 4.6 per cent of the GDP. Lower than expected tax revenues, stalled share sales of state-run firms and depressed market conditions are worrisome factors. Many economists are apprehensive that the deficit for 2011-12 may be over 5 per cent. The RBI has warned of inflationary risks becoming more serious if that happens. In RBI's January 2012 policy review, D. Subbarao flagged the inflationary risks stemming from the government's failure to contain fiscal deficit and said that a lack of credible fiscal consolidation would restrain RBI from lowering interest rates.

In its Monetary Policy Statement 2012-13, RBI admitted that "domestically, the state of the economy is a matter of concern. Inflation remains sticky and above tolerance level...." Recognizing the fact that high interest rates were affecting growth, RBI reduced repo rate and reverse repo rate by 50 basis points each, on 17 April 2012. While this was a welcome step for the industry, it was felt that it may not cut much ice after a string of increases in the preceding two years. Moreover, banks were not ready to pass on the benefit of this reduction immediately to the customers. Besides, this reduction can hardly be construed as a policy change as inflation that showed a sign of some let up in February and March 2012 reached uncomfortable levels in April 2012, with wholesale inflation rate surging to a worrisome 7.23 per cent and food inflation going as high as 10.49 per cent. It is pertinent to mention here that the softening of food prices in December 2011 and January 2012 was due to seasonal supply, and not the result of RBI's high interest rate policy. With the change of season, the prices of vegetables, fruits, etc. have gone higher, to their previous levels.

The much feared petrol prices hike also came towards the end of May 2012 which is likely to push the prices of many other commodities further up. Such a scenario may stall any further moves by RBI to cut interest rates.

However, interest rates cannot be kept high indefinitely without inviting serious troubles like sluggish growth, low investment, increasing unemployment, economic slowdown and a possible downgrade. It is therefore time to have a relook at the policy stance and take concrete steps to boost industry and put the economy again on a higher growth path. A flourishing industry will attend to the supply side problems, keeping the prices in check. There is also a call from many quarters to do away with, or at least reduce subsidies to control fiscal deficit. Populist measures and coalition politics like rolling back of petroleum price and Railway fare hike have no room for a developing economy like ours, especially when it is passing through a difficult phase.

The book delves into the problem of persistent high inflation in India for the last two years or so and looks at the measures taken by RBI in the form of increasing interest rates. It studies the impact of such a policy on India's GDP growth and industrial production and presents the current economic scenario which looks grim. It also suggests ways and means to tame inflation and to boost industry. A number of sources have been dwelt upon in writing this book. The opinions of industrial bigwigs have been given in the book to give it a broad base and authenticity. Speeches and addresses by RBI governor, deputy governor and other high officials have been included in the book. I am thankful to all these officials and the sources referred to.

The book will prove highly useful for policymakers, parliamentarians and those concerned with India's socio-economic prosperity. To those who wish to know about the problem of inflation in India, its causes and cures, the book will provide for a richly rewarding and stimulating reading.

K.R. Gupta

Contents

1

Interest Rate Hikes and Their Consequences

The Reserve Bank of India, on 25 October 2011 increased repo rate, the key interest rate by 25 basis points to check rising prices. This was the 13th time the central bank increased the interest rate since March 2010 as can be seen from Table 1.1. The repo rate, the rate at which the banks borrow from the RBI was increased from 8.25 per cent to 8.50 per cent. On 19 March 2010 it was 4.75 and was increased to 5.00 per cent. In the twelve more hikes including the one made on 25 October 2011, the repo rate had nearly doubled from March 2010 levels to 8.50 per cent.

The banks also raised their interest rates following the increase in cost of funds for banks. Interest rates were not reduced by RBI in 2011-12 despite a slow down in growth and it stated that "changing the policy stance when inflation is still far above the tolerance level entails risks to the credibility of the Reserve Bank's commitment to low and stable inflation."

The RBI felt that inflation will start cooling by December 2011 as it actually did, and was likely to come down to 7 per cent by March 2012. However, RBI kept repo rate and reverse repo rate unchanged though it lowered CRR by 50 basis points and 75 basic points on 24 January 2012 and 9 March 2012 respectively as shown in Table 1.1 below:

Commenting on the monetary policy announcements, Finance Minister Pranab Mukherjee said, "This decision has

Table 1.1: Hike in Key Rates, March 2010-Oct. 2011

Effective Date	Repo Rate	Reverse Repo Ratio	CRR	SLR	MSF Rate*
2009-10					
21 Apr. 2009	4.75	3.25	5.00	24.0	
7 Nov. 2009	4.75	3.25	5.00	25.0	
13 Feb. 2010	4.75	3.25	5.50	25.0	
27 Feb. 2010	4.75	3.25	5.75	25.0	
19 Mar. 2010	5.00	3.50	5.75	25.0	
2010-11					
20 Apr. 2010	5.25	3.75	5.75	25.0	
24 Apr. 2010	5.25	3.75	6.00	25.0	
2 Jul. 2010	5.50	4.00	6.00	25.0	
27 Jul. 2010	5.75	4.50	6.00	25.0	
16 Sep. 2010	6.00	5.00	6.00	25.0	
2 Nov. 2010	6.25	5.25	6.00	25.0	
18 Dec. 2010	6.25	5.25	6.00	24.0	
25 Jan. 2011	6.50	5.50	6.00	24.0	
17 Mar. 2011	6.75	5.75	6.00	24.0	
2011-12					
3 May 2011	7.25	6.25	6.00	24.0	
9 May 2011	7.25	6.25	6.00	24.0	8.25
16 Jun. 2011	7.50	6.50	6.00	24.0	8.50
26 Jul. 2011	8.00	7.00	6.00	24.0	9.00
16 Sep. 2011	8.25	7.25	6.00	24.0	9.25
25 Oct. 2011	8.50	7.50	6.00	24.0	9.50
24 Jan. 2012	8.50	7.50	5.50	24.0	9.50
9 Mar. 2012	8.50	7.50	4.75	—	—
17 Apr. 2012	8.00	7.00	4.75	—	9.00

**Note* : The MSF commenced from 9 May 2011.

Source : RBI

been taken by Governor to affirm RBI's commitment to tackle inflation as the headline inflation is still high. I do hope as a result of it, inflation would moderate in course of time". He, however, admitted "it would have some impact on growth also. But the situation is difficult and in difficult situations we cannot expect to have a simple solution".

The industry, which has been seeking a pause in interest rate hike, expressed concern, saying the rate hike would weaken

What is headline inflation?

It refers to the raw inflation figure as reported through the Consumer Price Index (CPI) released on a monthly basis by the Bureau of Labour Statistics. The CPI calculates the cost to purchase a fixed basket of goods as a way of determining how much inflation is occurring in the broad economy. The CPI uses a base year and indexes current year prices as per that year's values. Headline inflation is affected by areas of the market which may experience sudden inflationary spikes such as food or energy. Comparisons of headline inflation are made on a year-on-year basis.

Core inflation does not consider the CPI components that can exhibit large amounts of votability, notably food and energy, month to month.

What is CRR?

CRR is the proportion of deposits banks have to park with the RBI.

Why has the RBI slashed the CRR?

The CRR cut will inject an estimated ₹ 48,000 crore in the pool of banks' lendable resources. It is aimed at making more funds available with banks to match the rising demand from corporations to pay their advance taxes.

Will the reduction in CRR reduce borrowing rates for customers?

Maybe in a very indirect way. With more cash in hand following the cut in CRR, banks may not need to woo customers by offering higher interest rates to shore up their deposit base. Some banks may even consider lowering the interest they pay to customers on their fixed and savings deposits to cut costs. Lower costs, in turn, could prompt them to reduce their final lending rates.

What is repo rate?

It is the rate at which the RBI lends to banks. A higher repo pushes up banks' borrowing costs prompting them to increase interest rates for final home, auto and corporate borrowers.

What is reverse repo rate?

It is the rate at which RBI absorbs cash from the system. At higher reverse repo, the central bank would suck cash from the system to stymie demand and cool prices.

What is liquidity corridor?

The difference between the repo and reverse repo rates is the liquidity corridor or the liquidity adjustment facility (LAF).

What are policy rates?

The policy rates act as a guide for final lending rates that banks charge from borrowers.

In tight liquidity situations, the repo rate acts as the policy rate. In situations of excess liquidity, when banks park money with the RBI from their pool of lendable resources, the reverse repo rate acts as a policy rate.

What role do policy rates play in price control?

A higher repo rate would raise banks' borrowing costs, which in turn would raise interest rate on home, auto and corporate loans.

How does a higher reverse repo rate help in reducing prices?

A higher reverse repo rate would give banks incentive to park money with RBI, reducing liquidity and demand. A higher reverse repo means it would suck cash from the system to stymie demand and cool prices.

Can consumers expect their EMIs to come down?

Not immediately. A lower repo will bring down costs for banks, but banks usually offer lower interest rates only for new customers. Existing home loan borrowers who have borrowed money on floating rates will have to wait longer before banks actually bring down their EMIs.

What about loans on automobiles and consumer goods?

Automobile and consumer goods loans are all on fixed interest rates and, therefore, existing customers are not affected by changes in RBI's policy rates.[1]

economic growth. "Another interest rate hike by the RBI will further weaken economic growth and impact all other indicators", ASSOCHAM President Dilip Modi said. The lowering of forecast for annual GDP growth for 2011-12 from 8 per cent to 7.6 per cent and then to 6.9 bears testimony to the fact that rates have affected economic growth.

As stated earlier, the hike in October 2011 was the 13th since March 2010. The series of rate hikes has cumulatively increased interest rates by 425 basis points. The policy, according to RBI, is expected "to continue to anchor medium term inflation expectations", while stimulating investment activity to support growth.

Marginal Standing Facility Rate

A new policy rate called marginal standing facility rate was introduced by RBI in May 2011. Under this, banks will be able to borrow upto 1 per cent of their respective Net Demand and Time Liabilities. The rate of interest on the amount accessed from this facility will be 100 basis points (i.e. 1 per cent) above the repo rate. This scheme is likely to reduce volatility in the overnight rates and improve monetary transmission.

In its policy statement of 3 May 2011, RBI declared: "The stance of monetary policy is, among other things, to manage liquidity to ensure that it remains broadly in balance, with neither a large surplus diluting monetary transmission nor a large deficit choking off fund flows." And in the mid-quarter monetary policy review (15 March 2012), RBI declared as under:

Monetary and Liquidity Measures

On the basis of the current macroeconomic assessment, it has been decided to:

- Keep the cash reserve ratio (CRR) of scheduled banks unchanged at 4.75 per cent of their net demand and time liabilities; and
- Keep the policy repo rate under the liquidity adjustment facility (LAF) unchanged at 8.5 per cent.[2]

Recent Monetary Measures

In its Monetary Policy Statement 2012-13 dated 17 April 2012, the Reserve Bank announced the following policy measures.

Repo Rate

It was decided to reduce the repo rate under the liquidity adjustment facility (LAF) by 50 basis points from 8.5 per cent to 8.0 per cent with immediate effect.

Reverse Repo Rate

The reverse repo rate under the LAF, determined with a spread of 100 basis points below the repo rate, was adjusted to 7.0 per cent with immediate effect.

Marginal Standing Facility

In order to provide greater liquidity cushion, it was decided to raise the borrowing limit of scheduled commercial banks under the marginal standing facility (MSF) from 1 per cent to 2 per cent of their net demand and time liabilities (NDTL) outstanding at the end of second preceding fortnight with immediate effect.

Banks can continue to access the MSF even if they have excess statutory liquidity ratio (SLR) holdings, as hitherto.

The MSF rate, determined with a spread of 100 basis points above the repo rate, stood adjusted to 9.0 per cent with immediate effect.

Bank Rate

The Bank Rate was also adjusted to 9.0 per cent with immediate effect.

Cash Reserve Ratio

The cash reserve ratio (CRR) of scheduled banks was retained at 4.75 per cent of their NDTL.[3]

It is necessary to mention here that although RBI decreased repo rate and reverse repo rates by 50 basis points each on 17 April 2012, it was not considered enough as it will not make much effect after a series of hikes.

Flawed Approach to Contain Inflation

Keeping interest rates high, as has been done by RBI, can be called a flawed approach to contain inflation. The primary purpose of increasing policy rates is to decrease liquidity, curb demand and control inflation. Whether these measures will be successful in controlling inflation this time is to be seen. The truth is that our policy of increasing interest rates to control inflation has not succeeded in the last 50 years. With this approach, the interest rates in India have been one of the highest in the world. Same is the case with the inflation rate.

There are six main drivers of inflation: (i) the supply side constraints; (ii) the policy and bank interest rates; (iii) the unearned money, including black money; (iv) government actions; (v) the fiscal deficit; and (vi) the movements in international commodity prices.

So far as supply side constraints are concerned, inflation would tend to go up if the demand is less elastic and the supply side constraints are limiting the supplies. Food grains and agriculture-based commodities are prime examples of this. In 2010 when rainfall was lower than normal, agriculture production came down, which resulted in the continuous rise in prices of agriculture-based commodities.

Interest rates have short-term as well as long-term impacts on inflation. In the short-term, increase in interest rate makes money supply costly and more money flows towards bank fixed deposits and treasury bonds. This reduces supply of money for buying goods and services. This is the logic behind monetary measures to tame inflation. However, this impact is only for a short period. Demand for major items of consumption in India is less elastic than in developed countries. Soon people start buying and the impact fizzles out.

The long-term impact is that higher interest rates increase the cost of production due to the burden of high interest rates. High interest rates also make the investment in modernisation of plants expensive and unviable. They also make creation of new capacity difficult to justify. These three factors put together contribute to higher cost of production. This results in the supply not increasing as planned or envisaged, not able to meet the ever-increasing demand and thus hardening of prices.

As investments for modernisation get discouraged, companies are forced to continue with their outdated, inefficient plants. This is one of the factors that keeps Indian companies uncompetitive and makes them produce inferior goods, at a high cost, and renders them as marginal players in the international market. This is one of the reasons why our exports are not increasing, while imports rise steadily and we are in a state of trade deficit. Even with the repeated hikes in interest rates, high inflation continues in India barring short durations of price moderation of certain goods, particularly food articles due to steady seasonal supply.

Unearned money is the money available in the hands of people who have not put legitimate efforts to earn it. The bribes, payments received on false bills, money earned in a parallel economy, etc. are a major driver for inflation. Each of our Five Year Plans is of the order of ₹ 10 lakh-crore. A big chunk of the amount that goes out of the coffers of the government becomes unearned money in the hands of influential people due to corruption and mismanagement of funds. Besides this, counterfeit currency, whether it comes from neighbouring Pakistan or is printed in the country, adds to the pool of unearned money, which increases demand for various goods and services and pushes the prices up.

Prices of Petroleum Products

The government is repeatedly increasing the price of petroleum products instead of reducing the taxation to meet a spike in the cost of crude. With this, the cost of transportation and freight charges move northwards. This cascading effect results in fuelling the inflation. With the current cost of crude over $ 110/barrel, the cost of petrol/diesel excluding taxes comes to around ₹ 33-34/litre. It goes without saying that this escalation is bound to push inflation further up. The government is not reducing taxes and raised the price of petrol and diesel several times in the last one year as can be seen in Table 1.2.

Table 1.2: Prices of Petrol: Delhi, Mumbai, Kolkata and Chennai

(₹ Per Litre)

Date	Delhi	Mumbai	Kolkata	Chennai
1 December 2011	65.64	70.65	70.02	69.55
16 November 2011	66.42	71.47	70.84	70.38
4 November 2011	68.64	73.81	73.15	72.73
16 September 2011	66.84	71.92	71.28	70.82
1 July 2011	63.70	68.62	68.01	67.5
15 May 2011	63.37	68.33	67.71	67.22
16 January 2011	58.37	63.08	62.50	61.93
16 December 2010	55.87	60.46	59.90	60.65
9 November 2010	52.91	57.35	56.81	57.44
2 November 2010	52.59	57.01	56.47	57.09
17 October 2010	52.59	57.01	56.44	57.09
21 September 2010	51.83	56.25	55.69	56.31
8 September 2010	51.56	55.97	55.40	56.02
26 June 2010	51.43	55.88	55.32	55.92
1 April 2010	47.93	52.20	51.67	52.13
27 February 2010	47.43	51.68	51.15	51.59
2 July 2009	44.72	48.76	48.25	48.58
29 January 2009	40.62	44.55	44.05	44.24

The position given in Table 1.2 shows petrol prices in four major Indian cities of Delhi, Mumbai, Kolkata and Chennai since January 2009. It can be observed that the prices of petrol have been rising steadily in India since January 2009. The prices elsewhere in India are nearly the same as on the given dates. The price of petrol in Delhi in January 2009 was ₹ 40.62 per litre, which rose to ₹ 55.87 per litre in December 2010 and ₹ 65.54 per litre in December 2011. Actually, it had gone past ₹ 68 per litre, and it was only after the Prime Minister Manmohan Singh rolled back the 4 November increase that it came below ₹ 66 per litre. From January 2009 price, it was over 60 per cent increase in December 2011 (65.64). Similarly, in Mumbai the overall increase was from ₹ 44.55 per litre in January 2009 to ₹ 70.65 per litre in December 2011, which is an increase of nearly 60 per cent. The petrol prices in Kolkata and Chennai were ₹ 44.05 per litre and ₹ 44.24 per litre respectively in January 2009, which rose to ₹ 70.02 per litre and ₹ 69.55 per litre respectively in December 2011, an increase of nearly 60 per cent. Since the petrol prices of these cities can be taken as representative of those in other cities, we can say that the petrol prices in December 2011 in India have increased around 60 per cent over the prices of 2009.

Since petrol is a major fuel in travel and transportation, its price is directly linked with the cost of producing various types of goods and services as well as transportation of goods. A high cost of petrol naturally stokes inflation.

Similar is the case with diesel prices in India which have shown a rising trend since January 2009 as shown in Table 1.3.

Table 1.3: Prices of Diesel: Delhi, Mumbai, Kolkata and Chennai

(₹ Per Litre)

Date	Delhi	Mumbai	Kolkata	Chennai
1 July 2011	41.29	45.99	43.74	43.95
25 June 2011	41.12	45.84	43.57	43.80
2 November 2010	37.75	42.06	40.06	40.16
8 September 2010	37.75	42.06	40.02	40.16
26 June 2010	40.10	41.98	39.94	40.07
1 April 2010	38.10	39.88	37.99	38.05
27 February 2010	35.47	39.6	37.73	37.78
2 July 2009	32.87	36.70	35.03	34.98
29 January 2009	30.86	34.45	33.21	32.82

A look at Table 1.3 shows that diesel prices have risen in India. The price in Delhi, which was ₹ 30.86 per litre slood at ₹ 41.29 per litre in July 2011, which is an increase of over 25 per cent. Similarly, diesel prices which were ₹ 34.45 per litre, ₹ 33.21 per litre and ₹ 32.82. per litre in Mumbai, Kolkata and Chennai, respectively rose to ₹ 45.99 per litre, ₹ 43.74 per litre and ₹ 43.95 per litre, respectively, which is an increase of about 25 per cent. In case of diesel, the price increase has not been as high as in the case of petrol, but still ₹ 45 per litre or thereabout is a very high price. Since the efficiency of diesel is not as high as that of petrol, the economic cost of diesel is as high as that of petrol.

Diesel is widely used as a fuel in various manufacturing industries. Besides, it is the main fuel of transportation vehicles like trucks, buses and trains. Therefore, high price of diesel pushes the prices of various types of goods and services higher. An increase in diesel price also makes distribution of goods, including food grains costly for the government and other agencies.

Thus, as we have seen from Tables 1.2 and 1.3, the prices of petrol and diesel have gone up in India during the last two years, which has resulted in higher prices of commodities in general. Not just in India, the prices of crude oil have gone very high internationally and at present stand around US$ 115 per barrel as against around US$ 80 per barrel a year ago. The government in such a scenario has no option but to increase the prices of petroleum products including petrol and diesel. However, if inflation is to be kept under tolerable level, the government has to take some concrete steps like developing alternative sources of energy like electric energy, wind energy, nuclear energy, etc. in a big way. Unfortunately, the development made in this regard is not upto the mark.

The government at the centre is caught in a tricky situation. Whenever it tries to increase the prices of petrol and petroleum products, there is opposition from some of its coalition partners. Apprehensive that it may lose majority, the government either keeps the price hike in abeyance or rolls back the increased prices due to political pressures. This is increasing the burden of subsidies given to oil marketing companies and worsening the fiscal position, which is detrimental to economic growth.

Inflation cannot be controlled by keeping interest rates high, which instead will harm industry and hamper economic growth. If alternative sources of energy are not developed, and dependence on petrol and diesel as fuel is not decreased, the price of crude oil is not likely to come down substantially. India's oil marketing companies, which are hard pressed to sell petroleum at subsidized prices have accumulated huge under-recoveries as the subsidy provided by the government is not adequate enough for them to make profit. The government must therefore view the entire economic scenario in totality and frame such policies as address all the issues, instead of resorting to high interest rate policy which will do more harm than good.

Inclusive Growth, Populist Schemes and Inflation

Although Indian economy started growing fast since the 1990s, there is a problem of not achieving inclusive growth. As a result, inequality has risen. We compare our macroeconomic indicators like GDP growth with peers from the BRIC nations, viz. Brazil, Russia and China which have launched many schemes and programmes to bring an incluive growth as per their socio-economic indicators. So the Indian Government too has started several social development programmes like Mahatma Gandhi National Rural Employment Guarantee Scheme (MGNREGS), etc. However, some economists believe that these programmes actually increase aggregate demand and have stoked inflation. Hence, we have a problem of achieving inclusive growth and increasing the overall supplies which are already under pressure.

The government's non-plan expenditure is continuously rising due to its populist schemes like providing rice at ₹ 2-3/kg to BPL families, giving free or subsidised power to farmers, giving subsidised fertilizers to farmers and waiving off the bank debts of farmers. Another thing that should be noted is that the MGNREGS has a potential expense of ₹ 1,00,000 crore/year. The 2011-12 budget for this was ₹ 40,000 crore. Finance Minister Pranab Mukherjee was fully aware of worsening fiscal position due to food subsidy and schemes like MGNREGS. He proposed to cut the expenditure for MGNREGS in the Budget 2012-13. But experts feel that it will not be practically possible because of rising wages and due to the fact that the beneficiaries under such schemes are self-selecting and cannot be reduced. These schemes result in an additional burden on government finance, resulting in a fiscal deficit, which has to be bridged by printing notes or treasury bonds. This money pumped in the system becomes a driver for inflation.

Impact of International Commidity Prices

The movement in international commodity prices also affects inflation. Commodities like coal, gas and petroleum have a direct impact on our cost of imports. Movements in prices of gold and silver also have some impact on inflation. During the last one year or so, the prices of coal and petroleum have registered a large increase in international market. This has pushed the prices of other commodities up all over the world, including India.

Three Components of Interest Rate

According to K.K. Jain, there are three components in the interest rate. The first component is the real interest rate which is around 2-3 per cent. The second component is cover for risk. The third component is cover for inflation. Therefore, increase in interest rates would tend to increase the inflation since the real interest rates and the risk cover remain constant. In early 1990s, interest rates were 18-20 per cent, and consequently, inflation was close to 15 per cent. A few years ago when interest rates were brought down to 6-7 per cent, inflation came down to 3-4 per cent. This was lowest inflation in India in the last 50 years.

Depreciation of Rupee

During the early 1960s, the US dollar was equal to around ₹ 40 and one rupee could fetch 70 yen. Today, a dollar is equal to more than ₹ 50 and a rupee can fetch less than 1.8 yen. Thus, the rupee has depreciated more than 25 per cent against the dollar and more than 38 times against the yen in the past 50 years. Depreciation as compared to yen is higher because interest rates in Japan are even lower than that in the US. Depreciation of rupee means higher payment for goods imported. If these goods are used as raw material, cost of goods produced increases which leads to a corresponding increase in price. If the imported goods are sold directly in the market, a higher price is charged to keep a profit margin. Thus, the depreciation of rupee leads to inflation.

Thus, increase in interest rates alone is not likely to contain inflation and if we are serious about containing it, we need to address all the important causes mentioned above that drive inflation.

According to experts, treating inflation purely as a monetary phenomenon seems to be incorrect. The problem with the monetary authority, viz. Reserve Bank of India is that it is obsessed with increasing policy rates and showcasing to the Indian people that it has been doing its best to control inflation disregarding the fact that inflation in India is as much due to large amount of money with public to buy as due to shortage of supply. Improvement in supply cannot be brought about without giving a boost to production.

It is also time for the RBI to have a dialogue with the mandarins of the Finance Ministry on the need to control fiscal deficit. Fiscal deficit has still not been reigned in despite the huge Telecom auction deposits received by the government. Further, the neglect of supply side has aggravated the inflationary situation. The persisting inflation in India has already undermined the role of the RBI and it is time for the government to tackle it through non-monetary instruments.

Relationship between Interest and Inflation

Inflation is impacted by money supply in an economy. Central governments use the interest rate to control money supply and, consequently, the inflation rate. When interest rates go high, it becomes more expensive to borrow money and at the same time, savings become attractive. When interest rates are low, people find it proper to borrow and thus the banks are able to lend more, resulting in an increased supply of money. The resultant higher purchasing power pushes the prices of various goods and services up.

Changes in the rate of interest are used to control inflation by controlling the supply of money in the following ways:

(i) A high interest rate influences spending patterns and shifts consumers and businesses from borrowing to saving mode. This controls money supply.

(ii) An increase in interest rates boosts the return on savings in building societies and banks. Low interest rates encourage investments in shares. Thus, the rate of interest can impact the holding of particular assets. In this way there is a shift in demand across sectors and consequent changes in price levels.

(iii) A increase in the interest rate in a particular country fuels the inflow of funds. Investors with funds in other countries find investment in that country more profitable option than before. If such flow of funds is used to produce more goods, the supply will increase and prices will come down, otherwise the flow funds will increase purchasing power and push the prices up.

Inflation and Interest Rates: Effect on the Time Value of Money

Inflation has a significant impact on the time value of money (TVM). Changes in the inflation rate often result in changes in the rates of interest. Banks and companies anticipate the erosion of the value of money due to inflation over the term of the debt instruments they offer. To compensate for this loss, they have to increase the interest rates.

Ways to Control Inflation

Inflation management is not an easy affair. In India, which has been facing the challenge of rising prices for quite some time now, there are both demand and supply side issues. On the one side, there is rising demand because of regular increase in population and a rise in the standard of living of people in general with an increase in their earning, and on the other side, the supply factors have not kept pace. The rising demand and supply deficiencies in various sectors are responsible for a rise in prices.

Countries like China have managed to keep inflation low during the high growth phase because supply was never really a problem. It is believed that they created additional capacities and it is only now when the global food prices have risen, inflation has become a problem in China.

Unlike China, India has several supply-side issues and the result is spiralling inflation. The Indian Government's policy should focus on increasing supplies. Tampering with demand would lead to lower growth. Over a medium- to long-term period, we have to plan in such a manner that the supplies are sufficient enough to keep pace with demand. But, in the short-term, we have no other option but to soften demand through monetary tightening. The problem with RBI's policy is that it has kept on following tight money policy for so long that it has adversely impacted economic growth.

It is right to say that RBI can only control inflation which comes from demand factors. By raising interest rates, it has tried to lower money supply in the overall economy, which will have an overall effect of lowering the demand for goods and services in the country. Another drawback of monetary measures as a tool to control inflation is that they take a long time to make an impact, if at all. When the RBI hikes policy rates, some banks bring a corresponding increases in their interest rates, others do not make an immediate increase or make a small increase, yet some others may not take any decisions and keep a policy of wait and watch and see if they can absorb the RBI hike. Thus, it can never be expected that RBI's repo rate hike of say 50 bps will suddenly arrest or lower inflation.

It is pertinent to mention here that in Europe and America, central banks have kept interest rates very low. But banks did not lower the rates as much due to high risk and funding pressures. Monetary transmission has not been efficient in the global economic crisis. We see a similar situation in India as well. When RBI lowered rates in wake of crisis, the interest rates in banks did not come down as much. And now when it raised rates starting from March 10, 2011 the banks have started increasing their deposit and lending rates. Thus, banks also tend to follow what suits their proftability best, as much as RBI policy allows them.

The inflation rate in United States was 3.9 per cent in September of 2011. The Consumer Price Index for All Urban Consumers (CPI-U) increased 0.3 per cent in September 2011 on a seasonally adjusted basis, as reported by the US Bureau of Labor Statistics. Over the last 12 months, the all items index increased 3.9 per cent before seasonal adjustment. The position of inflation rates in the US from the year 1999 to 2012 (upto Feb.) is given in Table 1.4.

Increases in energy and food indexes were the main cause of the increase in the prices of seasonally adjusted all items in the US. The gasoline index continued to rise, and indexes for

Table 1.4: Table of Inflation Rates in the US by Month and Year (1999-2012)

Year	Jan.	Feb.	Mar.	Apr.	May	Jun.	Jul.	Aug.	Sep.	Oct.	Nov.	Dec.	Ave.
2012	2.9	2.9											
2011	1.6	2.1	2.7	3.2	3.6	3.6	3.6	3.8	3.9	3.5	3.4	3.0	3.2
2010	2.6	2.1	2.3	2.2	2.0	1.1	1.2	1.1	1.1	1.2	1.1	1.5	1.6
2009	0	0.2	-0.4	-0.7	-1.3	-1.4	-2.1	-1.5	-1.3	-0.2	1.8	2.7	-0.4
2008	4.3	4	4	3.9	4.2	5.0	5.6	5.4	4.9	3.7	1.1	0.1	3.8
2007	2.1	2.4	2.8	2.6	2.7	2.7	2.4	2	2.8	3.5	4.3	4.1	2.8
2006	4	3.6	3.4	3.5	4.2	4.3	4.1	3.8	2.1	1.3	2	2.5	3.2
2005	3	3	3.1	3.5	2.8	2.5	3.2	3.6	4.7	4.3	3.5	3.4	3.4
2004	1.9	1.7	1.7	2.3	3.1	3.3	3	2.7	2.5	3.2	3.5	3.3	2.7
2003	2.6	3	3	2.2	2.1	2.1	2.1	2.2	2.3	2	1.8	1.9	2.3
2002	1.1	1.1	1.5	1.6	1.2	1.1	1.5	1.8	1.5	2	2.2	2.4	1.6
2001	3.7	3.5	2.9	3.3	3.6	3.2	2.7	2.7	2.6	2.1	1.9	1.6	2.8
2000	2.7	3.2	3.8	3.1	3.2	3.7	3.7	3.4	3.5	3.4	3.4	3.4	3.4
1999	1.7	1.6	1.7	2.3	2.1	2	2.1	2.3	2.6	2.6	2.6	2.7	2.2

Source: http://www.usinflationcalculator.com/inflation/current-inflation-rates/

electricity and natural gas also registered an increase. Broad increases in food indexes also continued in September 2011 with the food at home index rising 0.6 per cent for the third month in a row but still it was not very high.

The US index for all items less food and energy increased 0.1 per cent in September 2011, its smallest increase since March. The index for apparel declined in September 2011 after a series of sharp increases, and the indexes for used cars and recreation also decreased. The indexes for new vehicles and household furnishings and operations were both flat. The shelter index rose, but posted its smallest increase since April 2011, while the indexes for medical care, airline fares, and tobacco all increased.

The 12-month change in the all items index, which was 3.8 per cent in August 2011, edged up to 3.9 per cent in September 2011. The 12-month change for all items less food and energy remained at 2.0 per cent for the second month in succession. The energy index has risen 19.3 per cent over the last year, while the food index has increased 4.7 per cent.

The above data shows that inflation is not a worrisome problem in the US at present. One of the reasons could be that the US has not recovered fully from the global recession of 2008-09. But it should be noted that the average inflation of the country, of the last 100 years, is just over 3 per cent. Its policies are based on industrial growth. A well-maintained supply chain, proper distribution system and absence of bottlenecks like hoarding, black marketing, etc. help in keeping the prices in check. In India on the other hand, there is rempant hoarding, black marketing and clandestine practices by middlemen, which often result in artificial shortage and high prices of certain goods.

World Interest Rates

While policymakers in India are increasing interest rates as a measure to curb money supply and control inflation, most of the developed countries are following a low interest rate policy. Federal Reserve System of the US has interest rate of just 0.25 per cent; Bank of England has interest rate of 0.50 per cent; Bank of Canada has interest rate of 1.00 per cent; and Bank of Japan has interest rates as low as 0.10 per cent.

A look at Table 1.5 reveals that interest rates in most of the countries are low. Interest rate of the respective central bank in each of the countries included in Table 1.5 is less than that in India with the exception of Brazil, which is an emerging economy like India. China has interest rate of 6.56 per cent against our 8 per cent. Egypt too has a high interest rate of 8.25 per cent but its last change was made in Sept. 2009, when a reduction of 25 basis points was made. It means that it has not made frequent changes in its policy rates unlike India which numerous changes. Making such frequent changes also means that India has focused only on monetary measures to control inflation and not taken collective steps using other measure as well, and secondly, it has not waited for sufficient time for these measures to make an impact.

It may be argued that most of the countries have not fully recovered from global recession and are facing the problems of high unemployment, low industrial growth, high fiscal deficit, etc. and are not registering good enough economic growth. India's economy on the other hand is still doing quite well, though not having the high GDP growth of pre-global crisis

Table 1.5: World Interest Rates

Country	Current Rate	Previous Rate	Change	Last Change
Australia	4.5%	4.7%	–0.2%	Nov 01 2011
Brazil	11.5%	12%	–0.5%	Oct 19 2011
Canada	1%	0.7%	0.3%	Sep 08 2010
Chile	3.5%	3.25%	0.25%	Nov 18 2010
China	6.56%	6.3%	0.26%	Jul 06 2011
Colombia	3.25%	3%	0.25%	Feb 28 2011
Czech Republic	0.75%	1%	–0.25%	May 06 2010
Denmark	0.75%	1%	–0.25%	Jan 15 2010
Egypt	8.25%	8.5%	–0.25%	Sep 22 2009
European Monetary Union	1.5%	1.2%	0.3%	Jul 07 2011
Hong Kong SAR	0.5%	1%	–0.5%	Dec 17 2008
Hungary	6%	5.7%	0.3%	Jan 24 2011
Iceland	4.5%	4.2%	0.3%	Aug 17 2011
India	8.5%	8.2%	0.3%	Oct 25 2011
Indonesia	6.75%	6.5%	0.25%	Feb 04 2011
Israel	3%	3.03%	–0.03%	Nov 01 2011
Japan	0.1%	0%	0.1%	Dec 19 2008
Korea, Republic of	3.25%	3%	0.25%	Jun 10 2011
Malaysia	2.75%	2.5%	0.25%	Jul 08 2010
Mexico	4.5%	4.75%	–0.25%	Jul 17 2010
New Zealand	2.5%	3%	–0.5%	Mar 09 2011
Norway	2.25%	2%	0.25%	May 12 2011
Philippines	4%	4.25%	–0.25%	Jul 09 2009
Poland	3.75%	3.5%	0.25%	Jun 03 2009
South Africa	5.5%	6%	–0.5%	Sep 10 2010
Sweden	2%	0%	2%	Sep 07 2011
Switzerland	0%	0.2%	-0.2%	Aug 03 2011
Taiwan	1.875%	1.75%	0.125%	Jul 01 2011
Thailand	2.5%	2%	0.5%	Jan 12 2011
Turkey	5.75%	6.2%	–0.45%	Aug 05 2011
United Kingdom	0.5%	1%	–0.5%	Mar 05 2009
United States	0.25%	1%	–0.75%	Dec 16 2008

Source: http://www.worldinterestrates.info/

period. It appears that RBI is compromising with growth in an attempt to control inflation, which, according to experts, is a bad bargain. Low economic growth will lead to many other attendant problems like low production, unemployment, layoffs, etc.

Policymakers in developed countries are keeping rates near zero and Federal Reserve Chairman Ben Bernanke has promised to keep it low till the middle of 2013. Most Asian central banks have left rates untouched for a long time and Turkey and Brazil have cut interest rates.

Low Industrial Production: An Impact of High Interest Rates

India's industrial output grew at a two-year low at 1.9 per cent in September 2011 due to a contraction in mining output and poor performance in manufacturing, the Central Statistical Office data revealed. The uncertainty in developed markets seemed to put the brakes on the economy's growth momentum, causing analysts to fear that external factors could have a greater impact on India.

The deceleration in industrial growth, partly ascribed to the high cost of funds, presents a strong case against the Reserve Bank of India's tight monetary policy, which it has been pursuing for the last 20 months.

Industrial growth fell to a two-year low to 1.9 per cent in September 2011, compared to 4.1 per cent in August 2011 against a Bloomberg UTV estimation of 3.8 per cent. Among the main industry segments, manufacturing activity declined to 2.1 per cent from 4.5 per cent a month ago. Mining sector growth was at –5.6 per cent as compared to –3.4 per cent in August 2011. This slow industrial output is due to RBI's policy of high interest rates as businesses found it difficult to carry on output in larger quantities due to high cost of funds.

In an interview with Bloomberg UTV, Taimur Baig, Chief Economist, Deutsche Bank AG said that wages are in tandem with rising inflation and that commodity pressure and rupee movement will keep pressure on the RBI. Baig also said that the central bank may not take a chance by cutting rates. But it will harm growth.

M.M. Miyajiwala, Executive VP-Finance, Voltas said, "Indian economy outlook is more bearish than 2008. Interest rates will have lag effect next year." He expects next year to be subdued. He also said, "Capital goods results indicate pressure on order inflows."

Venugopal Dhoot, CMD, Videocon, however, was not so pessimistic about the Indian economic scenario as he said that Indian economy was moving in a forward track. But lower GDP growth in 2011-12 as compared to the previous year hardly justifies this optimism.

"IIP for September is bad, but I do see a pick-up by the end of March. We had originally expected overall IIP at 7 per cent for the fiscal, but now it could be 6 per cent", C. Rangarajan, Chairman of the Prime Minister's Economic Advisory Council, said. He described the dip in factory output in September as "disappointing" and said industry may grow by just 6 per cent in the year 2011-12 as against the earlier projection of 7 per cent. The IIP for 22 major industry groups in the manufacturing sector is given in Table 1.6.

"The IIP numbers are disappointing. It is well below our expectation", Dr Rangranan said, adding, "...to some extent, the decline is contributed by negative growth in the mining sector." Mining output declined by 5.6 per cent in September 2011 as against a growth of 4.3 per cent in the same month in the previous year. During the first half of 2011-12, mining output dipped by 1 per cent, as against a growth of 7.2 per cent a year ago. IIP growth during the April-September period moderated to 5 per cent from 8.2 per cent in the corresponding period last fiscal.

"The government", Mr Rangarajan said, "should ensure that the fall in coal production is corrected and also investment in infrastructure, especially, roads, rail and power." Although the mining sector has been singled out as low, pushing the IIP down, yet the fact is that other industrial sectors have not fared any better barring a few. The impact of tight money policy will be seen in all sectors in the time to come.

In the manufacturing sector, the industrial groups like tabacco products, textiles, wearing apparel and fur, rubber and plastic products, machinery and equipment, electrical machinery and apparatus, wood and wood products, optical instruments, and furniture manufacturing slowed down in 2011 from the 2010 levels. Some other groups like motor vehicles and chemcial products had moderate growth.

Table 1.6: IIP-22 Major Industry Groups of Manufacturing Sector
(Base : 2004-05=100)

Industry Group	Industry	Weight	Annual April-August			Cumulative August		Monthly	
			2008 -09	2009 -10	2010 -11P	2010 -11	2011 -12P	2010 P	2011
		1	2	3	4	5	6	7	8
	Manufacturing Index	75.53	153.8	161.3	175.7	166.7	176.7	165.2	172.6
15	Food products and beverages	7.28	135.4	133.5	142.9	123.3	141.3	105.3	114.0
16	Tobacco products	1.57	102.7	102.0	104.1	108.8	104.4	111.4	88.6
17	Textiles	6.16	120.1	127.4	135.9	134.1	130.8	141.7	136.3
18	Wearing apparel; dressing and dyeing of fur	2.78	134.6	137.1	142.2	142.6	141.1	138.3	137.8
19	Luggage, handbags, saddlery, harness & footwear; tanning and dressing of leather products	0.58	104.4	105.8	114.3	112.2	119.8	114.3	122.8
20	Wood and wood products of wood & cork except furniture; articles of straw & plating materials	1.05	155.3	160.1	156.5	159.6	152.3	156.1	154.8
21	Paper and paper products	1.00	118.0	121.1	131.4	128.5	135.8	137.2	137.2
22	Publishing, printing & reproduction of recorded media	1.08	142.4	133.8	148.8	144.8	157.9	148.5	158.0
23	Coke, refined petroleum products & nuclear fuel	6.71	123.4	121.8	121.5	118.9	125.0	116.7	126.7
24	Chemicals and chemical products	10.06	115.0	120.7	123.1	122.4	124.7	124.5	126.3
25	Rubber and plastic products	2.02	142.6	167.4	185.2	185.4	183.6	178.3	176.9
26	Other non-metallic mineral products	4.31	134.9	145.4	151.4	148.6	153.1	142.2	150.4
27	Basic metals	11.33	159.0	162.4	176.7	165.1	189.7	171.5	190.7
28	Fabricated metal products, except machinery and equipment	3.08	144.0	158.6	182.8	157.3	179.4	167.5	186.9
29	Machinery and equipment n.e.c	3.76	171.0	198.0	256.3	234.6	230.4	218.4	216.8
30	Office, accounting & computing machinery	0.30	148.8	154.4	146.3	122.9	138.3	159.0	116.4
31	Electrical machinery & apparatus n.e.c	1.98	530.8	459.2	472.1	447.8	454.3	401.8	379.8
32	Radio, TV and communication equipment & apparatus	0.99	726.7	809.1	911.5	886.6	895.9	864.0	972.3
33	Medical, precision & optical instruments, watches and clocks	0.57	119.8	100.9	107.8	103.4	98.1	106.3	97.9
34	Motor vehicles, trailers & semi-trailers	4.06	138.0	179.1	233.3	212.4	245.3	225.0	243.3
35	Other transport equipment	1.82	134.0	171.1	210.7	193.4	227.1	208.8	234.1
36	Furniture, manufacturing n.e.c	2.99	142.5	152.7	141.2	140.5	142.1	134.5	132.6

Source: Central Statistics Office, Ministry of Statistics and Programme Implementation, Government of India

Table 1.6 shows the growth of 22 major industry groups of manufacturing sector. Overall, the manufacturing sector index showed a deceleration from 175.7 in 2010-11 to 172.6 in December 2011. While food products and beverages and tobacco products showed a decline, textile showed a small growth. Wearing apparel also declined as did wood and wood products. Paper and paper products grew from 131.4 to 137.2, while chemicals, etc. grew from 123.1 to 126.3. Rubber products declined substantially from 185.2 to 176.9. Only basic metals showed satisfactory growth from 176.7 to 190.7, from 2010-11 to December 2011. Machinery and equipment fell from 256.3 to 216.8, while growth in electrical machinery decelerated from 472.1 to 379.8 during that period. Thus, the 11P data showed a dismal position.

Planning Commission Deputy Chairman, Montek Singh Ahluwalia said that the IIP numbers were disappointing and the pace of growth in the economy has slowed down. "We have to ensure that the economic recovery takes place soon", added Ahluwalia. C. Rangarajan admitted that the manufacturing growth was extremely disappointing but added that interest rates were not the only reason for slowing of IIP growth. However, the industry experts feel that high interest rates had a major faction in pulling down grown.

Economists not Optimistic about Industrial Growth

September 2011 decline in industrial growth to a two-year low of 1.9 per cent has made the economists pessimistic. They are apprehensive and say it may take between 4 to 11 months for industrial production to improve and do not even rule out factory output contracting in the months to come. If that happens, the signs are not good for economic growth, as industry is 18-19 per cent of India's gross domestic product.

Economists are of the opinion that the contraction in mining output will jack up input prices of manufactured products. However, they are divided on whether these could be passed on to consumers at this stage of slackening demand. "If the trend continues, with electricity no longer supporting industrial production, the IIP will start contracting", said Anis Chakravarty,

Director, Deloitte, Haskins & Sells. As the effect of mining on electricity generation comes with a lag effect of three to four months, the electricity numbers will also start slowing, cautioned Arun Singh, senior economist with Dun & Bradstreet. He added: "In case the mining problem is not resolved soon, the IIP may stagnate or become negative, but that is in an extreme case." He expected industrial growth numbers to start heading up from August 2012 only, when the Reserve Bank of India is likely to begin cutting rates. RBI's tight monetary stance is being blamed for stifling growth numbers, while not impacting inflation much.

D.S. Joshi, Chief Economist CRISIL, said that the weak numbers would persist for another four to six months. Mr Joshi said rising input costs would eat into the margins of companies and not necessarily lead to inflation. "Demand-side pressure is down, so manufacturers will not be able to pass on the increased input costs to the users", he said. "The IIP numbers are disappointing...well below our expectation", he said, adding, "...to some extent, the decline is contributed by negative growth in the mining sector". However, it is not just the mining sector's poor performance that has dragged IIP down; many other groups in the industry have recorded a negative growth. Madan Sabnavis, Chief Economist, CARE Ratings, said IIP growth for 2011-12 would definitely be at sub-five per cent. Industrial growth was five per cent in the first half of financial year 2011-12. Thus, the impact of high interest rates on industrial production is quite clear.

Good performance by the farm sector is expected to offset slowdown in the industrial sector, Citi said. "While continued weakness in industrial production data could add downside risks to our FY'12 industry growth estimate of 6.5 per cent, these may be offset by higher agriculture growth, thus supporting our financial year 2011-12 GDP forecast at 7.6 per cent for now", Citi Investment Research & Analysis said in its issue of "India Macro Flash". But as we know, such hope was not echoed by the government which revised downward the economic growth expectation to 6.9 per cent for the year 2011-12. Reflecting slowdown, factory output growth slipped to a two-year low of

1.9 per cent in September compared to 6.1 per cent in the same month of 2010. This is the third consecutive month industrial growth has declined. During the April-September period of 2011-12 the growth of Index of Industrial Production (IIP) stood at 5 per cent as against 8.2 per cent in the same period last year.[4]

Industry experts have said that one of the biggest constraints for India's economic growth is high interest rates, and that the RBI should take measures to control supply-side bottlenecks rather than keeping the interest rates high.

"The biggest constraint that we have are high interest costs", said Tulsi R. Tanti, CMD, Suzlon Energy. "Interest costs have risen seven times and are at 13-14 per cent", he said. The corporate world fears that high interest rates are impacting GDP growth rate and consumption-based sectors. "The RBI needs to focus on easing supply-side constraints rather than rate hikes", Adi Godrej, Chairman, Godrej Group, said.

"Industrial growth outlook in the country has deteriorated over last few months. Uncertainty in economic environment has impacted business and consumer confidence which is reflected in the negative growth of capital goods and consumer non-durables", said Rajiv Kumar, Secretary General, Federation of Indian Chambers of Commerce and Industry (FICCI). Another industry lobby, the Confederation of Indian Industry (CII) said it was time the RBI gave thought to easing interest rates to support capital investment.

India Inc blamed the high interest rate regime for decline in industrial output growth. However, according to Planning Commission Deputy Chairman Montek Singh Ahluwalia, there is no connection between the two. "I would not draw any connection between the rate hike and decline in industrial production. The rate today is roughly what it was when the economy was growing at 9 per cent", Ahluwalia said when asked if RBI's tight monetary policy was hampering industrial production. It is pertinent to remember that the Reserve Bank has hiked interest by 3.75 per cent since March 2010 to tame inflation, which hovered around 10 per cent for most of the calendar year 2012. The high interest rate regime has made credit expensive for corporates as well as consumers, which the industry says has hit growth.

Montek Singh Ahluwalia, who was talking to reporters on the sidelines of a FICCI meet, said there are other global and domestic factors that are affecting factory production. "I do not think the slowing down (of industrial production growth) should be attributed to only the short-term interest rates", he said. "We are concerned that the pace of growth in the economy has gone down. But it (IIP data) is only a one month affair", Ahluwalia said. But as we know, Ahluwalia's statement has not been able to impress the industry and economic experts. There is, they feel, a direct connection with interest rates and industrial growth. High interest rates increase cost of production, erode profit margin, make expansion unviable and slow down production. Apex industry body CII also blamed the high interest rate regime for slowdown in IIP. "This probably reflects the impact of RBI's interest rate hikes together with the continuous rise in inflation. With the global economic scenario also deteriorating, the RBI should not only pause but begin to reverse its interest rate hikes", CII Director General Chandrajit Banerjee said.

The July-September 2011 quarter turned out to be the worst period for India Inc in nearly three years with a sharp fall in net profit and shrunk margins. A steep increase in fuel and interest costs, unfavourable foreign currency movement and higher depreciation were largely responsible for the overall poor performance of companies. Net profit of the over 1,200 listed companies that reported results for the said quarter, excluding banking, finance and oil and gas companies, fell by 28.5 per cent from the year ago. This was the first drop in at least nine quarters and sharper than the fall during the 2008 sub-prime crisis.

Even sectors like automobiles, petrochemicals, consumer durables and textiles, which had shown resilience during the economic meltdown, reported a fall in profit for the first time in several quarters. In addition, the lower than-expected growth of 1.9 per cent in industrial production in September 2011, is an indication that the performance of India Inc is likely to be subdued in the coming months.

The sharp fall in profit against the backdrop of 17.7 per cent top line growth reveals India Inc's inability to pass on rising costs to consumers without affecting their business. Firm raw material prices, buoyant staff costs and a spike in fuel prices show that operating costs rose faster than top line growth, thereby shrinking profits.

Operating margin for the July-September 2011 fell to an 11-quarter low of 16.8 per cent. Net margin after considering interest outgo and depreciation fell even more sharply to 8.7 per cent, the lowest in three years. An incessant rise in borrowing costs effected by the RBI in the past 18 months or so has started pinching India Inc. In the said quarter, the proportion of interest outgo in sales rose to 3 per cent, the highest since the December 2008 quarter.

The rupee's depreciation against hard currencies, including the dollar, the pound and the euro, adversely impacted bottom lines. Companies with overseas operations reported mounting forex losses, either due to restatement of international assets or because of losses on hedged revenue and cash flows.

Making matters worse for Corporate India is corruption. "Corruption is hurting India's image. It is having a major impact on GDP growth. Issues like these are not only reducing investment by foreign companies but also hurting sentiment among Indian investors. There is a need to dismantle discretionary government handling and have minimum requirements for smooth facilitation of business", Adi Godrej stated at the World Economic Forum.

Telecom companies reported yet another quarter of low profits due to higher interest cost and amortisation arising from the loans taken to acquire 3G licences.[5]

Business community is a worrisome lot these days as costs are rising and profits are falling. The cost of raw materials like leather and shoe uppers are rising rapidly.

As a result of interest rate hike by the RBI, the costlier borrowings have prompted consumers to defer purchases of goods such as cars, which are mostly bought through loans. Car sales growth in the Diwali month of October 2011 slid by 24 per cent, the slowest in a decade.

"The market condition continues to remain challenging as interest rates and rising fuel costs have led to consumers postponing their purchasing decisions. Only new launches and diesel cars are witnessing any demand and for existing models. It is a very difficult time", said Arvind Saxena, Director Sales and Marketing, Hyundai Motor India Ltd. "The prospect before the government is rather worrying: controlling prices may have hurt consumption demand, the edifice of the India growth story, at a time when the world is seeing a slowdown. The country seems to be losing its insulation", he added.

It can be observed from Table 1.7 that car sales of several companies went down in January 2012 in comparision with January 2011. Out of the total 62 brands of reputed car companies operating in India, the sale of as many as 38 brands showed a lower rate. High prices of cars because of higher import costs is one reason, while high interest rates on car loans is another major reason of low rates of car sales.

Slow manufacturing hurts corporate profits and employment prospects at India's 1,60,000-odd factories that employ about 110 million people. Many companies have withdrawn plans for share offerings. Two public sector companies (ONGC and Steel Authority of India) have postponed disinvestments, and 42 companies are waiting for an opportune time to sell shares. The strategy of the Reserve Bank of India, i.e. raise interest rates to mop up money, slow down the economy and lower inflation, is working only partially. The economy is indeed slowing but inflation was at its highest in September 2012.

The IIP data for December 2012 did not show any improvement as can be observed from Table 1.8.

Low industrial output has put the policymakers in a dilemma since the string of measures to cool prices has not tamed inflation but eroded growth in the broader economy, hurting employment prospects and investor sentiments.

Table 1.7: Year-on-Year Growth of Car Sales in India: Feb. 2011-Feb. 2012

Manufacturer	Model	Feb-11	Feb-12	YOY Growth (%)
Maruti Suzuki	800	2,712	2,193	-0.19
Tata	Nano	8,262	9,217	0.12
GM	Beat	3,183	4,675	46.87
GM	Spark	2,998	1,314	-56.17
Hyundai	i10	15,105	10,324	-31.65
Hyundai	Santro	8,070	5,924	-26.59
Maruti Suzuki	A Star	3,657	1,102	-69.87
Maruti Suzuki	Alto	33,015	32,909	-0.32
Maruti Suzuki	Wagon-R	14,131	12,900	-8.71
Maruti Suzuki	Estilo	4,469	1,378	-69.17
Ford	Figo	7,883	6,546	-16.96
GM	UV-A	118	20	-83.05
Honda	Jazz	400	356	-11.00
Hyundai	i20	6,834	4,844	-29.12
Maruti Suzuki	Ritz	5,882	5,782	-1.70
Nissan	Micra	2,030	2,198	8.28
Maruti Suzuki	Swift	10,936	20,739	89.64
Skoda	Fabia	1,466	916	-37.52
Tata	Indica	10,044	10,424	3.78
Volkswagen	Polo	3,303	3,839	16.23
Fiat	Linea	757	365	-51.78
Ford	Fiesta Classic	1,074	1,389	29.33
GM	Aveo	172	49	-71.51
Honda	City	3,668	6,052	64.99
Hyundai	Accent	1,224	580	-52.61
Hyundai	Verna	1,241	4,506	263.09
Mahindra Renault	Logan/Verito	1,151	1,632	41.79
Maruti Suzuki	Swift Dzire	9,490	15,068	58.78
Maruti Suzuki	SX4	3,534	2,033	-42.47
Tata	Indigo	8,966	8,595	-4.14
VW	Vento	3,548	2,174	-38.73
GM	Optra	359	273	-23.96
GM	Cruze	766	537	-29.90
HM (Mitsubishi)	Lancer + Cedia	19	47	147.37
Honda	Civic	512	208	-59.38
Toyota	Corolla Altis	985	996	1.12
Skoda	Laura	538	370	-31.23
Skoda	Superb	255	181	-29.02
Toyota	Camry	20	0	-100.00
Honda	Accord	242	94	-61.16

(Contd...)

Manufacturer	Model	Feb-11	Feb-12	YOY Growth (%)
Mahindra	Bolero	7,161	8,843	23.49
Maruti Suzuki	Gypsy	151	228	50.99
Maruti Suzuki	EECO	5,780	5,664	-2.01
Maruti Suzuki	Omni	7,756	7,641	-1.48
HM	Ambassador	302	200	-33.77
GM	Chevrolet Tavera	1,554	1,964	26.38
Mahindra	Scorpio	3,924	3,972	1.22
Mahindra	Xylo	2,287	2,796	22.26
Tata	Sumo	2,315	3,366	45.40
Toyota	Innova	4,515	6,271	38.89
GM	Chevrolet Captiva	133	25	-81.20
Ford	Endeavour	336	23	-93.15
HM (Mitsubishi)	Outlander	72	15	-79.17
Tata	Safari	1,850	1,711	-7.51
Tata	Aria	173	417	141.04
Honda	CR-V	21	100	376.19
Maruti Suzuki	Grand Vitara	5	2	-60.00
Hyundai	Santa-Fe	126	147	16.67
Toyota	Fortuner	991	1,346	35.82
HM (Mitsubishi)	Pajero	140	49	-65.00
HM (Mitsubishi)	Montero	11	5	-54.55
Skoda	Yeti	253	118	-53.36

Source: http://management-punditz.blogspot.in/2012/03/indian-car-sales-figures-february-2012.html

Output in the capital goods sector was worst hit. It contracted by 6.8 per cent showing signs that costlier borrowing and rising raw material costs are prompting companies to defer capacity expansion plans. Low industrial growth could result in fewer job opportunities and lower salary hikes as corporations, squeezed in by lower sales, and hold back investments.

"The continuous negative growth of textiles and apparel sector for the last few months would have serious implications for employment creation in the country as the sector is the second largest employer after agriculture", Rajiv Kumar, Secretary General of Federation of Indian Chambers of Commerce and Industry (FICCI), said.

"Employment growth at the top end will slow down in an economy that is still growing, simply because of cost issues", said Vikram Chhachhi, Executive Vice-president, DHR International, a US-based executive search firm.

"The conventional policy of interest rates...now you do have to rethink on that", chief economic advisor Kaushik Basu said

Table 1.8: Group-Wise Index Numbers of Industrial Production
(Base : 2004-05=100)
Production

Sr. No.	Industry	Weight	Annual			Cumulative April-December		Monthly December	
			2008-09	2009-10	2010P	2010-2011	2011-12 P	2010	2011 P
		1	2	3	4	5	6	7	8
	General Index	**100.00**	**145.2**	**152.9**	**165.5**	**161.0**	**166.8**	**175.7**	**178.8**
I.	**Sectoral Classification**								
1.	Mining and Quarrying	14.16	115.4	124.5	131.0	127.6	124.1	141.5	136.2
2.	Manufacturing	75.53	153.8	161.3	175.7	170.7	177.3	187.3	190.7
3.	Electricity	10.32	123.3	130.8	138.0	135.7	148.5	137.3	149.8
II.	**Use-Based Classification**								
1.	Basic Goods	45.68	128.1	134.1	142.2	138.7	147.2	148.5	154.5
2.	Capital Goods	8.83	240.6	243.0	278.9	272.6	264.6	313.6	261.8
3.	Intermediate Goods	15.69	127.6	135.3	145.3	143.8	142.6	152.0	147.8
4.	Consumer Goods	29.81	152.6	164.3	178.3	171.1	180.8	188.9	207.7
4(a).	Consumer Durables	8.46	215.4	252.0	287.7	277.9	292.6	283.5	298.4
4(b).	Consumer Non-Durables	21.35	127.7	129.5	135.0	128.8	136.6	151.4	171.7

Source: Central Statistics Office, Ministry of Statistics and Programme Implementation, Government of India

while referring to the high policy rates kept by the RBI. Costlier borrowings have prompted consumers to defer purchases of various types of goods and services. Shrinking demand from Europe, which is battling sovereign debt worries has affected exports, especially for India's handicrafts, gems and jewellery, leather and textile sectors. India's exports growth moderated to 10.8 per cent in October 2011 and experts say could contract in the coming months.

Weak Finances and Widening Deficit

A slowing economy is squeezing federal finances and analysts questioned the government's ability to restrict the fiscal gap for the financial year 2011-12 at the budgeted level of 4.6 per cent of gross domestic product (GDP).

Slowing tax revenues, along with stalled share sales in state-run firms hurt by depressed market conditions, have added to the government's woes.

Many private economists saw the deficit for the year overshooting the 5 per cent mark. The RBI warned of inflationary risks if the government's deficit for the year 2011-12 exceeded the budget target. As headwinds to global growth gain pace, several central banks around the world have begun to cut interest rates to shield their economies. But the Reserve Bank of India (RBI) has so far been an outlier and has continued with its tight monetary stance.

However, in an acknowledgement of mounting risks to economic growth, the RBI signalled towards the end of calendar year 2012, a pause in the rate tightening cycle after raising interest rates 13 times since March 2010 to control inflation that stayed above 9 per cent for nearly a year.

Low export numbers in October 2011 widened the trade deficit to a four-year high of $ 19.6 billion. The trade ministry saw the trade deficit for the full year to be in excess of US$ 150 billion, but expected a slowdown in imports in the last few months of the 2011-12.

This in turn could widen current account deficit for 2011-12 to 3 per cent of GDP from 2.6 per cent in 2010-11. The partially convertible rupee has been the worst performing currency in Asia for 2011-12, having shed more than 9 per cent against the dollar.

Because of the policies which the government has been pursuing in the past couple of years, our IIP will go down further in the coming year. It is time that interest rates are lowered and the efforts to bring down the prices are made towards increasing the supply side, eliminating middlemen's profit, hoarding, etc. It is time the machinery of collection of taxes, direct and indirect, is energised like tapping the accumulated pending taxes from various individuals like cine stars, sportsmen, politicians, corporates, etc. It is time government introduces dual pricing policy for petroleum products, issues smart cards to vehicle owners and restricts subsidised supply to an afixed quota and commercial establishments pay market rate for petroleum products.

The government should encourage the farming community to increase the yields. The farming land has contracted substantially during the last couple of years, either due to real estate or SEZ activities which will have direct impact on food grain production. Government should put restrictions on diverting farm land to commerical and real estate activities.

RBI with its regular hike of repo rates and reverse repo rates has been far ahead of most central banks in other countries and has done away with the unconventional monetary policies put in place after the crisis in 2008. In India, inflation has become a structural problem rather than a cyclical problem. There are many factors responsible for inflation and monetary policy alone cannot solve the problem.

India's Current Account Deficit

Any deficit is a problem, whether fiscal or current account. If expenditures are more than income, obviously you are under stress. Persistent current and fiscal deficit is a major problem to the growth of an economy. As India is a developing economy, the expenditures may be higher than incomes. But the critical question is how are the expenditures being financed? If it is largely financed by the short-term flows, then it is a reason to be worried. These sources can die any time and the country's economy can be under pressure.

Inflation further complicates the problem. Many developed countries like USA, UK, and Greece, Ireland, Portugal and Span had deficits and now are under stress with deeper problems. In the past, the South East Asian and Latin American economies had faced similar problems. Suddenly, there is one particular event that triggers a crisis resulting in the funds drying up and causing an economic collapse. So if we do not check fiscal deficit our economy may also see a debt crisis.

RBI's Monetary Policy Statement (2012-13) dated 17 April 2012 also admits high fiscal debt of the Central Government. It says: "The fiscal deficit of the Central Government has remained elevated since 2008-09. The fiscal slippage in 2011-12 was also significantly high. Even though the Union Budget envisages a reduction in the fiscal deficit in 2012-13, several upside risks to the budgeted fiscal deficit remain. In particular, containment of non-plan expenditure within the budget estimates for 2012-13 is contingent upon the Government's ability to adhere to its commitment of capping subsidies. Going by the recent burden-sharing arrangements with the oil marketing companies (OMCs), the budget estimate of compensation for under-recoveries of OMCs at the present level of international crude prices is likely to fall significantly short of the required amount. Any slippage in the fiscal deficit will have implications for inflation.

Further, the large fiscal deficit also has led to large borrowing requirements by the government. The budgeted net market borrowings through dated securities for 2012-13 at ₹ 4.8 trillion were even higher than the expanded borrowings of ₹ 4.4 trillion last year. Such large borrowings have the potential to crowd out credit to the private sector. Crowding out of the more productive private credit demand will become more critical if there is fiscal slippage.

After raising the policy rate by 375 basis points during March 2010-October 2011 to contain inflation and anchor inflation expectations, the Reserve Bank paused in its mid-quarter review (MQR) of December 2011. Subsequent growth-inflation dynamics prompted the Reserve Bank to indicate that no further tightening was required and that future actions would be towards lowering the rates."[6]

Savings Banks Deposit Rate Deregulation

Reserve Bank of India also deregulated savings bank interest rates in October 2011. In a statement, the RBI said banks are free to determine the savings bank deposit rate subject to two conditions: (i) Each bank will have to offer a uniform interest rate on savings bank deposits up to ₹ 1 lakh, irrespective of the amount in the account within this limit. (ii) For savings bank deposits over ₹ 1 lakh, a bank may provide differential rates of interest, if it so chooses. However, there should not be any discrimination from customer to customer on interest rates for similar amount of deposit.

Most experts said this was the most significant announcement in the RBI policy. C. Rangarajan said freeing the savings deposit rate would result in competition in banks but "would settle down". "Banks will have to take the cost of maintaining savings deposits (primarily because cheques can be issued and collected on these deposits) into account", he said, adding that "interest rates would be determined by the costs incurred by banks on these deposits". He said the savings rate might end up 1-2 percentage points above the current 4 per cent.

In India, savings deposits account for almost a quarter of total bank deposits. For decades, RBI has been setting interest rates on savings accounts and, starting last May and right up until this move, the rate was 4 per cent. In contrast, time deposits generally carry much higher nominal interest rates of 8.5 per cent to 9.5 per cent. Amid the current inflation of over 9 per cent, this implies that savers have substantial negative real return on their savings deposits.

It is believed that a direct consequence of this policy is that banks will offer higher interest rates to compete for savings deposits, thereby undermining the role these deposits play as a relatively stable and low-cost funding source. Beatrice Woo and Sally Yim at Moody's Investors Service expect the move to exacerbate already increasing pressure on net interest margins and asset quality. They said, "We expect public-sector banks to be the ones most negatively affected by this development. Collectively, they hold just over half of the system's savings deposits thanks to their large and wide branch networks across the country."[7]

For example, State Bank of India, the country's largest bank, controls 20 per cent of system deposits with savings accounts making up a third of its deposit base. Deregulation is likely to affect its probability if it increases its SB interest rates. With deregulation, it is likely that public-sector banks will need to pay significantly higher interest to maintain their deposit base, notwithstanding their distribution advantage in the rural areas.

Conversely, private banks, which are perceived to offer superior customer service and more advanced information technology, will use this pricing freedom as a new tool to gain market share. This is especially true for the newer and smaller players that are especially keen to develop stable funding bases. Yes Bank, for example, has announced that it will raise savings interest rates by 200 basis points to 6 per cent.

It is also believed that the measure of competition makes it unlikely that the banking sector including private and public banks, will be able to pass on the entire increase in funding costs to borrowers, implying narrowing interest margins ahead. And, to the extent that banks do raise lending rates to mitigate their increased funding costs, borrowers' debt-servicing capability and banks' asset quality may be undermined.

Bank deposits, which offer higher interest rates and greater liquidity, are apt to lure some customers away from buying savings-type insurance products. There will be no positive effect on insurers' investment income because bank deposits account for only a tiny portion of their portfolio, and insurers, as corporations, are allowed to keep money only in current account (earning zero interest) or term deposits, which already command higher negotiated interest rates.

Most experts have reacted to this deregulating decision favourably. Two arguments have been advanced to support the move. The first is that it would serve depositors well, since it would now allow them to earn a higher return on savings held in such deposits. The second argument is that RBI's efforts to use increases in interest rates to moderate inflation have not worked because the transmission of increases in the apex bank and/or repo rates to the loan rates charged by banks is muted. Since banks have access to funds in the form of savings deposits on which the interest rate is fixed, the cost at which they obtain capital does not rise in proportion to the increase in the RBI's intervention rates. So banks do raise interest rates on their loans, but not adequately, muting the effect of the policy on demand and inflation.

There is reason to believe that it is the second of these arguments that has influenced the RBI to resort to this move. Unwilling (and also unable) to restrict credit flow because of the fear that it will affect growth too adversely, the central bank has decided to maximise the impact of the thirteen interest rate hikes it has announced in recent months on demand. The RBI holds that the policy has been on the anvil, had been seriously considered a couple of times in the recent past and had been made effective now.

Savings bank deposits can be categorised in between current account deposits that pay no interest since they are maintained largely for transactions purposes, and term deposits or fixed deposits that are seen as pure savings products likely to be held till they mature, and are paid higher interest rates depending on their term. The longer the period for which the bank has a guarantee that it has access to the money deposited, the higher would be the interest rate paid to the depositor. For some time now, banks have had the freedom to set the interest rates they offer on term deposits.

Saving bank deposits, from which depositors are free to withdraw their money, are seen as being partly held for transaction purposes and partly for saving purposes, which makes them eligible for an interest rate that is lower than that offered on term deposits. In India's post-Independence financial regulatory framework, the RBI had imposed a flexible cap on interest rates on all deposits. However, while interest rates on fixed deposits were fully deregulated in 1997, the interest rate on savings deposits has remained under RBI control. That rate had remained at 3.5 per cent from March 2003 till April 2011, when it was raised to 4 per cent.

Regulation of deposit interest rates is not specific to India, but has been adopted in the past in many countries, and continues to prevail in many countries including China. In the US, interest rate controls under Regulation Q were introduced as part of the framework instituted by the Glass-Steagall Act in 1933, and were in place till the mid-1980s. The original intent of such regulation was to dampen price competition between banks. In case interest rates are free to be set by banks, they would compete with each other to attract deposits by raising interest rates. One difficulty banks face is that while a substantial part of their resources comes in the form of deposits that can be withdrawn more or less at will, they have to lend on terms that include a fixed maturity, which is inevitably longer than the average maturity of deposits.

If competition between banks to attract deposits raises the cost of funds, while banks are locked into loans charging interest rates that are not changeable till maturity, the interest rate spread gets squeezed, leading to lower profits or losses. Since savings deposits can be seen as partly savings products and not maintained just for transaction purposes, banks tend to treat these as part of their core deposits, which determines how much they lend. This is also justified because of the fact that some account holders withdraw money from their saving banks accounts, while many others deposit money in their accounts, and thus, the overall deposit with banks is not effected. It goes on increasing over a period of time with the opening of more accounts and deposit of more money in the savings bank accounts. Based on the average monthly minimum balance maintained on savings deposits, the RBI too identifies 90 per cent of savings bank deposits as core deposits. This means that the banks can lend relatively long against such deposits, increasing the probability of an interest-rate mismatch if deposit rates rise sharply due to competition. This would result in a situation where banks suffer losses, turn fragile and face closure.[8]

Savings deposits are only one form (and not the dominant form) in which households invest their savings. Since interest rates on term deposits are already free, the effect of liberalisation of rates on savings deposits is expected to be marginal and manageable. This, however, is not all truth. The access to cash or liquidity that savings deposits offer to depositors, have made them an important means of holding savings for households. The household sector accounts for close to 85 per cent of all savings deposits in India's banks, and these deposits account for about 13 per cent of the savings in financial assets of households. This compares with a total of 55 per cent of household savings in financial assets held as deposits with the banking system. Term deposits because of the higher return they offer are more popular. But 13 per cent of household savings is not a small amount. Given the substantial contribution of the household sector to aggregate savings, even this proportion makes savings deposits an important source of funds for banks, amounting to 22 per cent of all bank deposits.[9]

Impact of Savings Rate Deregulation

A likely outcome of interest rate liberalisation, according to C.P. Chandrasekhar would be a decline of the share of public banks in savings deposits. In order to wean depositors away from public banks, in the aftermath of interest rate liberalisation, private banks may hike interest rates on savings deposits, so as to increase their presence in the domestic market. Public sector banks would be forced to follow or lose a part of their business, or both. This could damage the profitability of the public banks, which even now bear a disproportionate share of the social obligations imposed on the banking system. Further, they would be forced into finding ways of reducing their commitment to financial inclusion. In sum, the likelihood is that the liberalisation of savings deposit rates would weaken the public banking system and be adverse from the points of view of growth, of financial inclusion and of stability.[10]

Dr. Subbarao defended the policy of savings bank rate deregulation saying that it will bring a healthy competition among the banks and benefit a large number of small depositors in the country. A large number of people will be lured to come in the mainstream financial system.

Along with regular hike in policy rates, savings bank rate deregulation is inter alia aimed at controlling money supply and curbing demand.

There was a mixed response to the deregulation. R.K. Bakshi, executive director of Bank of Baroda, said that this policy could be a landmark for the banking industry with regard to the savings rate deregulation and formation of working group for credit pricing. With respect to cost of funds and its impact on profits, which is likely to be a major concern of the banks, he said that it depends on how much the rate is hiked by. According to the latest policy, investment up to rupees one lakh will return with same interest rate. "I don't think up to rupees one lakh, even with the present 4 per cent rate of interest paid on daily balance basis, there is much scope to increase rate", Bakshi said.

Nilesh Shah of Axis Bank also praised the policy of deregulation. On banks, he said that they have a position to tackle whereby savings rate will get deregulated on one hand while on the other, there will be non-discrimination credit pricing coming into play. "Clearly, banks will have to take out some amount of productivity gains to ensure that both these factors don't impact the profitability and growth", Shah said. "They will have to price their products properly", he added.

Romesh Sobti, Managing Director and Chief Executive Officer, IndusInd Bank, agreed that banks could face margin compression in the near-term if savings rate is hiked. "But banks will also have the freedom to moderate their transaction cost", he said. "So to some extent, the cost increase will be absorbed through optimization of the cost of transactions", he continued to say. According to him, banks with bigger portfolios will need to rejig their business model accordingly.

Experts like Sanju Verma of Violet Arch Capital Advisors do not approve of the savings rate deregulation. "You cannot have savings rate deregulation without touching the other end of the spectrum with respect to transaction cost, recognition of NPAs, tweaking around with the SLR norms...all of which indirectly pad up the cost for banks", she pointed out. "I am slightly surprised that after having announced a ₹ 53,000 crore additional borrowing on the part of the government..., the RBI has still chosen to go ahead and do this", she added.

It is pertinent to note that the government had attributed the increased borrowing to the shrinkage of small savings to about ₹ 26,000-27,000 crore. "Now, if you are going to deregulate savings rate from the current 4 per cent odd, what are you going to do with the PPF rate, the EPFO rate, the postal savings rate, the rate attracted by RBI bonds, the rate attracted by other tax-free infrastructure bonds, because in some sense, all of these are linked and at least take a moral high ground from the savings rate", Verma said. "So if you are going to have this savings rate tomorrow at 6 or 7 per cent speaking hypothetically, are you saying the EPFO rate will be going up from current 9 per cent to 11 per cent? Are you saying that the National Housing Bond tax free rates will go up from 7-8 per cent to 9 per cent? What about the RBI bonds themselves?", she questioned and concluded this has been a hasty decision.[11]

RBI's policy in this regard is quite confusing, especially considering the fact that EPF rate for 2011-12 was reduced from 9.30 per cent to 8.25 per cent in March 2011.

Within hours of the central bank's announcement, Yes Bank, declared it was raising its savings rate to 6 per cent in a blatant effort to attract customers. It is being felt that large banks like State Bank of India and HDFC Bank stand to lose customers to comparatively smaller banks because of this deregulation.

Rana Kapoor, the Chief Executive of Yes Bank, felt that lured by higher rates and better service, Indians would save more and put more of their savings in banks, which could then be used to finance infrastructure and industry. "Let's face it, anywhere between one-third to 45 per cent of the savings are not in the banking system", he said. "And the savings propensity is sluggish, around 30 to 35 per cent. We need savings propensity to rise to 40 to 45 per cent in this decade." While Kapoor's prediction may seem aggressive, he is right when he speaks about the state of Indian savings. India's savings amount to 33.7 per cent of its gross domestic product. That is relatively high by world standards though lower than in China, which saves 50 per cent of its GDP.

One of the unintended outcomes of savings bank rates deregulation would be that since Indian rupee is trading at over 50 to the dollar, many expatriates will be lured to send money home to earn higher exchange value and a higher rate of interest when savings rates in many American and European banks are at or below one per cent. There will thus be more liquidity—a proposition not to the liking of our policymakers who have been using high interest rate as tool of controlling inflation. Thus, the RBI's decision of deregulating saving bank interest rates for controling inflation may not work.

If deregulation drives banks to push rates from 4 per cent into the 6 per cent range, it would increase the costs of banks. Their profits may fall by as much as 50 per cent. With banks already feeling the heat due to high interest rates and persistent inflation, the move comes as a huge blow. "Already banks are under pressure with slow growth in their loan books and high interest rates", said Jagannadham Thunuguntla, head of research at SMC Global. "Against that backdrop, deregulation on savings accounts will be a new bullet to bite for the banking system." The total savings bank balance in the entire banking system is around $ 292 billion, if the savings interest rate goes up just 1 per cent, the Indian banks will have to pay about $ 2.9 billion extra in interest.

"This is a major step that is likely to benefit the entire industry in the long-run", said Kuntal Sur, a director at KPMG India who saw the brighter side of the picture. "It will give customers as well as banks freedom to set rates at whatever level they think is most appropriate." But it is difficult to see how banks would recover high costs due to increased interest rates. If they increase lending rates, the industry, on which the growth of economy largely depends, will suffer.

According to some analysts, the end of decades of regulated interest rates will raise the cost of funds and squeeze margins, and leave their customer base in urban India open to better offerings from low-cost rivals from the private sector. The reform, one of the biggest in the industry for years, will favour banks with better technology, bold marketing strategies and the impulse to innovate. It will also play to private sector expertise and experience of other markets where fiercer rivalry for depositors' funds is the norm.

As said earlier, offering higher interest rates on saving deposits aims at luring people to save more and spend less, easing out the demand and bringing the prices down. But whether it will actually happen or not and if yes, to what extent, will be seen only in later times, somewhere in the second or third quarter of 2012-13.

Views of Industry Officials on RBI Interest Rate Hike

As stated earlier, RBI's policy of keeping interest rates high has not gone well with industry people. We have also seen how it has adversely impacted industrial production. Given below are the views of various industry officials on RBI's interest rate hikes in the recent past. Those views sum up the whole position and present comments on RBI's policy:

"We are confident that no further rate hikes will take place but worries about growth remain. The industry has been expecting a slowdown in the economy but RBI was not acknowledging it. Finally they have acknowledged there is a slowdown by revising down the growth forecast.

For the paints industry, the constant rate increases have severely affected demand as they have impacted the auto and housing industry. So we are hoping, if the rate rise cycle comes to an end with this, then demand can show signs of revival in a minimum of 6-10 months."

—H.M. Bharuka, Managing Director, Kansai Nerolac

"It's a difficult scenario, our margins are getting hurt because of higher interest costs. On the other hand, our consumers like real estate firms are in a tight spot too. This is hurting demand for our products. Also, containing inflation by raising interest rates seems to be having no impact as the inflation is largely because of supply side issues."

—Anil Gupta, Chairman and Managing Director, Kei Industries

"Every industry runs on cash flows, and by raising rates, the RBI is curbing this flow. Thankfully, the spending power of Indians is not dead like that of the people in the US and the banks are still strong. But this development will slow GDP growth...and by no means curb the rising inflation."

—D.S. Kulkarni, CMD, DS Kulkarni Developers

"The positive side is the language used by the RBI, indicating they will look at moderating. I think the government and the Reserve Bank are getting concerned that we can get into a period of high inflation and low growth. Still, at this point in time they could have put off the increase in my view, because the economy is likely to grow just above 7 per cent."

—Venu Srinivasan, Chairman, TVS Motor Co. Ltd.

"The corporate margins would be under pressure given the increase in interest rates, leading to a compression on spends in capex. For home buyers, this would result in an increase in outflow of EMI (equated monthly installments), which will lead to a compression in demand in new home purchases."

—N. Shridhar, Group Director,
Business Strategy & Finance, DB Realty

"So far, they have not been able to check inflation that remains unabated. They must look at some other means instead of just keep raising the repo rate. We all know it's a demand dampener. I hope it is the last one."

—Sunil Sikka, President, Havells India

"The industry is already reeling under high interest rates. Things will get even worse after this. Funding costs will rise as interest rates will have a spiralling effect on everything. In such a situation, the demand becomes lower, so your production goes down and costs go up. There will be pressure on profitability. Things are very difficult for the industry. The government seems to be thinking that only by increasing the rates they can bring down the inflation."

—Paban K. Kataky, Director, Exide Industries

"This might be the last rate hike. But corporates are unlikely to take any new investment decisions at these levels. They would rather wait for the rates to soften."

—B. Hariharan, Group Finance Director,
Ballarpur Industries

"This is definitely going to impact the sector. They are choking out whatever breath is left in the market. We don't see the logic behind the hike. The direct impact of the hike would be on the EMI (equated monthly installments) of buyers, so new home buyers would hesitate to enter the market. This could likely lead to a dip in sales."[12]

—Pravin Malkani, Managing Director,
Patel Realty India, a Unit of Patel Engineering

The views of these key industry officials are indicative of the fact that they are not happy with RBI's high interest policy which has adversely impacted almost every segment of industry.

They are asking for a change in this policy stance so that the businesses do not suffer further.

The Fall of Rupeee and Its Impact

The rupee depreciated against major currencies in the last quarter of 2011-12. Against the US dollar, it tumbled to a record low of ₹ 52.73 on 22 Nov. 2011. This made oil imports costlier and even if crude oil prices fall globally, the landed cost of oil in India will be much higher.

Since most Indian imports are in US dollar, imported raw material for all industries will get costlier and import-intensive industries like automobiles, capital goods and IT hardware may be particularly hit.

The virtual collapse of the rupee points to the fact that the Indian economy is going haywire. "Fiscal deficit is mounting, investments, both domestic and foreign, have been hit, GDP growth is slowing down, industrial production is weak, FII inflows have dried up."[13]

Describing the sharp depreciation of the rupee as disruptive, the Reserve Bank said in the last week of Nov. 2011 that any action to arrest the fall will be guided by medium-term considerations. "We don't really have a target or a rate in mind. It's moving as per market dynamics. It (fall in the value of the rupee) is disruptive, there is no question. There will be impact on our import bill, particularly for energy. It's having an impact on companies and it is a problem", Reserve Bank Deputy Governor Subir Gokarn said.

On the possibility of action by the central bank to arrest the fall of the rupee, Gokarn said, "Any action we take now will have to take into account the fact that these actions might have consequences a little further down the road. So we have got to balance out actions with risks or a potential increase in vulnerability later on...."[14]

The immediate impact of the fall in the value of rupee, he said, will be on the inflation rate, which has been hovering near the double-digit mark for several months.

Amid sustained fall in rupee's value, the Plan panel attributed the decline to volatility in the global currency market, but expressed the hope that the Indian currency would stabilize soon.

"It has been a period of enormous currency volatility and you are going to look at what has happened in the Indian currency market in the light of what is happening globally. I think it will settle down", Planning Commission Deputy Chairman Montek Singh Ahluwalia said.[15]

The Indian rupee is the fourth most depreciated currency in the world and the most depreciated in the Asian continent. The RBI has attributed the movement to demand-supply factors and said it is happening globally. A weaker rupee is a matter of concern for India as it depends on imports for over 70 per cent of its oil and gas requirements and the depreciation of the local currency has made imports more expensive. The depreciation of the rupee comes at a time when the headline inflation has remained above the 9 per cent mark for 11 consecutive months. Higher imports of raw material and saleable goods translate into higher prices for the consumers.

Meanwhile, Reserve Bank of India Deputy Governor Subir Gokarn said the central bank will weigh possibilities of action on rupee. He further said that action on rupee was not an easy judgement and such action will be aimed at volatility.

The finance ministry's signal that the central bank may not sell dollars aggressively to stem the local currency's depreciation also led to the fall. India's central bank also expressed hesitation about intervening to support the rupee, suggesting it may not even have the resources.

Criticising the Reserve Bank for not intervening in the currency markets, Surjit Bhalla, Managing Director of Oxus Research and Investments said, "The RBI has intervened several times in the past but in the last six months they have perhaps been preoccupied with different things." He said that RBI's move not to intervene would backfire and lead to higher inflation. "If they were worried about inflation, and thought that the rupee was a tool to arrive at controlling inflation, they should have stopped the depreciation because imported goods especially oil cost more", he said. "It's senseless that we need to be worried about inflation and hence not interfere in the currency markets", he added.

While exports will be cheaper, currencies of other countries have also fallen against the dollar, although not as much, diminishing India's advantage.

Numerous corruption scandals, accusations of policy paralysis and a worsening fiscal situation with the administration overshooting borrowing targets for the second half of the year by 32 per cent have put pressure on the rupee.[16]

Rupee Plunge may Negate India's Anti-inflationary Measures

It is believed that the rupee's slide vis-à-vis the US dollar may fuel inflationary pressures in the economy and weaken the central bank's defences against high prices as it offsets some of the moderating impact of last 21 months' rate hikes on domestic demand.

"It will be definitely blunt the high base impact. We will have to rework the inflation numbers, as we had not taken this into account. We had expected December 2011 inflation at 8.2 per cent", said Abheek Barua, chief economist at HDFC Bank. And as it turned out, it was actually above 8.2.

According to a Yes Bank report, every 10 per cent fall in the rupee is likely to lift the inflation rate based on the wholesale price index (WPI) by 40 basis points.

Traders have been buying the 'safe haven' dollar amid the prolonged debt crisis in the euro zone. Back home, demand for the greenback from oil companies, major importers of crude oil, further pulled the rupee down.

In its "Macroeconomic and Monetary Development Report", in October 2011, the RBI had also acknowledged that the depreciation of the rupee raises the risk of imported inflation. "The rupee has depreciated by about 11 per cent against the dollar during 2011-12. India's imports account for about 22 per cent of GDP and depreciation of the rupee raises the risk of imported inflation", the RBI had said in the October report.

Rupee depreciation has already started to push up prices in some sectors like automobile, consumer goods, and mobile phones. The makers of consumer durables have raised product prices by up to 10 per cent, as their import costs have gone up because of the rupee's depreciation.

State-owned oil marketing companies, which sell diesel and cooking fuels at government-controlled prices, are also piling up revenue losses as a falling rupee is pushing up the cost of oil imports. Every rupee's fall against the dollar pushes up the combined gross revenue loss for Indian Oil Corp. Ltd., Bharat Petroleum Corp. Ltd. and Hindustan Petroleum Corp. Ltd. by a staggering ₹ 8,000 crore. The current year's gross revenue loss of these oil companies is already pegged at a massive ₹ 1,30,000 crore, and the government will now be under pressure to bear at least a part of the jump in production costs.

If a barrel of oil is currently at $ 100 with rupee at 48 to a dollar, its domestic price will be ₹ 4,800. If the rupee falls to 50, the cost will rise to ₹ 5,000. However, if, at the same time, the price of crude eases to $ 97, the price will settle lower at ₹ 4,850 and negate the impact of rupee fall to an extent.

The RBI Deputy Governor Subir Gokarn said market forces must determine the level of the rupee, indicating that the central bank was not keen to intervene in the currency market.[17]

Falling Rupee Deters Investors

Falling rupee is bad news for Indian investors on two counts. First, a weak rupee would push up the fiscal deficit further. India imports around 70 per cent of its requirement of crude oil and the government will have to pay more for it in rupee terms. Due to the control on oil prices, the government may not be able to pass on the high prices to the consumers.

This will strain its finances and lead to an increase in fiscal deficit. Also, higher oil prices would push up inflation. Higher inflation is bad news for not just your wallet but also for companies because they will also have to pay more in rupee terms for their raw materials, despite the fall in global commodity prices, due to a depreciating rupee. More importantly, a weak rupee could negatively impact FII flows into the Indian markets.[18]

Falling Rupee and Food Prices

People will feel the impact of the weakening rupee, which hit a record low of 52 to a dollar in November 2011, most in terms of high food prices. India imports a number of food items such as pulses and edible oil, to meet domestic demand. A falling rupee simply makes imports costlier since India now has to pay more, in terms of rupees, for the same goods and services it imports.

According to a Reserve Bank report, a declining rupee and higher minimum support price (MSP) pose fresh risks to food prices. "Despite a normal monsoon during 2011 and record production of food grains in 2010, food price inflation may not moderate much in an environment of increase in rural wages, significant increase in MSPs and persistent input cost pressures in the farm sector", the central bank believed.

India imports 21 per cent of world's pulses to meet domestic demand, according to Pravin Dongre, president of the Mumbai-based Indian Pulses & Grains Association. "Prices of commonly consumed pulses, which have been so far stable, will go up somewhat on the back of a weaker rupee", Dongre said.

A weak rupee also directly cranks up the government's fuel expenses, which fans prices of most other goods. The value of oil imported by India, in dollar terms, has declined since July 2011 owing to a fall in global crude prices. In rupee terms, however, it has increased due to the domestic currency's depreciation.

There was no let up in the prices of goods which continued to rise or remain high. October's Retail Price Index went up by 0.88 per cent, according to figures released by the National Statistics Office. This primarily reflected an increase of 4.15 per cent in the clothing and footwear index, due to seasonally higher prices of garments. An upward movement in the prices of vegetables, fruit and fish caused the food index to go up by 2.70 per cent. Higher prices for non-durable household goods underlay an increase of 0.74 per cent in the other goods and services index. The household equipment and house maintenance cost index edged up by 0.58 per cent, mainly on account of a rise in the prices of household utensils. An increase of 0.13 per cent was recorded in the beverages and tobacco index, mainly due to price rises in non-alcoholic beverages.

Interest Rates and Bonds

Some experts believe that if the interest rates become market-linked, it will not be a big benefit to the investors. The government may fix the rate for the next 12 months, but if interest rates go down a year after, the rate will also follow suit.

Small savings interest rates have been increased by some banks, following the deregulation but the hike is not very significant. If you look at them from a short-term perspective of about 1-2 years, the open-ended debt fund will outperform the term deposits. Today, you will get 8.6 per cent on your PPF because the interest rates are high. At the same time, short-term debt funds are giving returns of 9-10 per cent. However, one year down the line, when interest rates go down to, say, 7 per cent, the PPF interest rate will also go down. In the case of a short-term fund, you will not only get the accrued interest but also the capital gain. Interest rates keep on changing as per economic conditions, but in other investments like in bonds and mutual funds they remain more or less constant. Besides, there is tax exemption in these investments, which is not available in case of saving banks interest.

The views of Technical Advisory Committee (TAC) on the RBI's monetary policy followed in the first half of financial year 2011-12 are given below:

The TAC members reviewed the recent global and domestic macroeconomic developments. They felt that the global macroeconomic situation continued to be fragile. Most members were not very optimistic about the immediate resolution of the euro area debt problem and felt that the probability of an event shock was high. The policy response by the authorities was too little and too late. The negative impact in the case of an event shock on emerging economies could be serious through the trade, financing and confidence channels. Members expressed concern over the slow growth in the US. They also observed that the growth was slowing down in emerging market economies.

Reflecting on the domestic macroeconomic developments, all members felt that the economic growth was moderating. In particular, investment activity was slowing down due to tight monetary policy and several other factors, including global uncertainty and delay in clearing the projects. A concern was also expressed about the services sector, which was showing signs of moderation. Some members felt that exports growth will slow down, as a result of which trade deficit may widen.

Some other members felt that inflation was driven by external/supply-side factors and, therefore, the monetary policy tightening was impacting investment and growth and not inflation. In view of slowing global economy, it was expected that the global commodity prices may soften gradually, which should help moderate inflation, going forward.

Some members raised concerns over the high fiscal deficit and the risk of it slipping in the financial year 2011-12. This, combined with the increase in borrowings by the government, will pose a major challenge for liquidity and monetary management for the Reserve Bank. If right policy measures are not adopted, the consequences may be dangerous for India's economy.

Notes

1. Gaurav Choudhary. *Hindustan Times*, 13 March 2012.
2. Reserve Bank of India. Press Release, 15 March 2012.
3. D. Subbarao (RBI Governor). "Reserve Bank of India Monetary Policy Statement", 2012-13, 17 April 2012.
4. *The Hindu*, 11 November 2011.
5. *Economic Times*, 15 Novermber 2011.
6. D. Subbarao (RBI Governor). "Reserve Bank of India Monetary Policy Statement 2012-13", 17 April 2012.
7. Beatrice Woo and Sally Yim. "India's Deregulation of Savings Interest Rates will Reduce Banks Profitability", *Capital Market*, 31 October 2011.
8. C.P. Chandrasekhar. "Interest Rates: Breaching the Last Dyke", *The Hindu*, 30 October 2011.

9. *Ibid.*
10. *Ibid.*
11. http://www.moneycontrol.com/news/economy/savings-rate-deregulation-may-bebad-idea-say-experts_605345.html
12. Press Trust of India, 22 November 2011.
13. Sanjeev Sharma Tribune News Service, New Delhi, 21 November 2011.
14. Press Trust of India, 22 November 2011.
15. *Ibid.*, 21 November 2011.
16. *The Express Tribune*, 21 November 2011.
17. *DNA Newspaper*, 22 November 2011.
18. *The Economic Times*, 19 September 2011.

ANNEXURE-I

Table A1: Wholesale Price Index and Rates of Inflation (Base Year: 2004-05=100)

Commodities/Major Groups/Groups/ Sub-Groups	Weight	WPI Feb., 2012	Latest month		Build up from March		Year on year	
			2010-11	2011-12	2010-11	2011-12	2010-11	2011-12
ALL COMMODITIES	100.00000	158.4	0.07	0.44	8.66	**5.95**	9.54	6.95
PRIMARY ARTICLES	20.11815	201.5	-2.92	0.90	14.29	**7.07**	15.89	6.28
Food Articles	14.33709	192.3	-5.77	0.47	10.82	**7.43**	10.95	6.07
Cereals	3.37323	178.0	0.86	0.17	5.11	**3.31**	3.43	1.71
Rice	1.79348	173.0	-0.12	0.06	4.35	**3.59**	3.84	1.53
Wheat	1.11595	169.7	1.08	0.35	2.49	**-1.96**	-1.28	-4.18
Pulses	0.71662	208.7	1.84	-1.32	-2.77	**9.27**	-5.24	7.91
Vegetables	1.73553	160.7	-39.37	8.22	19.92	**12.14**	14.38	1.52
Potato	0.20150	105.9	-15.85	7.08	2.75	**-0.94**	-10.86	-2.22
Onion	0.17794	134.2	-57.93	-11.30	52.13	**-25.07**	5.17	-48.50
Fruits	2.10717	169.8	5.50	-1.39	17.24	**-7.97**	17.48	-0.53
Milk	3.23818	201.5	0.61	0.20	7.89	**15.41**	12.54	11.70
Egg, Meat & Fish	2.41384	230.4	-0.62	0.52	11.56	**17.91**	12.74	20.00
Non-Food Articles	4.25756	186.7	5.39	2.13	27.48	**-2.46**	34.36	-2.56
Fibres	0.87737	197.0	20.03	-1.60	85.97	**-30.54**	89.23	-29.89
Oil Seeds	1.78051	164.3	3.66	0.67	10.28	**8.81**	7.90	9.39
Minerals	1.52350	329.6	1.19	1.57	13.60	**23.54**	17.72	25.28
FUEL & POWER	14.91021	173.2	1.45	0.23	9.56	**9.90**	12.37	12.83
Liquefied petroleum gas	0.91468	147.3	0.00	0.00	14.99	**14.27**	14.99	14.27
Petrol	1.09015	177.7	2.65	0.00	23.14	**12.04**	28.73	12.04
High speed diesel	4.67020	167.8	0.00	0.00	6.22	**9.24**	12.45	9.24
MANUFACTURED PRODUCTS	64.97164	141.7	1.06	0.35	6.18	**4.50**	6.26	5.75
Food Products	9.97396	153.4	-0.14	0.00	2.40	**5.72**	0.00	5.72
Sugar	1.73731	176.4	-2.08	-0.28	-7.73	**3.46**	-15.43	4.13
Edible Oils	3.04293	139.2	1.73	-0.14	13.51	**8.07**	13.01	7.57
Beverages, Tobacco & Tobacco Product	1.76247	166.8	0.60	1.28	6.69	**7.96**	8.60	10.10
Cotton Textiles	2.60526	139.8	4.90	0.43	25.22	**-9.63**	26.74	-3.92
Man Made Textiles	2.20573	119.4	2.47	-0.33	10.98	**-2.21**	13.60	-0.75
Wood & Wood Products	0.58744	163.5	0.53	0.18	3.21	**7.78**	3.78	8.21
Paper & Paper Products	2.03350	132.3	1.26	-0.08	7.28	**2.16**	7.10	3.20
Leather & Leather Products	0.83509	130.6	0.49	-0.46	-2.83	**4.06**	-1.20	5.49
Rubber & Plastic Products	2.98697	134.1	1.00	-0.15	9.14	**0.83**	9.60	2.13
Chemicals & Chemical Products	12.01770	137.9	1.43	0.36	6.06	**6.65**	6.59	7.99
Non-Metallic Mineral Products	2.55597	155.9	1.32	-0.19	2.17	**5.12**	2.53	6.71
Cement & Lime	1.38646	160.2	1.96	-0.12	0.00	**4.23**	0.47	5.95
Basic Metals Alloys & Metal Product	10.74785	161.9	2.16	0.75	10.39	**9.17**	11.14	10.44
Iron & Semis	1.56301	161.1	3.96	1.64	12.36	**14.83**	14.30	15.82
Machinery & Machine Tools	8.93148	125.9	0.16	0.32	2.51	**2.11**	3.38	2.78
Transport Equipment & Parts	5.21282	125.5	0.08	0.16	2.96	**2.53**	2.96	3.21

Source: http://eaindustry.nic.in/cmonthly.pdf

Table A2: Global Inflation Indicators

Country/ Region	Key Policy Rate	Policy Rate (as on April 13, 2012)	Changes in Policy Rates (basis points)			CPI Inflation (y-o-y, per cent)	
			Sep15, 2008 to Aug 23, 2009	Aug. 23, 2009 to Oct 25, 2011	Since Oct 25, 2011	Mar-11	Mar-12
1	2	3	4	5	6	7	8
Advanced Economies							
Australia	Cash Rate	4.25 (Dec. 7, 2011)	(-) 400	175	(-) 50	2.7#	3.1#
Canada	Overnight Rate	1.00 (Sep. 8, 2010)	(-) 275	75	0	2.2$	2.6$
Euro area	Interest Rate on Main Refinancing Operations	1.00 (Dec. 14, 2011)	(-) 325	50	(-) 50	2.7	2.6
Japan	Uncollateralised Overnight Call Rate	0.0 to 0.10 (Oct. 5, 2010)*	(-) 40	(-) 10	0	-0.5$	0.3$
UK	Official Bank Rate	0.50 (Mar. 5,2009)	(-) 450	0	0	4.4$	3.4$
US	Federal Funds Rate	0.0 to 0.25 (Dec.16,2008)*	(-) 200	0	0	2.7	2.7
Developing Economies							
Brazil	Selic Rate	9.75 (March 8, 2012)	(-) 500	275	(-)175	6.3	5.2
India	Repo Rate	8.50 (Oct. 25, 2011)	(-) 425 (-400)	375 (100)	0 (-125)	8.8$	7.6$
China	Benchmark 1-year Deposit Rate	3.50 (Jul. 7, 2011)	(-) 214	100	0	5.4	3.6
	Benchmark 1-year Lending Rate	6.56 (Jul. 7, 2011)	(-) 241 (-200)	100 (600)	0 (-100)		
Indonesia	BI Rate	5.75 (Feb. 9, 2012)	(-) 275	0	(-) 75	6.7	4.0
Israel	Key Rate	2.50 (Jan. 23, 2012)	(-) 375	275	(-) 75	4.2$	1.7$
Korea	Base Rate	3.25 (Jun 10, 2011)	(-) 325	125	0	4.1	2.6
Philippines	Reverse Repo Rate	4.00 (March 1, 2012)	(-) 200	25	(-) 50	4.8	2.6
	Repo Rate	6.00 (March 1, 2012)	(-) 200	25	(-) 50		
Russia	Refinancing Rate	8.00 (December 26, 2011)	(-) 25	(-) 250	(-) 25	9.5$	3.7$
South Africa	Repo Rate	5.50 (Nov. 19, 2010)	(-) 500	(-) 150	0	3.7$	6.1$
Thailand	1-day Repurchase Rate	3.00 (Jan. 25, 2012)	(-) 250	225	(-) 50	3.1	3.5

*: Change is worked out from the minimum point of target range.

#: Q4 of 2011.

$: February.

Note: Figures in parentheses in column (3) indicate the effective dates when the policy rates were last revised.

Figures in parentheses in column (4, 5 & 6) indicate the variation in the cash reserve ratio during the period.

For India, data on inflation pertain to CPI for Industrial Workers.

Source: Websites of respective central banks/statistical agencies

Table A3: Comparative Movement of Oil Price and Exchange Rate Since July 2011

	July 2011	December 2012	Fortnight March 16-31, 2012	Change in per cent (July 2011-December 2012)	Change in per cent (December 2012-March 16-31, 2012)
1	2	3	4	5	6
Crude oil Indian Basket (US$)	112.5	107.2	123.2	-4.7	14.9
Exchange Rate (₹/US$)	44.4	52.7	50.8	18.6	-3.6
Crude Indian Basket (₹)	4995.8	5646.8	6253.1	13.0	10.7

Note: The composition of Indian Basket of Crude Oil represents the Average of Oman & Dubai for sour grades and Brent (Dated) for sweet grade in the ratio of 67.6:32.4.

Source: Petroleum Planning and Analysis Cell

2

High Interest Rates and GDP Growth

Recent data and reports indicate that India's GDP growth rate has moderated due to the high interest rate policy adopted by the RBI. Growth is slowing sharply in India, with some economists predicting it to remain below 7 per cent in 2012-13. The industrial output growth rate has dropped to a single digit in the recent months. Industrial production for August 2011 rose by a weaker-than-expected 4.1 per cent, continuing the slide from last year's double-digits.

Analysts feel a slower economic growth rate is acceptable in the short-term, provided it reduces the inflationary pressures. However, the steps taken by the RBI are not yielding the expected results. On the other hand, the measures have started slowing down the economic growth rate, which is a matter of concern.

Inflation vs Growth

The RBI accepted in mid-October 2011 that inflation was 'sticky' and said that GDP growth in the fiscal year 2011-12 was expected to be lower than the earlier envisaged 8 per cent. "Inflation risk persists. The baseline inflation path still remains sticky and broadly unchanged from earlier projections", said the RBI. "In this backdrop, the monetary policy trajectory will need to be guided by the emerging growth-inflation dynamics even as transmission of the past actions is still unfolding", added the regulator. The regulator has hiked policy rates by 3.5 percentage points since March 2011 to choke demand and contain inflation, which stubbornly remained at 9.7 per cent in September 2011.

RBI said growth risks had increased on account of 'global headwinds'—a reference to prospects of a recession in the US and a credit crisis in Europe. "On current assessment, growth in 2011-12 is likely to moderate slightly from that projected earlier", it said. RBI had earlier projected GDP growth for 2011-12 at 8 per cent, down from 8.5 per cent in the previous year. The central bank said planned investment in new projects has fallen 'significantly' since the second half of the fiscal year that ended in March 2011 and remained low in the April-June quarter of 2011-12. "Consequently, the pipeline of investment is likely to shrink, putting growth in 2012-13 at risk", the report said.

Higher Risks to Growth

It is believed that RBI was well aware that its past policy actions are moderating growth and it will be still quite some time when the full effects of cumulative policy action is seen on the growth front. Given that inflation is much above comfort level, the RBI would not have liked to be seen as not doing anything. Hence, there were hikes in policy rates. Given the past hikes, the RBI could have signalled its concern on the inflation front through a much smaller dose of rate hikes or by posturing a hawkish stance. It is well known that monetary policy is more effective in curbing demand in a high-growth scenario than lifting demand in a low-growth environment. It has taken two years for the RBI to compress demand, and we can very well imagine the time it would take to lift demand, if growth were to take a severe hit.

The Finance Minister, Mr Pranab Mukherjee, said that Reserve Bank's rate hikes, aimed at curbing price rise, will also have some impact on economic growth. Talking about the repo rate hike in October 2011, he said, "I do hope that the decision of the RBI to enhance the repo rate and reverse-repo rate by 25 basis points would have its impact on inflation. Of course, it would have some impact on growth also."

Later, in a statement, Mr Mukherjee said the RBI's policy "would help in getting us back to a more comfortable inflation situation soon while leaving scope for growth to pick up in the second half of fiscal year 2011-12". He said the decision had been taken by the RBI to affirm its commitment to tackle inflation as the headline inflation is still high.

The Press Information Bureau (PIB), Government of India, presented its Advance Estimates of National Income, 2011-12 on 7 Feb. 2012. These estimates are based on anticipated level of agriculture, industry and performance of other key-sectors like transportation, communication, banking, insurance, etc. PIB's press note is reproduced below:

The Central Statistics Office (CSO), Ministry of Statistics and Programme Implementation has released the advance estimates of national income at constant (2004-05) and current prices, for the financial year 2011-12.

2. These advance estimates are based on anticipated level of agricultural and industrial production, analysis of budget estimates of government expenditure and performance of key sectors like railways, transport other than railways, communication, banking and insurance.... The advance estimates at current prices are derived by estimating the implicit price deflators (IPDs) at sectoral level from the relevant price indices. The salient features of these estimates are detailed below:

I. ADVANCE ESTIMATES OF NATIONAL INCOME, 2011-12

Estimates at Constant (2004-05) Prices

Gross Domestic Product

3. Gross Domestic Product (GDP) at factor cost at constant (2004-05) prices in the year 2011-12 is likely to attain a level of ₹ 52,22,027 crore, as against the Quick Estimates of GDP for the year 2010-11 of ₹ 48,85,954 crore, released on 31st January 2012. The growth in GDP during 2011-12 is estimated at 6.9 per cent as compared to the growth rate of 8.4 per cent in 2010-11.

4. The growth rate of 6.9 per cent in GDP during 2011-12 has been due to the growth rates of over 8 per cent in the sectors of 'electricity, gas and water supply', 'trade, hotels, transport and communication', and 'financing, insurance, real estate and business services'. There may be slow growth in the sectors of 'agriculture, forestry and fishing' (2.5 per cent), manufacturing (3.9 per cent) and construction (4.8 per cent). The growth in the mining and quarrying sector is estimated to be negative (–2.2 per cent).

Agriculture

5. The 'agriculture, forestry and fishing' sector is likely to show a growth 2.5 per cent in its GDP during 2011-12, as against the previous year's growth rate of 7.0 per cent. According to the information furnished by the Department of Agriculture and Cooperation (DAC), which has been used in compiling the estimate of GDP from agriculture in 2011-12, production of food grains is expected to grow by 2.3 per cent as compared to 12.2 per cent growth in the previous agriculture year. The production of cotton and sugarcane is also expected to rise by 3.3 per cent and 1.6 per cent, respectively, in 2011-12. Among the horticultural crops, production of fruits and vegetables is expected to increase by 3.5 per cent and 2..1 per cent, respectively, during the year 2011-12.

Industry

6. The manufacturing sector is likely to show a growth of 3.9 per cent in GDP during during 2011-12 as against the growth of 7.6 per cent during 2010-11. According to the latest estimates available on the Index of Industrial Production (IIP), the index of manufacturing and electricity registered growth rates of 4.1 per cent and 9.5 per cent, respectively during April-November 2011-12, as compared to the growth rates of 9.0 per cent and 4.5 per cent in these sectors during April-November 2010-11. The mining sector is likely to show a negative growth of 2.2 per cent in 2011-12 as against growth of 5 per cent during 2010-11. The IIP mining registered a decline of 2.5 per cent. The construction sector is likely to show a growth rate of 4.8 per cent during 2011-12 as against growth of 8 per cent in the previous year. The key indicators of construction sector, namely cement production and steel consumption have registered growth rates of 5.3 per cent and 4.4 per cent, respectively during April-December 2011-12.

Services

7. The estimated growth in GDP for the trade, hotels, transport and communication sectors during 2011-12 is placed at 11.2 per cent as against growth of 11.1 per cent in the previous year. This is mainly on account of growth during April-

November 2011-12 of 15.5 per cent in passengers handled in civil aviation. Further, private corporate sector registered significant growth in trade, hotels and restaurant and business services during first half of 2011-12 . There has been an increase of 28.0 per cent in stock of telephone connections as on December 2011. The sales of commercial vehicles witnessed an increase of 19.2 per cent in April-December 2011. The sector, 'financing, insurance, real estate and business services', is expected to show a growth rate of 9.1 per cent during 2011-12, on account of 16.9 per cent growth in aggregate deposits and 15.9 per cent growth in bank credit during April-December 2011 (against the respective growth rates of 28.0 per cent and 19.2 per cent in the corresponding period of previous year). The growth rate of 'community, social and personal services' during 2011-12 is estimated to be 5.9 per cent.

National Income

8. The net national income (NNI) at factor cost, also known as national income, at 2004-05 prices is likely to be ₹ 45,68,249 crore during 2011-12, as against the previous year's Quick Estimate of ₹ 42,68,715 crore. In terms of growth rates, the national income is expected to rise by 7.0 per cent during 2011-12 in comparison to the growth rate of 7.8 per cent in 2010-11.

Per Capita Income

9. The per capita income in real terms (at 2004-05 prices) during 2011-12 is likely to attain a level of ₹ 38,005 as compared to the Quick Estimate for the year 2010-11 of ₹ 35,993. The growth rate in per capita income is estimated at 5.6 per cent during 2011-12, as against the previous year's estimate of 6.4 per cent.

Estimates at Current Prices

Gross Domestic Product

10. GDP at factor cost at current prices in the year 2011-12 is likely to attain a level of ₹ 82,79, 976 crore, showing a growth rate of 15.7 per cent over the Quick Estimates of GDP for the year 2010-11 of ₹ 71,57,412 crore.

National Income

11. The NNI at factor cost at current prices is anticipated to be ₹ 73,28,878 crore during 2011-12, as compared to ₹ 63,25,039 crore during 2010-11, showing a rise of 15.9 per cent.

Per Capita Income

12. The per capita income at current prices during 2011-12 is estimated to be ₹ 60,972 as compared to ₹ 53,331 during 2010-11, showing a rise of 14.3 per cent.

The estimates give an indication how the economy was behaving in the year 2011-12. An impact of RBI's high interest rates is obvious from the estimates, as shown below:

(i) The GDP growth for 2011-12 was slated to be 6.9 per cent as against 8.4 per cent in 2010-11.

Table 2.1: Advance Estimates of National Income and Expenditures on GDP, 2011-12

(At 2004-05 Prices)

Item	2009-10	2010-11 (QE)	2011-12 (AE)
A. ESTIMATES AT AGGREGATE LEVEL			
1. NATIONAL PRODUCT (Rs. Crore)			
1.1 Gross National Income (GNI) at factor cost	4,479,973	4,833,178 (7.9)	5,171,538 (7.0)
1.2 Net National Income (NNI) at factor cost	3,959,653	4,268,715 (7.8)	4,568,249 (7.0)
2. DOMESTIC PRODUCT (Rs. Crore)			
2.1 Gross Domestic Product (GDP) at factor cost	4,507,637	4,885,954 (8.4)	5,222,027 (6.9)
2.2 Gross Domestic Product (GDP) at market prices	4,780,179	5,236,823 (9.6)	5,627,685 (7.5)
2.3 Net Domestic Product (NDP) at factor cost	3,987,317	4,321,491 (8.4)	4,618,739 (6.9)
B. ESTIMATES AT PER CAPITA LEVEL			
Population (million)	1,170	1,186	1,202
Per capita NNI at factor cost (Rs.)	33,843	35,993 (6.4)	38,005 (5.6)
Per capita GDP at factor cost (Rs.)	38,527	41,197	43,444

Note: The figures in parenthesis show the percentage change over previous year

QE: Quick Estimate; AE: Advance Estimate

(ii) Agriculture was likely to grow at 2.5 per cent in 2011-12 as against 7 per cent in 2010-11.

(iii) Industrial growth was estimated at 3.9 per cent in the GDP in 2011-12 as against 7.6 per cent in 2010-11.

(iv) Services were likely to maintain about the same growth rate, i.e. 11.2 cent in 2011-12 compared with 11.1 per cent a year earlier.

It is quite clear that RBI's high interest rate policies have affected all the major sectors, particularly the industrial sector. The advanced estimates also show that the growth rates of national income and per capita income have gone down as compared with previous year's growth rates.

Statement I of the estimates given as Table 2.1 gives advanced estimates of national income and expenditure on GDP for 2011-12, at 2004-05 prices.

Table 2.2: Advance Estimates of National Income for the Year 2011-12
(At Current Prices)

Item	2009-10	2010-11 (QE)	2011-12 (AE)
A. ESTIMATES AT AGGREGATE LEVEL			
1. NATIONAL PRODUCT (Rs. Crore)			
1.1 Gross National Income (GNI) at factor cost	6,053,585	7,078,512 (16.9)	8,198,276 (15.8)
1.2 Net National Income (NNI) at factor cost	5,395,688	6,325,039 (17.2)	7,328,878 (15.9)
2. DOMESTIC PRODUCT (Rs. Crore)			
2.1 Gross Domestic Product (GDP) at factor cost	6,091,485	7,157,412 (17.5)	8,279,976 (15.7)
2.2 Gross Domestic Product (GDP) at market prices	6,457,352	7,674,148 (18.8)	8,912,179 (16.1)
2.3 Net Domestic Product (NDP) at factor cost	5,433,588	6,403,939 (17.9)	7,410,578 (15.7)
2.4 Gross National Disposable Income	6,665,252	7,837,248	9,113,410
B. ESTIMATES AT PER CAPITA LEVEL			
Population (million)	1,170	1,186	1,202
Per capita NNI at factor cost (Rs.)	46,117	53,331 (15.6)	60,972 (14.3)
Per capita GDP at factor cost (Rs.)	52,064	60,349	68,885

Note: The figures in parenthesis show the percentage change over previous year

QE: Quick Estimate; *RE*: Revised Estimate

Statement 2 of the estimates, given as Table 2.2 provides advanced estimates of national income for 2011-12 at current prices.

Table 2.2 provides comparative figures of national income for 2009-10, 2010-11 and 2011-12 (estimates) at current prices. It shows that the percentage growth of national income for national product and domestic product has been slower in 2011-12 as compared with 2010-11.

Statement 3 of the estimates given as Table 2.3 provides advanced estimates of GDP for 2011-12 of factor cost by economic activity at 2004-05 prices.

Table 2.3: Advance Estimates of GDP at Factor Cost by Economic Activity (at Constant 2004-05 Prices)

Rs. Crore

Industry	2009-10	2010-11 (QE)	2011-12 (AE)	Percentage change over previous year	
				2010-11	2011-12
1. Agriculture, forestry & fishing	662,509	709,103	727,161	7.0	2.5
2. Mining & quarrying	104,225	109,421	107,029	5.0	-2.2
3. Manufacturing	719,728	774,162	804,256	7.6	3.9
4. Electricity, gas & water supply	88,266	90,944	98,464	3.0	8.3
5. Construction	355,717	384,199	402,610	8.0	4.8
6. Trade, hotels, transport and communication	1,197,213	1,330,455	1,479,748	11.1	11.2
7. Financing, insurance, real estate & business services	769,883	849,995	927,546	10.4	9.1
8. Community, social & personal services	610,096	637,675	675,213	4.5	5.9
9. GDP at factor cost	4,507,637	4,885,954	5,222,027	8.4	6.9

Table 2.3 shows that the estimated GDP growth in 2011-12 declined from 2010-11 in five industrial sectors: (i) agriculture; (ii) mining and quarrying, where it has registered a negative growth; (iii) manufacturing; (iv) construction; and (v) financing, insurance, etc. In trade, hotels, transport and communication, the growth was almost stagnant at 11.2 per cent in 2011-12 as compared with 11.1 per cent in 2010-11. This is a measure of the impact of RBI's tight money policy to control inflation.

Statement 4 of the estimates given as Table 2.4 provides advanced estimates of GDP for 2011-12 at factor cost by economic activity at current prices.

Table 2.4: Advance Estimates of GDP at Factor Cost by Economic Activity

(at Constant Prices)

Rs. Crore

Industry	2009-10	2010-11 (QE)	2011-12 (AE)	Percentage change over previous year 2010-11	2011-12
1. Agriculture, forestry & fishing	1,079,365	1,269,888	1,430,418	17.7	12.6
2. Mining & quarrying	157,400	191,207	219,978	21.5	15.0
3. Manufacturing	907,032	1,040,345	1,163,653	14.7	11.9
4. Electricity, gas & water supply	112,522	124,038	135,452	10.2	9.2
5. Construction	502,190	585,265	670,778	16.5	14.6
6. Trade, hotels, transport and communication	1,485,476	1,755,531	2,084,171	18.2	18.7
7. Financing, insurance, real estate & business services	962,186	1,170,522	1,395,853	21.7	19.3
8. Community, social & personal services	885,314	1,020,616	1,179,672	15.3	15.6
9. GDP at factor cost	6,091,485	7,157,412	8,279,975	17.5	15.7

Table 2.4 again presents a dismal picture of six sectors in 2011-12 as compared with 2010-11. It is quite clear that RBI's policy of keeping interest rates high to control inflation has adversely impacted the country's GDP growth. Various sectors of the economy have found it difficult to maintain optimum level of production due to high cost of funds. The cost of raw material and labour have also gone high during the last two years, eroding the profit margins. It is apprehended that if RBI continues with its tight money policy, economic growth will be further affected.

Economic surveys up to the financial year 2010-11 had highlighted the growing divergence between the two measures of GDP, namely GDP at factor cost at constant prices (production or value-added method) and GDP at constant market prices (demand-side GDP), arising from the global financial crisis and the policy responses which included fiscal stimuli. As per the latest revisions to GDP announced by the CSO in the Quick

Estimate of national income released on 31 January 2012, demand-side GDP is estimated to have grown by only 3.9 per cent in 2008-09 and the recovery in 2009-10 and 2010-11 was sharper at 8.2 per cent and 9.6 per cent respectively. The revisions indicate that the global crisis in 2008-09 was mainly reflected in negative growth in gross capital formation, with the slowdown in private final consumption expenditure being modest. More importantly, post-crisis growth in gross fixed capital formation has been lukewarm. As per the Advance Estimates, the growth of GDP at market prices is expected to be 7.5 per cent in 2011-12. The growth in real terms of consumption expenditure, gross fixed capital formation, exports and imports works out to 6.0 per cent, 5.6 per cent, 14.3 per cent, and 17.5 per cent respectively for the year 2011-12. The growth in these indicators in 2010-11 was 8.1 per cent, 7.5 per cent, 22.7 per cent, and 15.6 per cent respectively.[1] The data clearly indicates a decline in growth in 2011-12.

The growth rate of investment in the economy is estimated to have registered a significant decline during the year 2011-12. The year has been witnessing a sharp increase in interest rates that resulted in higher costs of borrowings, and other rising costs affecting profitability and, thereby, internal accruals that could be used to finance investment.

Agriculture and Food

Agriculture including allied activities accounted for 13.9 per cent of GDP at 2004-5 prices in 2011-12 as compared to 14.5 per cent in 2010-11. In terms of composition, out of a total share of 14.5 per cent in GDP in 2010-11, agriculture alone accounted for 12.3 per cent, followed by forestry and logging at 1.4 per cent, and fishing at 0.7 per cent. Notwithstanding the declining trend in agriculture's share in GDP, the importance of the sector to the economy is best understood with reference to its share in employment and in terms of its criticality for macroeconomic stability. While the former was well known, the latter became manifest with rising growth in incomes since the mid-2000s.[2]

Hence, growth in agriculture and allied sectors remains an important objective and a 'necessary condition' for inclusive growth. The average annual growth in agriculture and allied sectors realized during the Eleventh Plan period was 3.3 per cent against the targeted growth rate of 4 per cent. The sector recorded slightly lower average growth than targeted in the Eleventh Plan period, due to severe drought experienced in most parts of the country during 2009-10 and drought/deficient rainfall in some states, namely Bihar, Jharkhand, eastern UP, and West Bengal in 2010-11. However, timely and corrective measures taken by the government helped boost agricultural production, and growth in the sector reached 7.0 per cent in 2010-11, the highest growth rate achieved during the last six years. In 2011-12, agriculture and allied sectors are estimated to achieve a growth rate of 2.5 per cent,[3] which is a matter of concern.

Industry and Infrastructure

Industrial growth, measured in terms of the index of industrial production (IIP), shows fluctuating trends. Growth had reached 15.5 per cent in 2007-08 and then started decelerating. Initial deceleration in industrial growth was largely on account of the global economic meltdown. There was, however, a recovery from 2.5 per cent in 2008-09 to 5.3 per cent in 2009-10 and 8.2 per cent in 2010-11. Fragile economic recovery in the US and Europe and moderately subdued expectations at home affected the growth of the industrial sector in the year 2011-12. Overall growth during April-December 2011 reached 3.6 per cent compared to 8.3 per cent in the corresponding period of the previous year.

There was a contraction in production in the mining sector, particularly the coal and natural gas segments. Contraction in output also resulted in its contribution to growth turning negative. The electricity sector witnessed an improvement in growth in 2011-12. This sector contributed 22.6 per cent to overall industrial growth, which was more than twice its weight in the IIP. Growth moderated in the manufacturing sector, from 9.0 per cent in April-December 2010 to 3.9 per cent in April-December 2011, which, given its large share in the IIP, led to a slowdown in the industry sector as a whole.[4] Here again the adverse impact of RBI's high interest rate policy is clearly visible.

As a matter of fact, industrial output in India has continued to be affected by what is known as policy paralysis. The industrial output declined by 3.5 per cent in March 2012 as compared to an expansion of 9.4 per cent in March 2011. Corporate India is hard pressed by high interest rates, rising input costs, sliding margins and most importantly, policy delays. Shrinking demand has hit companies hard at a time when they are looking for options to keep revenues high, maintain reasonable profits and minimal layoffs.

The data released by the Central Statistics Office (CSO) on 11 May 2012 revealed that while the overall industrial output fell 3.5 per cent in March 2012, the manufacturing sector was down 4.4 per cent in March 2012 compared to 11 per cent growth in March 2011 while the mining sector fell 1.3 per cent against an expansion of 0.4 per cent in the same year-ago period. The industrial sector rose 4.1 per cent in February 2012 but poor performance of the crucial infrastructure sector has hurt overall growth.

Industrial growth in 2011-12 stood at 2.8 per cent compared to 8.2 per cent in the previous year and almost near similar levels in the aftermath of the global financial crisis in 2008-09. Data also suggested that some sectors such as garments, where production is estimated to have declined 57 per cent, are under stress. Some other consumer demand driven segments such as inverters (78 per cent decline) and air conditioners (49 per cent drop) too felt the heat. Data glitches have dogged official statistics prompting the government to scale down January industrial growth in the current financial year 2012-13.

The global economic slowdown and slowing domestic demand have also contributed to the moderation in industrial output. The sudden decline in March output came as a surprise for analysts who were expecting the sector to post growth in the 1-2 per cent range. Economists also said slowdown in the industrial sector would hurt overall economic growth which was estimated at 6.9 per cent for 2011-12.

The decline in the industrial sector rattled the financial markets, hurting the rupee and the sensex. Analysts said the government must act to reverse the situation and take steps to revive growth. Some said RBI may not reduce interest rates sharply due to the persisting inflationary pressures, which is not a good news for industry.

"In a normal business cycle, weak industrial activity offers scope for cutting policy rates if the inflation outlook justifies it. However, the situation in India is far from normal. The government's policy inaction is hurting business confidence and investment spending. Also, inflationary pressures, especially due to inadequate supply-side response and the chronic suppressed inflation, are still alive," Rajeev Malik, senior economist at CLSA in Singapore, said.[5] "The IIP figures of March 2012 are disappointing.... Continued weak global business sentiments are also adversely impacting recovery in domestic private investment," he added.

According to experts, both manufacturing and services are hit by the moderation, due to slow growth in exports because of slowing European economies. The weakest links are the capital and intermediate goods segments.

Weak investment demand due to tight monetary conditions and slow policy reforms have led to a sharp decline in output growth in these sectors. Output in the capital goods sector contracted by 21.3 per cent (–) as against a growth of 14 per cent in the same month last year. Output growth in basic goods, which is comprised of infrastructure sectors such as cement, steel, coal and power, appear to be slowing down considerably. According to Pranab Mukherjee, "Domestic investment recovery remains frail.... Though RBI's monetary stance has been reversed in last policy announcement, it will take some more time for interest costs to come down."[6] But the economists feel that instead of playing the waiting game, the government should take some concrete steps to control inflation by tending to the supply side, and boost industrial production by reducing interest rates, otherwise the situation may become from bad to worse, hurting the economy more and affecting FDI, employment, exports, stock market and halting the overall economic growth.

Services Sector

The share of services in India's GDP at factor cost (at current prices) increased from 33.5 per cent in 1950-51 to 55.1 per cent in 2010-11 and 56.3 per cent in 2011-12 as per Advance Estimates. Trade, hotels, and restaurants as a group, with 16.9 per cent share, is the largest contributor to GDP among the various services sub-sectors, followed by financing, insurance, real estate, and business services with 16.4 per cent share. The services sector growth rate at constant prices has always been above the overall GDP growth rate since 1996-07 except for 2003-04. The compound annual growth rate (CAGR) of the services sector at 10.2 per cent for the period 2004-5 to 2010-11 has been higher than the 8.6 per cent GDP growth rate during the same period. In the years 2009-10 and 2010-11, the services sector registered a growth rate of 10.5 per cent and 9.3 per cent respectively. In 2011-12, as per the Advance Estimates, the growth rate of services has been placed at 9.4 per cent.[7] Growth in this sector can be stated as satisfactory and it has not been affected by tight money policy. However, in this sector, private players have done better than public undertakings. Credit growth in private banks has been higher than that in public sector banks, which is not a good trend.

Against the backdrop of global and domestic macroeconomic conditions, outlook and risks, the policy stance for 2012-13 has been guided by the two major considerations.

First, growth decelerated significantly to 6.1 per cent in Q3 of 2011-12, though it was expected to have recovered moderately in Q4. Based on the current assessment, the economy is clearly operating below its post-crisis trend.

Second, as earlier projected, headline WPI inflation as well as non-food manufactured products inflation moderated significantly by March 2012. During December-January, inflation softened on account of a decline in food prices. However, in the following two months, inflation softening was driven largely by moderation in the core components reflecting a slowdown in demand.

Against this backdrop, the stance of monetary policy is intended to:

- Adjust policy rates to levels consistent with the current growth moderation.
- Guard against risks of demand-led inflationary pressures re-emerging.
- Provide a greater liquidity cushion to the financial system.[8]

Guidance

The reduction in the repo rate is based on an assessment of growth having slowed below its post-crisis trend rate which, in turn, is contributing to a moderation in core inflation. However, it must be emphasized that the deviation of growth from its trend is modest. At the same time, upside risks to inflation persist. These considerations inherently limit the space for further reduction in policy rates.[9]

We can conclude by saying that during the finanial year 2011-12, GDP growth has declined to 6.67 per cent as compared to 8.4 per cent a year earlier, i.e. in 2010-11. The government has blamed this on the European crisis and the overall slack business conditions in most parts of the world. But the fact is that low GDP is the result of RBI's high interest rate policy which is detrimental to industrial growth. However, the RBI has stuck to this policy for too long. Even if the inflation eased out in December 2011 onwards, RBI merely reduced CRR by 125 basis points and left the other rates untouched till the close of the financial year.

In its Monetary Policy Statement 2012-13, RBI admitted that "domestically, the state of the economy is a matter of growing concern. Though inflation has moderated in recent months, it remains sticky and above the tolerance level, even as growth has slowed. Significantly, these trends are occurring in a situation in which concerns over the fiscal deficit, the current account deficit and deteriorating asset quality loom large. In this context, the challenge for monetary policy is to maintain its vigil on controlling inflation while being sensitive to risks to growth and other vulnerabilities."[10]

RBI decreased repo rate and reserve repo rate by 50 basis points each, but it was not considered enought after a string of hikes during 2011-12. RBI has predicted a marginal growth GDP in the current financial year, i.e. 2012-13 from 6.69 (projected) in 2011-12 to 7.03. Industry experts feel that interest rates should be reduced substantially to boost industrial production, increase credit growth to both food and non-food sectors, to put the economy again on high growth path.

RBI is right in believing that the "growth in the index of industrial production (IIP) decelerated to 3.5 per cent during 2011-12 (April-February) from 8.1 per cent in the corresponding period of the previous year. In terms of use-based classification, while capital goods and intermediate goods sectors registered negative growth of 1.8 per cent and 0.9 per cent, respectively, the growth of the consumer durables sector decelerated to 2.7 per cent. These trends suggest that industrial activity may have expanded slower than 6.9 per cent in Q4 implied in the advance estimates of GDP." But it is only the right policy that will make the economy emerge stronter from this difficult situation as it has done in the past.

Notes

1. *Economic Survey 2011-12.*
2. *Ibid.*
3. *Ibid.*
4. *Ibid.*
5. Times News Network: *The Times of India*, 12 May 2012.
6. "March Industrial Ouput Shrinks". *Hindustan Times*, 12 May 2012
7. *Ibid.*
8. D. Subbarao (RBI Governor). "Reserve Bank of India Monetary Policy Statement 2012-13", 17 April 2012.
9. *Ibid.*
10. *Ibid.*

3

Monetary and Liquidity Conditions

Broadly speaking, high inflation is too much money chasing too few goods. In other words, demand for goods and services is more as people have a high purchasing power, but the supply in unable to match the demand, leading to hardening of prices. The Reserve Bank of India has been trying to decrease liquidity in the market, with its policy of keeping deposit rates as well as lending rates high.

In the second quarter of 2011-12, liquidity conditions remained in deficit mode, in line with the policy objective of the Reserve Bank. Base money decelerated as currency growth moderated. Money (M3) growth, however, accelerated moderately as the money multiplier increased. While credit growth is above the indicative trajectory, it will moderate as growth decelerates. Going forward, the global uncertainty and fiscal pressures pose challenges to effective monetary policy management.

The RBI has been pursuing a tight monetary policy stance since early 2010 in response to sustained inflationary pressures. Inflation, which initially emerged from supply side constraints, increasingly became generalised and the RBI had to calibrate its policy response to anchor inflation expectations, while at the same time ensuring that the growth of the economy was not hampered. In continuation of this policy stance, the Reserve Bank raised the policy repo rate by 50 basis points in July 2011 and again by 25 basis in September 2011 as shown in Table 1.1

(chapter 1). The level of policy rate and inflation presently are broadly comparable to the levels prevailing in September 2008.

Liquidity Remained in Deficit Mode

The average liquidity adjustment facility (LAF) injection, which was around ₹ 49,000 crore in the first quarter of 2011-12, dropped marginally to around ₹ 47,000 crore in the second quarter of 2011-12 mirroring the increase in centre's cash deficit. Liquidity deficit largely remained within (+/–) 1 per cent of

Table 3.1: Liquidity Position 2010 and 2011

(₹ Crore)

Outstanding as on last Friday	LAF	MSS	Centre's Surplus@	Total
1	2	3	4	5=(2+3+4)
2010				
April	35,720	2,737	-28,868	9,589
May	6,215	317	-7,531	-999
June	-74,795	317	76,431	1,953
July	1,775	0	16,688	18,463
August	11,815	0	20,054	31,869
September	-30,250	0	65,477	35,227
October	-1,17,660	0	86,459	-31,201
November	-1;03,090	0	93,425	-9,665
December	-1,13,415	0	1,44,437	31,022
2011				
January	-76,730	0	1,18,371	41,641
February	-72,005	0	77,397	5,392
March*	-1,06,005	0	16,416	-89,589
April	-39,605	0	-35,399	-75,004
May	-75,795	0	-9,544	-85,339
June	-96,205	0	8,339	-87,866
July	-48,555	0	-25,983	-74,538
August	-49,215	0	-21,192	-70,407
September	-82,645	0	-24,387	-1,07,032
October (on 14th)	-54,270	0	-32,883	-87,153

@ : Excludes minimum cash balances with the Reserve Bank in case of surplus.
* : Data pertain to March 31

Note: 1. Negative sign in column 2 indicates injection of liquidity through LAF.
2. Negative sign in column 4 indicates WMA/OD availed by the Central Government.

Source: http://www.rbi.org.in

NDTL of the banks, in line with the stated policy objective of the RBI. The liquidity deficit, which had witnessed some stress in June 2011 due to quarterly advance tax payouts, eased in early July 2011, reflecting the drawdown of Central Government cash balances and transition to WMA/OD as shown in Table 3.1. above.

Since the introduction of the new operating procedures of monetary policy in May 2011, injection of liquidity under the marginal standing facility (MSF) has been limited to two occasions (₹ 100 crore on June 10 and ₹ 4,105 crore on July 15, 2011), which is indicative of the liquidity position not getting overtight. This has perhaps tired down the effect of high interest rates which tended to suck liquidity out of the market.

Growing Endogeneity of Money Keeps Money Supply Above Trajectory

While the base money growth has decelerated sharply, the money supply growth accelerated moderately as the money multiplier rose as shown in Table 3.2 below. This divergent trend in base money and broad money arises out of increasing endogeneity of money supply as banks respond to strong credit demand, which is met through recourse to additional borrowings, including that from the RBI.

Table 3.2: Monetary Indicators

Item	Outstanding Amount (₹ crore) Oct. 07, 2011	2010-11	FY variations (per cent) 2011-12	Y-o-Y Oct. 08, 2010	Variations (per cent) Oct. 07, 2011
1	2	3	4	5	6
Reserve Money (M0)*	13,84,833	6.2	0.6	21.4	12.8
Broad Money (M3)	69,62,822	6.9	7.1	15.8	16.2
Main Components of M3					
Currency with the Public	9,49,232	8.6	3.8	18.9	13.8
Aggregate Deposits	60,11,223	6.6	7.7	15.3	16.7
of which: Demand Deposits	6,51,919	-5.9	-9.2	14.3	-3.5
Time Deposits	53,59,304	8.8	10.2	15.5	19.7
Main Sources of M3					
Net Bank Credit to Govt.	21,57,973	5.2	8.8	22.5	22.9
Bank Credit to Commercial Sector	44,44,825	7.3	4.9	19.8	18.7
Net Foreign Assets of the Banking Sector	15,42,066	5.1	10.7	1.1	14.5

Note: 1. Data are provisional.
2. * : Data pertain to October 14, 2011.

Source: http://www.rbi.org.in

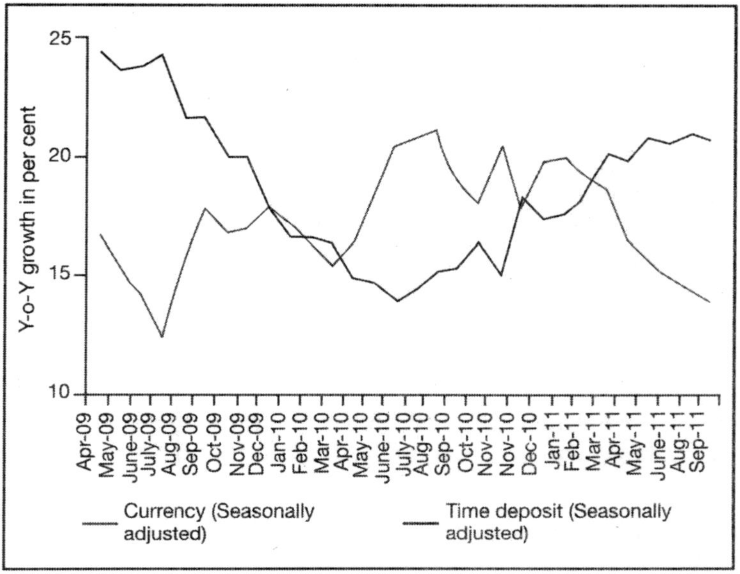

Fig. 3.1: Currency Growth

Strong Growth of Deposits

Bank deposits registered a robust growth since December 2010 due to successive hikes in interest rates. The opportunity cost of saving in lower interest bearing instruments like small savings increased, resulting in a shift from small savings to term deposits as shown in Fig. 3.1 above.

Credit Expansion still above Indicative Trajectory but may Decrease

Credit expansion, which had witnessed a sharp deceleration in the first quarter of 2011-12, continued the trend in the initial period of the second quarter, partly reflecting the high base of 2010. Notwithstanding this deceleration, credit expansion remained above the indicative trajectory of 18 per cent set out by the RBI in the July 2011 review, mainly due to high nominal GDP growth. But with the moderation of growth coupled with fiscal money policy, which RBI continues to pursue, it is likely to decline in the next six months or so, which is neither good for industrial expansion nor economic growth.

During the first three quarters of 2010-11, the divergence between credit growth and deposit growth was high and growing. As the cost of funds under LAF increased progressively with the rise in the repo rate, banks raised their deposit and lending rates. This stronger transmission of monetary policy helped in narrowing the divergence between deposit and credit growth. The gap between the two declined from 9 percentage points in mid-December 2010 to 5.6 percentage points in March 2011 and further to 2.1 percentage points in October 2011. This can be attributed to the fact that with high interest rates on deposits, more money is coming to banks as term deposits from the public. But, at the same time, credit growth is declining as people are not borrowing much due to high lending rates. Banks' lending sources have also declined due to high SLR and CRR they have to maintain.

Non-Banking Sources Dominate Credit Expansion

The non-bank sources have occupied the space that was vacated by banks in meeting the credit requirements of the economy during 2011-12. This is reflected in the increase in the share of non-bank sources in total flow of financial resources from about 46 per cent in April-September 2010 to 54 per cent in April-September 2011, with both domestic and foreign funding sources showing significant increase. Within domestic sources, net issuance under CPs, NBFCs-ND-SI and housing finance companies (HFCs) increased. The resource flow from external sources rose on account of higher mobilisation through FDI and ECBs. This again is one of the fall-outs of RBI's tight money policy. With frequent increases in repo rates, bank's lending rates have gone very high. Besides, with increases in cash reserve ratio, the funds with the banks for lending purposes have reduced. Needy borrowers are approaching non-bank sources to raise loans. Thus, private financiers are making huge profit by lending at high rates. High cost of funds, moreover, does not allow manufacturers and traders to sell at low rates. This keeps inflation high.

The credit deceleration has been diffused over a wide range of sectors that include chemical and chemical products, engineering, power, telecommunications and consumer durables. The slowdown in credit growth may have been prompted by deceleration in investment demand that could have impacted term loans. Further, the top rated corporates resorted to relatively cheap sources of borrowings including ECBs and CPs.

Flow of Financial Resources to Commercial Sector

RBI's tight money policy has led to a decrease in the flow of finance to the commercial sector as shown in Table 3.3.

Table 3.3: Flow of Financial Resources to the Commercial Sector

(₹ Crore)

Item	April-March		April-September	
	2009-10	2010-11	2010-11	2011-12
1	2	3	4	5
A. Adjusted Non-Food Bank Credit (NFC)	4,78,614	7,11,031	2,59,692	2,29,157+
(i) Non-Food Credit	4,66,960	6,81,501	2,27,006	2,07,483+
of which: petroleum and fertilizer credit	10,014	-24,236	-24,130	1,573&
(ii) Non-SLR Investment by SCBs	11,654	29,530	32,686	21,674+
B. Flow from Non-banks (B1+B2)	5,88,784	5,14,495	2,20,690	2,70,441
B1. Domestic Sources	3,65,214	2,95,573	1,23,652	1,37,838
1. Public issues by non-financial entities	31,956	28,520	10,054	6,205
2. Gross private placements by non-financial entities	1,41,964	67,436	-	-
3. Net issuance of CPs subscribed to by non-banks	26,148	17,207	41,875	59,693*
4. Net Credit by housing finance companies	28,485	38,386	8,775	11,110&
5. Total gross accommodation by 4 RBI regulated AIFIs-NABARD, NHB, SIDBI & EXIM Bank	33,783	40,007	15,282	8,558
6. Systematically important non-deposit taking NBFCs (net of bank credit)	60,663	67,937	35,209	39,784$
7. LIC's net investment in corporate debt, infrastructure and Social Sector	42,215	36,080	12,457	12,488&
B2. Foreign Sources	2,23,570	2,18,922	97,038	1,32,603
1. External Commercial Borrowings / FCCB	15,674	52,899	27,635	41,809
2. ADR/GDR Issues excluding banks and financial institutions	15,124	9,248	7,250	1,783
3. Short-term Credit from abroad	34,878	50,177	19,707	13,721#
4. Foreign Direct Investment to India	1,57,894	1,06,598	42,446	75,290&
C. Total Flow of Resources (A+B)	10,67,398	12,25,526	4,80,382	4,99,598
Memo:				
Net resource mobilisation by Mutual Funds through Debt (non-Gilt) Schemes	96,578	-36,707	3,266	3,426

+: up to October 7, 2011 *: up to August 15, 2011 $: up to July 2011 #: up to June 2011 &: up to August 2011

-: Not available

Note: FDI Data include equity capital of incorporated entities for the period April-August and does not include reinvested earnings, other capital and equity capital of unincorporated entities.

Source: http://rbi.org.in/

Table 3.3 shows that non-food credit declined from ₹ 2,59,692 crore in the half-year April-September 2010-11, to ₹ 2,29,157 crore in the half-year April-September 2011-12, a decrease of ₹ 30,000 crore. This is primarily because of high interest rates and low lendable funds with the banks due to high statutary liquidity ratio (SLR) and cash reserve ratio (CRR) which the banks have to maintain.

On the other hand, flow of finance to commercial sector increased from ₹ 2,20,690 crore in half year April-September 2010-11 to ₹ 2,70,441 crore in the half year April-September 2011-12. This is an increase of app. ₹ 50,000 crore. This means private financiers have taken a good advantage of RBI's tight money policy by lending more than before and earning more money as interest. Obviously, high SLR and CRR have kept the banks at a disadvantage. If RBI does not substantially reduce these rates, banks will continue to suffer due to their disadvantaged position.

Monetary Overshooting a Risk in the Face of Fiscal Pressures

Even though there has been only moderate injection of primary liquidity through LAF transactions, broad money growth has stayed above the indicative trajectory, operating on the impetus provided by the endogenous factors like high deposit growth, bolstered by substitution from currency to deposits. Going forward however, credit growth could moderate as growth decelerates and inflation moderates as has been estimated by the RBI. However, even with some deceleration expected in credit growth, containing monetary growth remains a challenge in the face of large market borrowing.

This means that money supply in India is likely to remain large. It is difficult to guage how much money will find its way into bank deposits in the lure of earning high deposit interests prevailing now, and how much of it will be used in spending. Also, the earnings of people are increasing, which will give them more spending power. Thus, the prices of goods and services are likely to remain high, contrary to what RBI believes. It is pertinent to mention here that the easing out of food prices in December 2011 and January-February 2012 was the result of high seasonal supply of vegetables, etc. and should not be construed to be the result of RBI's policies.

Table 3.4: Credit Flow from Scheduled Commercial Banks

(Amount in ₹ Crore)

Item	Outstanding as on October 7, 2011	Variation (y-o-y)			
		As on Oct 8, 2010		As on Oct 7, 2011	
		Amount	Per cent	Amount	Per cent
1	2	3	4	5	6
1. Public Sector Banks	30,38,986	4,24,615	19.8	4,70,704	18.3
2. Foreign Banks	2,21,422	17,923	11.4	45,898	26.1
3. Private Banks	7,86,334	1,25,973	24.5	1,45,213	22.6
4. All Scheduled Commercial Banks*	41,48,598	5,84,064	20.2	6,75,538	19.5

Note: 1. Data as on October 7,2011 are provisional.
2. *Including Regional Rural Banks.

Source: http://rbi.org.in

Table 3.4 shows the position of credit flow from scheduled commercial banks as on 8 October 2010 and 7 October 2011. Year-on-year variations in public sector banks have been lower (18.3) than those in foreign banks (26.1) and private banks (22.6). This reveals that RBI's policy of keeping SLR and CRR high has affected the lending of public sector banks.

Credit Growth Slows Down due to High Interest Rates

Credit offtake slowed down substantially in 2011-12, because of high interest rates. Year-on-year credit growth up to March 23, 2011-12 was 17 per cent as against 21.5 per cent in the same period of the previous fiscal, RBI data showed.

According to CARE Ratings, liquidity condition is likely to remain tight due to high net borrowing programme (₹ 4,79,000 crore) of the government. The upward pressure on interest rates will continue to be felt in the first half of 2012-13 as 65 per cent of the budgeted borrowings will be done during this period.

The growth rate for bank credit in 2010-11 crossed the 18 per cent target fixed by RBI on account of higher borrowings by telecom players to make spectrum auction payments. In 2011-12, the credit disbursement crossed the revised target of 16 per cent but remained lower than the original target of 18 per cent fixed at the beginning of the financial year. Credit offtake has slowed down due to higher cost of borrowings and shelving of investment decisions by the companies, said CARE Ratings.

High deposit interest rates increased banks' cost of funds. Banks also increased lending rates to protect profit margin. In 2011-12, banks' base rate—the benchmark lending rate—increased from 8.25 per cent to 9.50 per cent, to 10 per cent, and to 10.75 per cent.

Because of steep rise in interest rates companies preferred to remain on the sidelines, keeping financing of working capital at the minimum necessary level. At the same time, weaker global and domestic economic conditions prompted postponement of investment and expansion plans, which lowered demand for credit.

According to RBI, the overall slowdown in economic activity, risk aversion by banks and monetary policy actions taken so far have led to a general deceleration in credit growth. The deceleration in credit growth of the public sector banks was particularly sharp, said the RBI.

This reflected a rising aversion of banks that is leading to a portfolio switch to investments in risk-free government securities on the back of large government borrowing. The credit growth of foreign banks which had witnessed sharp decline during October 2008-October 2009 period, has witnessed a rebound since then.

The deceleration in non-food credit was contributed to by all sectors including industry, personal loans, services and especially agriculture, while the deceleration in agriculture is partly on account of definitional changes effected during February-March 2011. The high growth of NPAs in the farm sector also possibly contributed to the slowdown.

RBI also said in its Monetary Policy Statement 2012-13 that "money supply (M3) growth, which was 17 per cent at the beginning of the financial year 2011-12, reflecting strong growth in time deposits, moderated during the course of the year to about 13 per cent by end-March 2012, lower than the Reserve Bank's indicative trajectory of 15.5 per cent, mirroring both tightness in primary liquidity and lower credit demand during most part of the year."[1]

On non-food credit growth, RBI stated that "it decelerated from 22.1 per cent at the beginning of 2011-12 to 15.4 per cent by February 2012 reflecting slower economic activity. However, it picked up to 16.8 per cent in March, higher than the indicative projection of 16 per cent. Disaggregated data up to February 2012 showed that the deceleration in credit growth was broad-based across agriculture, industry, services and personal loans. The pick-up in non-food bank credit towards the year-end was on account of increased credit flow to agriculture and industry. Net bank credit to the Central Government increased at a significantly higher rate of 15.7 per cent in 2011-12 as compared with 8.4 per cent in the previous year reflecting higher borrowings."[2]

Liquidity conditions according to RBI, "remained in a deficit mode throughout 2011-12. However, beginning November 2011, the liquidity deficit went beyond the comfort level of (+)/(–) one per cent of net demand and time liabilities (NDTL) of banks. Average net injection of liquidity under the daily liquidity adjustment facility (LAF) increased from around ₹ 0.5 trillion during April-September 2011 to around ₹ 1.4 trillion during February 2012 and further to ₹ 1.6 trillion during March 2012, partly reflecting a build-up in government cash balances. In order to mitigate the liquidity tightness, the Reserve Bank took steps to inject primary liquidity of a more durable nature. It conducted open market operations (OMOs) aggregating around ₹ 1.3 trillion between November 2011 and March 2012. Further, the cash reserve ratio (CRR) was reduced by 125 basis points (50 basis points effective January 28, 2012 and 75 basis points effective March 10, 2012), injecting primary liquidity of about ₹ 0.8 trillion. Reflecting these measures, combined with decline in government cash balances, the net injection of liquidity under the LAF, which peaked at ₹ 2.0 trillion on March 30, 2012, declined sharply to ₹ 0.7 trillion on April 13, 2012."[3]

Liquidity Crunch: Pledging of Shares by Corporation

India inc is in a tight position these days. According to a news report, promoters of 100 out of BSE-500 companies have pledged their shares to raise funds as liquidity has tightened for crisis-hit sectors like infrastructure, real estate and aviation in the previous financial year, 2011-12 and the current year, 2012-13. As many as 60 companies saw their promoters pledging more that 50 per cent of their holdings, which is a clear reflection of the strain that the corporate in India are undergoing.

According to Kishore Ostwal, MD, CNI Research, an equities research provider, "There is a big liquidity problem and so promoters are forced to sell their shares or pledge them. Several companies have seen a drop in promoter holdings and an increase in preferential allotments." He felt that any relief from the high interest rates is unlikely in the near future.

J. Thunuguntla, head, research, SMC Global Securities believes that the climate is tough for fund raising and promoters are not getting an easy access to funds, and they have no choice but to pledge their shares. Promoters of Kingfisher Airlines, who had pledges 50.5 per cent of their stake at the end of the previous fiscal, have given 90.1 per cent of their holdings as security in 2012-13. The percentage of holdings of SpiceJet increased from 18.4 in 2010-11 to 47.6 in 2011-12. However, there are some companies like those of the Tata Group whose pledged shares dropped in 2012-13 from the previous year, but this may be a one-off case, and by and large India inc is the victim of high interest rates and low liquidity. And since the RBI is not likely to reduce interest rates in near future as high inflation has tended to resurface after going down in Jan-Feb 2012, it is apprehended that the industry will continue to suffer during 2012-13 and probably beyond.

Borrower Defaults Increase

Another fall-out of RBI's high interest rate policy is that default rates among corporate borrowers have increased. As a matter of fact they hit a 10-year high of 3.4 per cent in 2011-12, as companies are finding it increasingly difficult to pay loans because of high interest rates, elevated commodity prices and slackening demand following the Eurozone crisis.

A review by Crisil has shown that the environment changed dramatically in the second half of 2011-12 after S&P downgraded the US Government. The downgrade increased risk aversion among global financial institutions and created a shortage of dollar liquidity, which cut-off financing from international markets.

Crisil stated that highly indebted industries like textiles, steel, construction and engineering account for one-fourth of the defaults. Downgrades exceeded upgrades in the second half of 2011-12 with 266 debt issuers being upgraded as against 292 downgrades. This marked a reversal from the first half when 313 entities were upgraded and only 207 were downgraded.

The report said that downgrades are expected to exceed upgrades in the current fiscal, 2012-13 too as demand is expected to be hit because of slower growth.

The companies in India across various sectors continue to suffer as interest rates have remained high for much longer period than expected. Rising defaults will not only increase the Non-Performing Assets (NPAs) of banks—not good for their balance sheets—but also make the companies liable to pay penal interest, worsening things further.

NPA Management

The asset quality of banks is one of the most important indicators of their financial health. It also reflects the efficacy of banks' credit risk management and the recovery environment. It is important that the signs of distress in all stressed accounts are detected early and those which are viable are also extended restructuring facilities expeditiously to preserve their economic value. During annual financial inspection (AFIs), it has been observed that the restructuring facilities are not readily extended to small accounts. To improve the banks' ability to manage their non-performing assets (NPAs) and restructured accounts in an effective manner and considering that almost all branches of banks have been fully computerised, it is proposed:

- to mandate banks to put in place a robust mechanism for early detection of signs of distress, and measures, including prompt restructuring in the case of all viable accounts wherever required, with a view to preserving the economic value of such accounts; and
- to mandate banks to have proper system generated segment-wise data on their NPA accounts, write-offs,

compromise settlements, recovery and restructured accounts.[4]

RBI has emphasised that banks should have an efficient NPA management system, a strong mechanism and granular data. It may be argued that most banks do have strong NPA management systems in place. NPAs are increasing as there are more defaults because of high interest burden on the borrowers. If interest rates are reduced to a comfortable level and economy has a growth momentum, only then businesses can flourish, defaults decrease and NPA position of banks improve.

Table 3.5 shows sectoral deployment of credit. Year-on-year variations as on 24 September 2010 over 25 September 2009; and as on 23 September 2011 over 24 September 2010 in various sectors have been given. Half-yearly variations as on 24 September 2010 over 26 March 2010; and as on 23 September 2011 over 25 March 2011 have been given. It is observed that

Table 3.5: Sectoral Deployment of Credit

(Per cent)

Sector	Outstanding	Y-o-Y Variation		Financial Year Variation	
	Credit as on Sept. 23, 2011 (₹ crore)	Sept. 24, 2010 over Sept. 25, 2009	Sept. 23, 2011 over Sept. 24, 2010	Sept. 24, 2010 over Mar. 26, 2010	Sept. 23, 2011 over Mar. 25, 2011
1	2	3	4	5	6
Non-food credit	37,96,893	18.7	18.7	5.2	3.5
Agriculture and allied activities	4,33,791	19.3	7.9	-3.4	-5.8
Industry	17,42,163	24.4	22.9	8.1	7.5
of which, Chemical & chemical products	96,670	15.3	9.4	3.1	2.3
All engineering	1,01,632	27.8	22.5	12.4	8.9
Infrastructure	5,64,958	47.4	20.3	23.6	7.3
of which, Power	3,00,752	46.9	32.2	21.1	11.7
Telecommunications	89,964	94.7	-10.2	68.8	-10.4
Roads	1,03,545	28.3	31.9	6.7	11.9
Services	9,12,413	17.4	19.3	5.2	1.3
of which, Commercial Real	1,14,459	7.9	12.6	10.3	2.3
NBFCs	1,83,761	18.5	46.2	10.8	4.7
Personal Loans	7,08,526	8.6	15.2	5.0	3.4
of which, Consumer durables	8,492	12.5	-6.5	9.5	-16.4
Housing (incl. Priority sector)	3,66,889	10.4	15.7	5.4	6.0
Education	48,339	23.6	18.1	11.1	10.6
Vehicle loans	83,981	16.1	19.3	10.3	5.9

Note: Based on data collected from select SCBs that account for 95 per cent of the total non-food credit extended by all SCBs. These data are being disseminated every month from November 2010.

Source: http://www.rbi.org.in

the flow of credit to agriculture has registered a negative growth in the half year 24 September 2010 over 26 March 2010 (–3.4) and in the half year 23 September 2011 over 25 March 2011 (–5.8), and as can be seen, the decelaration is increasing. This shows the following:

(i) Interest rates being high, few farmers are willing to avail loans from banks. This adversely impacts agriculture as many farmers, in the absence of funds are unable to buy inputs like fertilizers, quality seeds, pesticides, etc., which translates into lower yield.

(ii) Banks having less funds, have reduced their lending, which is not desirable in a developing economy.

(iii) As interest rates on loans for agriculture and allied activities are comparatively low, banks are unwilling to lend liberally to this sector as it affects their profitability.

Besides agriculture, credit to telecommunication and consumer durables has also registered a negative growth in the half year 23 September 2011 over 25 March 2011. Some other sectors like chemical industry, services, personal loans, etc. have shown a slender growth, much lower than the corresponding period of previous year.

It is quite clear from the figures given in Table 3.5 that RBI's tight money policy has reduced banks' lendable funds as they have to maintain high SLR and CRR. Thus, growth deployment of credit to various sectors has declined, which has resulted in lower production as we have seen in the IIP data earlier. There is an urgent need to reduce SLR, CRR and repo rate substantially, so that the growth momentum of the economy is regained.

Interest Rates in 2012

It is being anticipated that RBI Governor D. Subbarao will reverse Asia's steepest increase in interest rates in the current year as the third largest developing economy slows, money-market indicators show.

The fixed payment to lock in borrowing costs for a year fell to 38 basis points below the central bank's 8.5 per cent repurchase rate, showing that swap traders are betting on monetary easing, data compiled by Bloomberg showed. Similar spreads were 45 basis points below benchmark rates in China and 180 in Brazil, the two biggest emerging markets. India's economy probably grew 6.8 per cent in the quarter January-March 2012, the least in two years, according to the median estimate in a Bloomberg survey report.

The Reserve Bank's rate increases during 2011 and 2012 have caused bond sales by Indian companies to drop 22 per cent as borrowing costs climbed. Downgrades in corporate debt ratings are approaching upgrades for the first time since 2009, after earnings at 40 per cent of firms in the benchmark stock index missed analysts' estimates in the past quarter.

"The RBI will be required to reverse its monetary stance to avoid a hard landing", Vivek Rajpal, a fixed-income strategist at Nomura Holdings Inc., Japan's biggest brokerage, said. "Growth is likely to slow further due to the impact of monetary tightening and headwinds from weakening demand in advanced countries", he added.

RBI is the only central bank in the biggest emerging markets which increased borrowing costs in October-December quarter of 2011-12, even as Europe's debt crisis worsened. It last raised the repo rate by 25 basis points, or 0.25 percentage point, on October 25, taking the total increase since March 2010 to a record 375 basis points, the steepest surge among Asia's ten biggest economies. Brazil's central bank has cut its Selic rate by a total 100 basis points since August to 11.5 per cent, while Bank Indonesia lowered its reference rate by 75 since September 30 to 6 per cent.

Towards the end of calendar year 2012, RBI indicated that the possibility of further increase in policy rates was low. "If we do see inflation rates coming off as we expect, we could be looking at the peaking of the cycle", Reserve Bank Deputy Governor Subir Gokarn said, referring to the monetary authority's policy outlook. But monetary easing is what the corporate world in India is looking for.

Monetary easing will push the average worldwide central bank interest rate, weighted for gross domestic product, to

1.79 per cent by June 2012 from 2.16 per cent in September 2011, the largest drop in two years, according to data and projections compiled by JPMorgan Chase & Co., which tracks 31 central banks. The number of authorities loosening credit is the most since the third quarter of 2009, when 15 institutions cut rates, the data showed.

Liquidity conditions for a large part of 2011-12 remained broadly around the comfortable level of liquidity deficit (1 per cent of NDTL of the banking system), with occasional stress on account of quarterly tax flows or divergence between deposit and credit mobilization. However, there has been rapid tightening of liquidity since November 2011. This was on account of pressure created by foreign exchange outflows and quarterly advance tax collections in December 2012. The RBI responded with a number of measures aimed at addressing the tightness in the foreign exchange market, including the conduct of open market operations (OMOs) to address rupee liquidity concerns.

RBI Governor D. Subbarao has stated that "On liquidity, conditions are steadily moving towards the comfort zone of the Reserve Bank, as reflected in the decline in banks' borrowings from the LAF and the behaviour of money market rates. The increase in the MSF limit will provide additional liquidity comfort. However, should the situation change, appropriate and proactive steps will be taken with the objective of restoring comfort zone conditions."[5]

Measures of Money Supply and Liquidity Aggregates

In order to provide a complete information on how money supply and liquidity aggregates are calculated in India, we are reproducing a relavant portion from Economic Survey 2011-12.[6]

- Reserve Money (M_0) = Currency in Circulation + Bankers' deposits with the RBI + 'Other' deposits with the RBI.
- Narrow Money (M_1) = Currency with the Public + Demand Deposits with the Banking System + 'Other' Deposits with the RBI.

- $M_2 = M_1$ + Savings Deposits of Post Office Savings Banks.
- Broad Money (M_3) = M_1 + Time Deposits with the Banking System.
- $M_4 = M_3$ + All Deposits with Post Office Savings Banks (excluding National Savings Certificates).
- While measures M_0, M_1 and M_3 are widely used in India, M_2 and M_4 are rarely used. The RBI initiated publication of a new set of monetary and liquidity aggregates as per the recommendations of the Working Group on Money Supply.

Following the submission of its report in June 1998, while no changes were made in the definitions of M_0 and M_1, new monetary aggregates NM_2 and NM_3 as well as liquidity aggregates L_1, L_2, and L_3 were introduced, the components of which are elaborated as follows:

- NM_1 = Currency with the Public + Demand Deposits with the Banking System + 'Other' Deposits with the RBI.
- $NM_2 = NM_1$ + Short-term Time Deposits of Residents (including and up to the contractual maturity of one year).
- $NM_3 = NM_2$ + Long-term Time Deposits of Residents + Call/Term Funding from Financial Institutions.
- $L_1 = NM_3$ + All Deposits with the Post Office Savings Banks (excluding National Savings Certificates).
- $L_2 = L_1$ + Term Deposits with Term Lending Institutions and Refinancing Institutions (FIs) + Term Borrowing by FIs + Certificates of Deposit issued by FIs.
- $L_3 = L_2$ + Public Deposits of Non-banking Financial Companies.
- Data on M_0 are published by the RBI on a weekly basis, while those for M_1 and M_3 are available on fortnightly basis. Among liquidity aggregates, data on L_1 and L_2 are published monthly, while those for L_3 are disseminated once in a quarter.

Trends in Monetary Aggregates

During the year 2011-12, the growth rates of reserve money (M_0) and narrow money (M_1) have been lower than in the preceding year while broad money (M_3) growth has been higher as shown in Table 3.6 below. The moderation in growth of M_1 as against M_3 is on account of decline in the growth of demand deposits and currency, while time deposits have accelerated in response to hike in the deposit rates of banks.[7]

Table 3.6: Movement of Select Monetary Parameters

(Per Cent)

	Parameters Growth Rates as on 2 December 2011 Position					
	Yearly variation		Financial-year basis		Year-on-year basis	
	2009-10	2010-11	2010-11	2011-12	2010-11	2011-12
M_0	17.0	19.1	6.4	0.7	22.3	12.8
M_1	18.2	9.8	4.0	-0.5	17.0	5.0
M_3	16.8	16.0	8.5	8.8	15.7	16.3

Source: RBI

RBI credit to the Central Government (as on 2 December 2011) has been ₹ 1,49,994 crore vis-à-vis an increase of ₹ 1,83,896 crore a year earlier.

Narrow Money (M_1)

During 2011-12, the growth in M_1 has been generally lower compared to that in 2010-11. On financial-year basis, M_1 declined by 0.5 per cent during the current year (up to 2 December 2011) compared to an increase of 4.0 per cent during the corresponding period of the previous year. On year-on-year basis, as on 2 December 2011, M_1 growth was 5.0 per cent as compared to 17.0 per cent a year earlier as shown in Table 3.7. During the current financial year (up to 2 December 2011), growth in 'currency with the public' decelerated to 6.4 per cent (₹ 58,262 crore), compared to an increase of 13.0 per cent (₹ 1,00,092 crore) during the corresponding period of the previous year. The other important component of M_1, namely demand deposits with banks, registered a decline of 9.2 per cent during the current financial year (up to 2 December 2011) as against a decline of 5.7 per cent during the corresponding period of the previous year. On

Table 3.7: Sources of Change in Money Stock (M3)

	Growth Rate (Per Cent)				
	31 March 2010 to 31 March 2011	31 March 2010 to 3 December 2010	31 March 2011 to 2 December 2011	4 December 2009 to 3 December 2010	3 December 2010 to 2 December 2011
I. M_1 (1+2+3)	9.8	4.0	-0.5	17.0	5.0
1. Currency with the public	19.1	13.0	6.4	18.8	12.1
2. Demand deposits with banks	0.0	-5.7	-9.2	14.9	-3.7
3. 'Other' deposits with RBI	-3.3	11.6	-29.6	16.0	-39.0
II. M_3 (M_1+4)	16.0	8.5	8.8	15.7	16.3
4. Time deposits with banks	18.2	10.2	12.0	15.2	20.2
III. Sources of change in money stock (M_3)					
1. Net bank credit to government	18.8	9.3	12.6	19.7	22.3
of which: Other banks credit to government	8.8	7.6	15.0	8.0	16.3
2. Bank credit to commercial sector	21.3	11.0	7.0	22.6	17.0
of which: Other banks' credit to commercial Sector	21.3	11.0	7.1	22.8	17.0
3. Net foreign exchange assets of the banking sector	8.7	7.0	13.7	1.7	15.6
4. Government's currency liabilities to the public	12.9	8.7	4.6	13.2	8.6
5. Banking sector's net non-monetary liabilities	32.2	18.1	14.7	27.4	28.5
IV. Memo Items					
1. Money multiplier (M3/M0)	4.72				
2. Velocity of money 1.21					
3. Net domestic assets	18.2	9.0	7.5	20.5	16.6
4. Net domestic credit	20.5	10.5	8.8	21.7	18.7

Source: RBI

year-on-year basis, as on 2 December 2011, the growth in 'currency with the public' was lower at 12.1 per cent as compared to 18.8 per cent during the corresponding period of the previous year. Over the same period, demand deposits registered a decline of 3.7 per cent as compared to a growth of 14.9 per cent a year earlier.[8]

Low growth of narrow money during the year 2011-12 is the result of RBI's tight money policy, which has reduced the money in circulation. Growth in demand deposits with banks declined because people preferred to keep more money in fixed deposits due to high interest rate offered by banks. However, growth in saving banks deposits is likely to improve because of deregulation of SB deposit rates with balance above rupees one lac.

Thus, as we have seen from the data given in the Economic Survey (2011-12), growth in liquidity was curtailed during the year 2011-12. RBI's high SLR and CRR rates reduced the lendable resources of banks. With high interest rates on loans, less people were inclined to avail loans from the banks, which adversely impacted industry and the growth of the economy moderated to 6.9 per cent per 2011-12. As banks offered high interest rates on time deposits, more people preferred to keep their funds in fixed deposits. This sucked liquidity from the market. This happened because of RBI's tight money policies to contain inflation. Low liquidity means lower demand for goods and services and thus lower prices. This is the principle on which the RBI has been framing its policies for the last two years or so. But low demand for goods and services because of low liquidity also hurts industry, which is forced to cut down on production. Lower production means lower economic growth. Although if the RBI continues with this approach, it is apprehended that our economy will also slow down like those of most countries of Europe leading to large lay-offs, unemployment and other attendant problems.

Notes

1. D. Subbarao (RBI Governor). "Reserve Bank of India Monetary Policy Statement 2012-13", 17 April 2012.
2. *Ibid.*
3. *Ibid.*
4. *Ibid.*
5. *Ibid.*
6. *Economic Survey* 2011-12.
7. *Ibid.*
8. *Ibid.*

4

Easing Out of Inflation

Headline year-on-year WPI inflation after remaining persistently high over the past two years started to show signs of moderation in the latter half of financial year 2011-12. It started with 9.7 per cent, and briefly touched double digits in September 2011 before coming down to 6.6 per cent in January 2012. Consumer price inflation (CPI) for the major indices declined to below 7 per cent in December 2011, and fell further in January 2012 as shown in Table 4.1 below.

Table 4.1: Annual Inflation as per Different Price Indices

(Per Cent)

	WPI		CPI-IW		CPI-AL		CPI-RL	
Month	2010-11	2011-12	2010-11	2011-12	2010-11	2011-12	2010-11	2011-12
April	10.88	9.74	13.33	9.41	14.96	9.11	14.96	9.11
May	10.48	9.56	13.91	8.72	13.68	9.63	13.68	9.63
June	10.25	9.51	13.73	8.62	13.02	9.32	13.02	9.14
July	9.98	9.36	11.25	8.43	11.02	9.03	11.24	9.03
Aug.	8.87	9.78	9.88	8.99	9.65	9.52	9.66	9.71
Sept.	8.98	10.00	9.82	10.06	9.13	9.43	9.34	9.25
Oct.	9.08	9.87	9.70	9.39	8.43	9.36	8.45	9.73
Nov.	8.20	9.46	8.33	9.34	7.14	8.95	6.95	9.14
Dec.	9.45	7.47P	9.47	6.49	7.99	6.37	8.01	6.72
Jan.	9.47	6.55P	9.30	5.32	8.67	4.92	8.69	5.27
Feb.	9.54	8.82	8.55	8.55				
Mar.	9.68	8.82	9.14	8.96				
Average	9.56	10.45	10.00	10.01				

Note: P : Provisional; CPI : Consumer Price Index; IW : Industrial Workers; AL : Agriculture Labour; RL : Rural Labour.

Source: The Office of the Economic Adviser (OEA), Department of Industrial Policy and Promotion (DIPP)

Headline WPI inflation remained relatively sticky at around 9 per cent during the calendar year 2011. The factors contributing to this situation and their relative importance have been changing over time. Some of the contributory factors during this period were: (i) higher primary articles prices driven by vegetables, eggs, meat, and fish due to changing dietary pattern of consumers; (ii) increasing global commodity prices, especially metal and chemical prices, which ultimately led to higher domestic manufactured prices; and (iii) persistently high international crude petroleum prices in the last two years averaging around US$ 111 per barrel in the calendar year 2011 as compared to US$ 80 per barrel in 2010. However, the rates of inflation showed a comfortable position as can be seen from Table 4.2.

Table 4.2: Wholesale Price Index and Rates of Inflation

[Base Year: 2004-05]

Week Ending 14th January, 2012 (Base: 2004-05)

Commodities/ Major Groups/ Groups/Sub-Groups	Weight	WPI Jan 14, 2012	Latest week over week		Build up from end March		Year on year		52 week Average
			2010-11	2011-12	2010-11	2011-12	2010-11	2011-12	
Primary Articles	20.12	199.1	0.57	0.00	17.29	5.68	18.35	1.89	11.12
Food Articles	14.34	191.4	0.89	0.26	17.64	6.87	17.14	-1.03	8.10
Cereals	3.37	178.2	0.41	0.85	4.64	3.91	1.52	2.71	3.96
Rice	1.79	173.3	0.06	0.23	4.60	3.90	3.39	1.58	3.15
Wheat	1.12	169.2	0.81	1.01	2.34	-0.82	-4.16	-3.37	-1.42
Pulses	0.72	212.8	0.86	-0.47	-5.74	12.35	-14.65	12.77	-0.38
Vegetables	1.74	142.1	1.21	-1.11	106.94	-0.91	70.63	-47.06	0.53
Potato	0.20	97.7	-2.17	-0.41	23.65	-8.95	-15.83	-22.46	-3.85
Onion	0.18	144.7	3.05	-12.41	341.65	-14.23	157.82	-79.10	-14.22
Fruits	2.11	173.0	3.13	-1.42	13.21	-7.14	18.35	5.17	19.06
Milk	3.24	201.6	0.06	0.75	5.34	15.86	14.03	12.25	9.38
Egg, Meat & Fish	2.41	230.2	0.47	1.05	9.31	16.62	14.48	20.33	11.48
Non-Food Articles	4.26	179.9	-0.22	-1.48	18.79	-6.16	24.15	0.56	16.07
Fibres	0.88	197.5	0.04	-5.41	49.51	-31.18	51.50	-13.03	35.18
Oil Seeds	1.78	163.6	-0.07	0.86	5.59	8.42	2.14	14.01	11.71
Minerals	1.52	325.1	0.00	0.71	12.35	21.94	16.21	24.94	22.65
Fuel & Power	14.91	172.7	0.00	0.00	7.71	9.37	10.87	14.45	13.36
Liquefied Petroleum Gas	0.91	147.3	0.00	0.00	14.99	14.27	14.99	14.27	13.83
Petrol	1.09	177.7	0.00	0.00	17.78	12.04	25.06	17.14	25.02
High Speed Diesel Oil	4.67	167.8	0.00	0.00	6.22	9.24	14.71	9.24	8.63

Source: http://eaindustry.nic.in/

Inflation in primary articles declined drastically, falling to 2.25 per cent by January 2012, after remaining in double digits for almost two years. However, inflation in fuel continued to remain high during 2010-11 and 2011-12. Inflation in manufactured products had started to accelerate since January 2011, remaining range-bound between 7 and 8 per cent in 2011, due to a surge in metal and chemical prices, but it has also recently started to moderate.

Compared to a relatively benign and stable inflationary period in the earlier part of the last decade, average headline WPI inflation started to rise in 2008-09 and persisted. The pressure was mainly from primary and fuel products with the average inflation in these commodities remaining persistently in double digits for a major period since 2008-09. In comparison, inflation in manufactured products remained relatively stable, dropping sharply in 2009-10 because of the global economic crisis and impacts in India, before it started to pick up and exceed its long run average of around 5 per cent in early 2011-12. Among individual product groups, inflation in food products, beverages, textiles, chemicals, and basic metals remained elevated mainly on account of high global commodity prices and cost push pressures[1] as shown in Table 4.3.

Fuel Prices

Fuel was another contributory factor behind high headline inflation in the 2010-11 and 2011-12. The sharp rise and volatility of prices of oil and petroleum products in international markets has become a matter of global concern. Crude oil prices remained volatile during financial year 2011-12 because of political upheaval in the major oil-exporting countries coupled with increasing uncertainty in the global economic environment. Crude oil prices have been increasing steadily since December 2008. International crude oil (Brent) prices have moved up very sharply from US$ 75 per barrel to over US$ 114 per barrel in June 2011, a 52 per cent year-on-year increase. It stood at US$ 125 a barrel on 20 March 2012.

The average price of the Indian basket of crude oil which was US$ 69.76 per barrel in 2009-10 has gone up to US$ 85.09

Table 4.3: Annual Average Inflation by Major Heads in WPI

(Per Cent)

Commodities	Weight	2005-06	2006-07	2007-08	2008-09	2009-10	2010-11 (Apr.-Jan.)	2011-12 (Apr.-Jan.)P
All commodities	100.00	4.47	6.59	4.74	8.05	3.80	9.55	9.11
Primary articles	20.12	4.30	9.62	8.33	11.05	12.66	18.41	9.91
Food articles	14.34	5.38	9.62	6.97	9.09	15.27	16.75	7.15
Non-food articles	4.26	-3.32	5.80	11.86	12.87	5.47	20.49	12.27
Minerals	1.52	15.15	18.64	11.84	22.08	8.79	26.74	24.15
Fuel & power	14.91	13.58	6.46	0.03	11.57	-2.11	12.24	13.67
Coal	2.09	17.60	0.09	3.38	24.30	3.43	5.07	13.26
Mineral oils	9.36	16.73	9.14	-0.90	12.35	-4.29	16.03	17.12
Electricity	3.45	2.57	2.66	0.84	0.19	0.96	5.74	1.17
Manufactured products	64.97	2.42	5.66	4.78	6.16	2.22	5.46	7.58
Food products	9.97	1.19	5.29	3.54	8.69	13.49	4.26	7.35
Beverages, tobacco & products	1.76	4.66	5.10	6.52	9.52	6.11	7.08	11.81
Textiles	7.33	-1.06	1.88	0.73	1.62	3.43	11.05	9.51
Wood & wood products	0.59	5.74	5.84	6.69	9.49	9.60	4.03	8.00
Paper & paper products	2.03	3.63	4.60	2.96	4.20	2.20	4.84	5.94
Leather & leather products	0.84	4.25	7.95	3.06	5.47	4.93	-0.92	1.76
Rubber & plastic products	2.99	1.91	5.61	4.28	4.53	0.74	5.98	6.82
Chemicals & their products	12.02	3.79	4.96	3.57	4.64	-0.26	5.00	8.74
Non-metallic mineral products	2.56	3.41	1.58	11.19	2.63	6.97	2.59	5.52
Basic metals, alloys & products	10.75	2.23	9.28	10.29	11.96	-6.12	8.10	11.12
Machinery & machine tools	8.93	3.58	6.31	3.65	2.89	0.46	2.73	3.11
Transport, equipment/parts	5.21	2.69	2.22	2.47	5.36	3.08	2.96	3.54

Source: OEA, DIPP. P: Provisional

per barrel in 2010-11 and further to US$ 109.97 per barrel in 2011-12 (up to December 2011). The pass-through of higher international crude oil prices on the domestic front was clearly evident as inflation in non-administered mineral oil, which consists of aviation turbine fuel, bitumen, furnace oil, and naphtha, recorded an increase of 41 per cent between September 2010 and January 2011.[2]

Global prices of crude oil and petroleum products play a decisive role in the domestic pricing of petroleum products because over 75 per cent of the country's crude oil requirement is met through imports. The price of crude oil and petroleum products in the international oil markets therefore has considerable impact on domestic prices of petroleum products. With the dismantling of administered petrol prices (with effect from 26 June 2010), prices of petrol have risen by 12.46 per cent during 2011-12 (April-December) from ₹ 58.37 per litre (April 2011) to ₹ 65.64 per litre (December 2011).[3]

Despite the increase in international oil prices, Indian consumers have been partially insulated from the adverse impact of price rise, as the prices of three important petroleum products, namely public distribution system (PDS) kerosene, LPG, and diesel continued to be administered by the government and the price rise has been passed on only partially. During April-December 2011-12 with the increasing subsidy burden and mounting under-recoveries of oil marketing companies (OMCs), the prices of PDS kerosene were moderately revised upwards from ₹ 12.73 per litre to ₹ 14.83 per litre, i.e. an increase of 16.50 per cent, and diesel from ₹ 37.71 per litre (April 2011) to ₹ 40.91 per litre, i.e. 8.49 per cent increase. The prices of domestic LPG cylinders have also been increased by 15.53 per cent from ₹ 345.35 per cylinder to ₹ 399 per cylinder. As a result, domestic fuel inflation was 14.21 per cent in January 2012.[4]

But even after these increases, the products remain heavily subsidised, with prices lower than in most countries, including among regional neighbours such as Sri Lanka and Bangladesh. The OMCs are incurring huge under-recoveries owing to non-revision of selling prices of diesel, domestic LPG, and PDS kerosene in line with their prevailing international prices.

According to RBI, "Fuel inflation moderated from over 15 per cent in November-December 2011 to 10.4 per cent in March 2012 even as global crude oil prices rose sharply, reflecting the absence of commensurate pass-through to domestic consumers. However, mirroring the high international crude oil prices, inflation in respect of non-administered mineral oils remained elevated at 19.8 per cent in March."[5] The problem is that high oil subsidies are worsening the already bad fiscal position. Government's main focus should be taking measures to control fiscal debt from rising above comfortable position rather than using only interest rate as a mechanism to control inflation.

"Notably, consumer price index (CPI) inflation (as measured by the new series, base year: 2010) increased sharply from 7.7 per cent in January to 8.8 per cent in February reflecting a reversal in food inflation. CPI, excluding food and fuel, was in double digits, suggesting that price pressures were still high at the retail level. Driven by food prices, inflation based on other CPIs reversed its declining trend of previous four months to increase in February 2012. According to the latest round of household survey conducted by the Reserve Bank, inflation expectations, although still elevated, have moderated after rising for the previous three quarters."[6]

Food Inflation

The food price index consists of two sub-components, viz. primary food articles and manufactured food products. The overall weight of the composite food index in the WPI is 24.31 per cent (primary food articles: 14.34 per cent and manufactured food products: 9.97 per cent). The primary food article inflation has been a cause of serious concern for the government during 2009-11. It remained at an average level of 16.75 per cent in 2010-11 and 15.27 per cent in 2009-10 (April-January) mainly due to increase in (a) fruits and vegetables prices, and (b) prices of protein-rich items such as milk, eggs, fish, and meat. However, in the current financial year (April-January 2011-12), average inflation in food articles has significantly declined to 7.15 per cent. This was mainly on account of sizeable drop in fruits and vegetables prices, as a result of which inflation in these commodities has now turned negative in December 2011 and January 2012 as shown in Table 4.4.

Inflation for 31 essential commodities including cereals pulses, milk, fish, meat, edible oils, kerosene oil, etc. for both WPI and CPI tracked each other closely. Year-on-year inflation in this particular category, according to Economic Survey

Table 4.4: WPI-based Year-on-Year Inflation in Major Subgroups

(per cent)

	Food-grains	Fruits & vegetables	Milk	Eggs, meat, & fish	Suga	Edible oils
Weight	4.09	3.84	3.24	2.41	1.74	3.04
Apr. 2010	11.05	14.32	27.91	38.61	24.55	0.09
Apr. 2011	2.15	26.48	2.87	11.14	3.45	13.47
May 2011	2.61	15.23	6.11	6.59	5.53	15.47
Jun. 2011	2.08	7.49	11.52	9.88	7.53	15.80
Jul. 2011	2.53	11.62	10.77	9.56	3.96	14.76
Aug. 2011	3.33	18.29	9.41	10.42	6.28	14.72
Sept. 2011	3.91	15.06	10.28	11.88	7.38	13.87
Oct. 2011	5.48	13.48	11.12	12.43	7.31	12.93
Nov. 2011	4.59	8.96	10.91	11.40	6.18	11.82
Dec. 2011P	4.11	-14.89	11.02	11.88	4.34	11.52
Jan. 2012P	4.08	-21.83	12.16	18.63	2.25	9.59

Source: OEA, DIPP. P: Provisional.

2011-12, declined from about 24 per cent in January 2010 to about 5 to 6 per cent in November and December 2011.

According to RBI, "Food articles inflation, which was 8.1 per cent during April-December 2011, briefly turned negative in January 2012 reflecting the seasonal decline in food prices, particularly of vegetables, combined with a high base effect. However, it increased sharply to 6.1 per cent in February and further to 9.9 per cent in March 2012 with the wearing-off of the base effect and rise in vegetables prices. Inflation in protein-based items—'eggs, fish and meat', milk and pulses remained high, reflecting persistent structural demand-supply imbalances."[7]

Main Drivers of Food Inflation

The major drivers of food inflation during 2011-12 were milk, eggs/meat/fish, and edible oils. In comparison with the previous year when cereals, vegetables, and sugar were the main contributors to food inflation, 2011-12 witnessed higher contribution from manufactured food products, especially edible oils due to higher global prices of soyabean oil, palm oil, etc. India's edible oil requirement is estimated at 16-17 million tonnes, about 50 per cent of which is met through imports of crude palm oil, sunflower oil, soyabean oil, and refined, bleached and deodorised palmolein. An increase in global prices thus has led to higher domestic prices of these commodities.

The government claims that in order to arrest the adverse impact of food inflation on the common man, the policy has continued to lay emphasis on the PDS, import-export policy, distribution of essential commodities at below market prices through state public-sector units (PSUs), anti-hoarding operations, and strengthening of supply chain efficiency. Even more important, the response of farmers to better prices and two consecutive years of good monsoons have resulted in increased production. But these claims do not hold good on many accounts. Firstly, the PDS itself has failed to assure regular supply to poor sections at lower rates in many regions. Secondly, those who do not get food grain at cheap rates, continued to suffer due to high prices. Thirdly, farmers did not get higher prices for their produce. Lastly, the middlemen got a chunk of profit.

According to RBI, "Non-food manufactured products inflation, which was 8.4 per cent in November 2011, decelerated significantly to 5.8 per cent in February and further to 4.7 per cent in March 2012. This reflected both a slowdown in domestic demand and softening of global non-oil commodity prices. The momentum indicator of non-food manufactured products inflation (seasonally adjusted 3-month moving average inflation rate) also showed a declining trends."[8] But non-food inflation was also likely to rise from April 2012, especially after the impact of Budget 2012-13 in which taxes on some non-food items have been raised. An example of prices of cars which stand increased w.e.f. April 2012 onwards. The inflation figures that came in May 2012 actually showed a rising trend.

Some expert views on January 2012 inflation data are given below:

Nirav Dalal, President and Managing Director, Debt Capital Markets, Yes Bank, Mumbai

"These numbers are not heartening if you look at them on a sequential basis. The core manufacturing is still growing at the same pace it did in the month ago period. Unless there is a decisive pause sequentially in inflation, I would be surprised if RBI hurriedly cuts rates. I expect the 10-year benchmark yield to hold around 8.10-8.15 per cent unless RBI announces open market operations in the two-most liquid bonds of 8.79 per cent, 2021 bonds, and 9.15 per cent, 2024 bonds."

Anubhuti Sahay, Economist, Standard Chartered Bank, Mumbai

"As core inflation has also come well below 7 per cent, both on elevated base effect and lower price pressure, it is likely to provide the RBI more comfort on easing interest rates."

Deven Choksey, Managing Director, K.R. Choksey Shares & Securities, Mumbai

"The biggest factor for inflation coming down seems to be lower contribution from food commodities because of the bumper crop. We expect inflation to remain at moderate levels in the near future, and if it settles around 6 per cent, it will be a happy situation. I don't think the RBI will be in a hurry to cut rates, but we expect them to monitor the situation. One of the factors they may be concerned about is the high crude prices."

Risks Remain Despite Easing Out of Inflation

Fall in inflation increases the chances of monetary easing by RBI but it has warned that macroeconomic risks could reverse trend. India's most closely watched inflation rate declined to its lowest level in 26 months in January, improving the odds for a round of monetary easing by the RBI. The Wholesale Price Index (WPI)-based inflation dropped to 6.55 per cent in January 2012 from 7.47 per cent in December 2011 as prices fell across the board. Such decline was more than expected. A Bloomberg survey had forecast inflation to slow to 6.7 per cent in January, while the Reserve Bank of India (RBI), in its monetary policy review had predicted that inflation will fall to 7 per cent only by the close of the fiscal year at end-March 2012. However, the analysts have cautioned against premature optimism, especially given that the decrease was largely because of the base effect of higher inflation in the year-earlier period and the fact that underlying macroeconomic risks could reverse the trend.

Finance Minister Pranab Mukherjee was confident that the inflation rate would moderate further in the coming months, although a "softening in the prices of manufactured goods, despite the rapid decline in non-food primary inflation, may be more gradual". As stated earlier, Mukherjee expected the March-end inflation rate to be close to 6 per cent. Mukherjee said the main worry centred on the prices of edible oils, milk and some animal proteins that may fuel food inflation as required institutional reforms in agricultural marketing and improvements in storage and cold chain systems will take place after a lag.

Food inflation contracted 0.52 per cent in January 2012 on the back of falling vegetable prices, compared with a 0.74 per cent rise a month ago. Core inflation, a measure of price increases in non-food manufactured items, declined to a year's low of 6.7 per cent from 7.7 per cent a month ago. The November inflation figure was revised to 9.5 per cent from the 9.1 per cent reported earlier, indicating an upward bias to the provisional data. Although the drop in the January 2012 inflation rate seems to have enthused the market, it's not yet convincing enough proof that prices are falling by the desired extent, the experts felt.

"What is important is to note that despite recording an average monthly inflation of 9.5 per cent for two years at a stretch, the index (WPI) has not come off from the elevated levels, thereby indicating that it is merely the base effect at play rather than prices actually coming off", said Kunal Kumar of Roubini Global Economics.

Rajeev Malik, senior economist at CLSA Singapore, said that the easing out of inflation in January 2012 should be interpreted with caution as local fuel prices have not been adjusted due to the ongoing state legislative elections. He said food inflation in December and January was affected favourably by seasonal factors. "The favourable base effect will reverse from February 2012 onwards and food composite inflation will probably settle in the 5-6 per cent range", Malik said.

According to apex bank's latest inflation expectations survey of households for the October-December quarter, the proportion of respondents who expect prices to rise by "more than the current rate" in next one year has increased to 76.9 per cent from 73.5 per cent in the previous round.

Citigroup India economists Rohini Malkani and Anushka Shah wrote in a report that despite the decline in WPI, inflation would remain well above RBI's comfort zone of 4-5 per cent due to the structural factors influencing the rate, suppressed fuel prices, and interplay of commodity prices and currencies.

Crisil Research said on the basis of an analysis that it expects inflation for 2012-13 at 5.8 per cent. "Lower inflation vis-à-vis 2011-12 is mainly due to a high base and low pricing power of corporates led by sluggish domestic demand", its report said. "Likely upward revision of domestic fuel prices and an expected reversal in the seasonal decline in food prices from April 2012 onwards will, however, exert pressure on inflation, the report added."

While the dip in inflation was sharper than expectations, analysts said RBI is unlikely to advance its rate cut cycle based on this data.

Analysts said they expected the government would breach its fiscal deficit target of 4.6 per cent of gross domestic product in the year ending 31 March 2012 by at least one percentage point because of underestimation of subsidies in the budget and lower-than-anticipated revenue collections.

RBI, in its February 2012 monetary policy review, signalled a shift in focus towards boosting economic growth, from combating inflation. In January, the central bank had cut CRR by half a percentage point to 5.5 per cent while keeping policy rates unchanged.

The central bank cautioned that in the absence of credible fiscal consolidation, it will be constrained from lowering the policy rate in response to decelerating private consumption and investment spending.

Mukherjee, who presented the annual budget on 16 March 2012 faced the unenviable task of cutting the high fiscal deficit without hurting growth momentum.

India's headline inflation slowed to its lowest level in more than two years in January as food prices fell, sparking hopes that the central bank will start cutting interest rates sooner or later to battle economic slowdown.

The data released in March 2012 by the government, was broadly in line with the 6.60 per cent average forecast in a Reuters poll, after a rise of 7.47 per cent in December 2011. According to A. Prasanna, an economist at ICICI Securities Primary Dealership in Mumbai, "Usually prices rise in January, but that has not happened to such an extent this time. The manufacturing and core manufacturing inflation have slowed down more than expected. This has raised chances of a 25-basis point rate cut in March (rather) than in April. The rupee's rebound in January also partially helped inflation to ease." The Reserve Bank of India was widely expected to start cutting interest rates in the quarter beginning 1st April as it looks to stimulate an economy that is headed for its slowest growth in three years.

The Reserve Bank of India ran a 20-month interest rate tightening cycle until October 2011 to slow down inflation to 7 per cent by March 2012. Economists expect the RBI, during 2012, to cut its policy rate by 100 basis points from the then 8.5 per cent, with a cut of 50 basis points in the April-June quarter.

In keeping its policy rate unchanged in March 2012 month, the RBI cited risks to inflation from global crude oil prices and the weak rupee, as well as India's yawning fiscal deficit. The rupee fell nearly 16 per cent last year against the dollar, before rebounding about 7.5 per cent in 2012 till March.

It is important to note that although inflation remained below 7 per cent in March 2012, food inflation rose to 9.9 per cent from 6.07 per cent in February 2012. Non-food inflation was also expected to rise due to raise of taxes on some items in Budget 2012-13.

The fiscal deficit, however, is widely expected to be almost a percentage point higher than the government's target of 4.6 per cent of gross domestic product for the fiscal year ending March 31, largely reflecting a slowdown in economic growth.

The Indian economy has lost momentum as lingering Euro zone debt woes together with high interest rates at home have hit capital investments. The government cut the economic growth forecast for the current fiscal year to 6.9 per cent, the slowest pace in three years. "If inflation number stays soft going ahead and the GDP print also comes soft in February then together, there is a chance that RBI may cut rates early", said Siddhartha Sanyal, chief India economist at Barclays Capital. Annual food prices in January 2012 fell 0.52 per cent from 0.74 per cent rise in December 2011, helped by improved supplies of vegetables. However, prices of protein-rich food items such as eggs, fish and meat, milk and pulses remained high, suggesting that food inflation remains a potential problem area.

Finance Minister Pranab Mukherjee said edible oils and milk are among items that "may continue to threaten food inflation". The minister, who said inflation remains "unacceptably high" said he expects it to keep moderating in coming months although softening in prices of manufactured goods "may be more gradual".

However, the situation in March 2012 was completely changed. Food inflation, which had gone in the negative territory in January 2012, came back with a vengenance to be close to 10 per cent in March. This only shows that easing of food prices was due to seasonal supply of vegetables, etc. and not the result of RBI's high interest rate policy.

Data released in mid-May 2012 showed that food inflation has surged higher as supply failed to keep pace with demand. The index for food articles group rose by 4.9 per cent to 206.4 in April 2012 from 196.8 for the previous month due to higher prices of fruits and vegetables (19 per cent), barley (5 per cent), tea (4 per cent), masur, maize and bajra (3 per cent each) and ragi and wheat (2 per cent each) and fish-marine, gram, rice and milk (1 per cent each). The government also revised upwards the inflation number for February to 7.4 per cent from the previously reported 6.9 per cent, which analysts said showed that inflationary pressures remained strong.

Such inflation data could also force the government to postpone any increase in fuel prices. The easing global crude oil prices could help, but any move to resist raising prices could upset its plans to repair government finances.

Rate Rise Cycle at its Peak: RBI

Saying that the January headline inflation at 6.55 per cent is in line with its expectations, Reserve Bank Deputy Governor Subir Gokarn said the data underlines that the rate hike cycle is at its peak. "It (headline inflation) is in our trajectory...till it matches our projection, it reinforces our belief that rate cycle has peaked", he said. Gokarn who is incharge of monetary policy at Mint Road, stated that in RBI's view, inflation is "trending down from the highs of nine per cent plus to something closer to seven per cent". The data released in Feb. 2012 said overall inflation had fallen to the 26-month low of 6.55 per cent due to a deflation in the food basket. The apex bank, which ushered in a series of 13 consecutive hikes over a 19-month period till December last year to tame the uncomfortably high inflation, has put a year-end target of headline inflation at 6 per cent. However, in its monetary policy announcement on 24 January 2012 where it cut the cash reserve ratio but kept its overnight lending rate unchanged, the RBI articulated a shift in focus from inflation to growth in its monetary stance. Gokarn mentioned jump in oil prices and the possibility of food inflation going back into positive territory as the future potential difficulties. The non-food manufacturing inflation, which stood at 6.49 per cent year-on-year, was also broadly in line with RBI projection, Gokarn said. In its February 2012 policy review, the RBI had cut CRR or the percentage of deposits banks have to park with RBI, by 0.50 per cent due to pressure on liquidity, and analysts are expecting it to cut its policy rate at its future reviews.

Despite some relief on the price front, the virtual drying up of investments is a source of worry. The annual wholesale price inflation rate has fallen to 6.55 per cent in January, marking a fourth straight month of decline from the 10 per cent high of September. Much of it—which was probably in line with the Reserve Bank of India's view—had to do with softening food prices from a bumper kharif harvest aided by good monsoon rains. Food inflation had, indeed, fallen far more spectacularly than the general inflation rate: from a level of 9.62 per cent in September 2011 to minus 0.52 per cent in January 2012. Experts felt that if this is more of a one-time phenomenon, it could well be reversed if the next monsoon turns out to be bad (which is what some of the global weather models are indicating). This view has also been reinforced by the RBI's latest Inflation Expectations Survey of Households. It points to a higher proportion of respondents who believe that prices would rise by "more than the current rate" in the next three quarters, even while maintaining a more favourable outlook for January-March. In other words, the inflation expectations beyond the near-term continue to be high.

The above view was quite right as inflation figures of April 2012 proved. The return of high inflation explains the RBI's obvious reluctance to ease its hard money stance. But the main issue is about identifying the problems confronting the Indian economy including high fiscal deficit, low industrial growth, decrease in credit growth, drying up of investments, etc. A low capital goods production index is yet another worry as this sector has registered negative year-on-year growth for four consecutive months from September to December, indicative of hardly any new orders for plant and equipment being placed by companies. It has implications for not only future growth, but even inflation, which requires a durable solution that can come only from augmenting supply. In the event of no extra productive capacities being created, any revival in demand only increases the chances of prices going up. It is all the more necessary, then, not to have policies that in the name of fighting inflation actually end up stifling supply response.

That being the case, the right policy to adopt in the present circumstances is one of fiscal consolidation, redirecting government expenditures away from consumption to investment. This, in combination with much-needed lowering of interest rates and credible measures signalling the government's commitment to reforms, would put an end to the current 'famine' as far as green field projects are concerned. A revival of investment may ultimately have a benign impact on prices as well. But the question is whether the government is willing to follow this plan of action or not.

Table 4.5 shows trends in inflation related to non-food manufactured products like textile, paper, wood, leather, rubber, chemicals, etc. A comparison between figures of December 2011 with those of February 2012 shows that inflation has eased out, which presented a case for reducing policy rates.

RBI Shifts Focus to Growth, Cuts CRR by 50 bps

Reserve Bank of India cut cash reserve requirements for banks by 50 basis points on 9 March 2012 to ease tight liquidity conditions, signalling a shift in policy towards reviving growth after two years of fighting inflation. With core inflation still stubbornly high at that time, the Reserve Bank of India, as expected, left its policy repo rate unchanged at 8.50 per cent for the second consecutive review. The RBI had raised rates 13 times between March 2010 and October 2011, making it one of the most hawkish central bank anywhere. "The growth-inflation balance of the monetary policy stance has now shifted to growth, while at the same time ensuring that inflationary pressures remain contained", RBI Governor Duvvuri Subbarao said in his policy statement. Subbarao said the "current inflation trajectory" made it premature to cut the policy rate, disappointing markets looking for definitive guidance on an interest rate cut. But since the economic growth rate has now decreased to below 7 per cent, RBI's reluctance to cut policy rates and interest rates during the financial year 2011-12 did not go well for industry which was expecting a cut.

Economists and other experts also felt that the RBI had kept to its hawkish stance long after most central banks around the world have shifted their focus to growth.

Annual headline inflation, measured by the wholesale price index, slowed to a two-year low of 7.47 per cent in December 2011, thanks to a sharp decline in food inflation. However, manufactured product inflation edged up from the previous month, and the RBI said in a report that the two drivers of rate policy would be core inflation and the impact of exchange rate changes on inflation. Thus, the cut in cash reserve ratio was a reaction to the acute liquidity deficit that was persisting.

Subbarao reiterated his call for more fiscal discipline from New Delhi, which was widely expected to fall far short of its deficit-cutting target for the year 2011-12.

"In the absence of credible fiscal consolidation, the Reserve Bank will be constrained from lowering the policy rate in response to decelerating private consumption and investment spending", Subbarao said in his report. C. Rangarajan was of the opinion that the RBI should cut interest rates only when there are definite signs that non-food inflation was easing. The RBI said it expected a 'modest' recovery in growth in the fiscal year 2012-13 and said that while inflation may ease, price pressures persist. "Upside risks to inflation arise from global crude oil prices, the lingering impact of rupee depreciation and slippage in the fiscal deficit", it said.

According to D. Subbarao, three considerations went into forming our policy decision. First was that growth has decelerated for a number of reasons which included: global environment, domestic environment and earlier monetary policy tightening. The second consideration was that inflation, as measured by wholesale price index (WPI) was moderating. However, he pointed out that food inflation which is seasonal was largely responsible. The third consideration was the liquidity situation. RBI has infused liquidity through open market operations (buying government bonds from banks) but it has also drained liquidity because of forex intervention (selling dollars and receiving rupees). Ultimately, it was a net drain from the system and there was a structural shortfall in liquidity. Banks felt the cut would improve their ability to lend to productive sectors of the economy and the cost of the money to them will come down.

The CRR cut should be seen as a signal of easing interest, Subbarao said, although he was non-committal on the timing or extent of potential rate cuts. "The reduction can also be viewed as a reinforcement of the guidance that future rate actions will be towards lowering them", Subbarao said.

With inflation showing signs of finally easing and risks to growth on the rise, the RBI was widely expected to cut interest rates by the end of June, if not sooner. It has already signalled that it is finished raising rates after 13 increases between March 2010 and October 2011. Headline inflation slowed down to a two-year low of 7.47 per cent in December, but that was due almost entirely to a drop in food inflation at that time. The non-food manufactured inflation at 7.7 per cent in December remained way above the central bank's comfort zone.

High Fiscal Deficit Restraining Policy Rate Cut: RBI

In his January policy review, the RBI Governor flagged the inflationary risks stemming from the government's failure to contain its fiscal deficit and had said a lack of credible fiscal consolidation would constrain him from lowering rates. He had urged the government to use the March 2012 budget to signal fiscal consolidation.

"In the absence of credible fiscal consolidation, the Reserve Bank will be constrained from lowering the policy rate in response to decelerating private consumption and investment spending", Reserve Bank Governor D. Subbarao said after announcing RBI's third quarter policy review.

The RBI Governor said that strong signs of fiscal consolidation are necessary to create a space for lowering policy rate without the risk of resurgent inflation. He also made a case for freeing of diesel prices to control the subsidy burden. "As the food subsidy bill is expected to rise, it will be prudent to fully deregulate diesel prices to contain both aggregate demand and trade deficit", he said. Finance Minister Pranab Mukherjee had earlier said that the government's subsidy burden could exceed budgeted target by ₹ 1 lakh crore on account of petroleum subsidy. "The gross fiscal deficit for 2011-12 will overshoot the budget estimate substantially", he said. The government pegged the fiscal deficit target at 4.6 per cent of the GDP for the year 2011-12.

Subbarao said the slippage in fiscal deficit would add to inflationary pressure. The RBI in its macroeconomic review of the economy released ahead of third quarter review of monetary policy had said that the higher expenditure on petroleum subsidy could drive up the fiscal deficit by around 0.8 percentage points of GDP for 2011-12.

The government will face additional pressures on account of food subsidies when the proposed Food Security Bill is enacted and implemented, RBI said, adding, the government needs to control its expenditure on petroleum subsidies.

The RBI's statement came against the backdrop of a worsening fiscal situation. The government has said that meeting the fiscal deficit target for the financial year 2011-12 would be a tough challenge. Finance ministry officials and analysts said the fiscal deficit in the year was likely to be in the range of 5.2 per cent to about 6 per cent, up from the estimated 4.6 per cent of GDP. Adding to the pressure is new spending commitments and rising subsidies that analysts say could worsen the overall fiscal situation and widen the consolidated deficit—both at the centre and states.

Subbarao Ignored Panel Advice on Rate Cut in January

The minutes of the meeting of a panel that advises the Reserve Bank of India on monetary policy show that the central bank was under pressure to cut rates as fears of a slowdown increased. However, D. Subbarao decided to hold rates and instead addressed only liquidity issues through a cut in cash reserve ratio. This is not the first time that Subbarao has not gone by the recommendations of the advisory panel. In July 2011, the central bank raised interest rates by 50 basis points although a few members were in favour of a pause in rate hikes and others wanted the hike restricted to 25 basis points. Subsequently, in the October 2011 meeting too, as many as five members were of the view that RBI should not hike the repo rate, yet the central bank went ahead with a 25 basis point hike. In January, RBI left the repo rate unchanged but reduced cash reserve ratio by 50 basis points. The minutes of the 18 January 2012 meeting of the technical advisory committee show that most members wanted a cut in interest rates.

Managing Director, HDFC Bank, Aditya Puri feels that the act of keeping interest rates high has been going on for a long time, calling it "policy paralysis". He said, "I don't believe in this policy paralysis business in the sense you can't have 7.5 per cent growth with policy paralysis. It is being overdone. Some

Table 4.5: Trends in Inflation Related to Non-Food Manufactured Products

	Weight	Y-o-Y Inflation				M-o-M	Buildup*
		Dec 2011		Jan 2012	Feb 2012	Feb 2012	Feb 2012
		Initial	Revised	Initial	Initial	Initial	Initial
Non Food Manufactured	**55.00**	**7.7%**	**8.0%**	**6.7%**	**5.7%**	**0.4%**	**3.4%**
Beverages, Tobacco, Tobacco Prod.	1.8	13.2%	14.1%	9.4%	10.1%	1.3%	7.5%
Textiles	7.3	4.1%	4.3%	1.4%	-0.7%	0.4%	-5.0%
Wood & Wood Products	0.6	9.3%	8.9%	8.6%	8.2%	0.2%	6.8%
Paper & Paper Products	2.0	5.2%	5.3%	4.6%	3.2%	-0.1%	1.1%
Leather & Leather Products	0.8	2.9%	3.0%	6.5%	5.5%	-0.5%	3.1%
Rubber & Plastic Products	3.0	4.4%	4.9%	3.3%	2.1%	-0.1%	0.4%
Chemicals & Chemical Products	12.0	9.8%	9.9%	9.1%	8.0%	0.4%	5.3%
Non-Metallic Mineral Products	2.6	8.4%	8.6%	8.3%	6.7%	-0.2%	4.7%
Basic Metals, Alloys & Metal Prod.	10.7	13.0%	13.5%	12.0%	10.4%	0.7%	8.4%
Machinery & Machine Tools	8.9	2.9%	3.1%	2.6%	2.8%	0.3%	1.6%
Transport, Equipment & Parts	5.2	4.5%	4.5%	3.1%	3.2%	0.2%	2.4%

Source: Office of the Economic Advisor, Ministry of Commerce and Industry, GoI, ICRA Estimates, * Buildup with reference to April 2011

industries which have had problems may have had some paralysis but that also if you are not in line with the laws and regulations." But he did agree with demands that the government needs to boost overall sentiments and suggested that tax policy can be used to contain inflation. "We need decisions on fiscal policy to control inflation, which the RBI has been saying for a while, because if you control only through monetary policy you are quite likely to bring growth below acceptable parameters. That has ramifications on tax collections, fiscal deficit, on the rupee and on business sentiments. And, it may not, as we have seen, in the full control of inflation."

According to D. Subbarao, maintaining the right balance between growth and bringing down inflation within acceptable limits will be a challenging task for the central bank. "There are several challenges, first is striking the right balance between growth and price stability", he said.

Defending the RBI's aggressive monetary tightening, which has drawn criticism for its impact on growth, Dr Subbarao said, "It is a legitimate concern that inflation has not come down appreciably despite hikes in interest rate...but it has to be noted that the rate of price rise would have been even higher had monetary tightening steps not been taken. Inflation rate could have been higher at 12-13 per cent, unlike 9.7 per cent at present."

In spite of low growth due to the sovereign debt crisis in Europe, India was not into recession, D. Subbarao said, "There is a projection that Europe will grow by minus two per cent in 2012. Lot of people are talking about recession. Our growth rate might have fallen, but to say it is a recession would be to challenge textbook economics", he pointed out.

Easing Growth may Lower Inflation: RBI

The Reserve Bank of India said that the moderation of economic growth would help in containing inflation, which is still a cause for concern for policymakers as well as the common man. "Higher oil prices clearly play a role as does the currency movement, but there is also the growth moderation, which we are seeing, which might actually help contain inflation from the demand side", said Subir Gokarn, Deputy Governor, RBI.

However, the experts feel that easing of growth in itself is not a good news for India's economy. With its high interest rate policy, the RBI seems to have compromised economic growth, which is not a good bargain. Lower growth means lower production, lower employment generation, lower per capita income and slower overall development.

The monetary policy focus during 2011-12 has been on controlling inflation and containing inflationary expectations. As an indication of strong anti-inflationary stance, the Reserve Bank of India raised policy rates 13 times from March 2010 to October 2011. The measures helped contain inflation and anchor inflationary expectations for some time. The task was rendered difficult due to supply-side factors contributing to food inflation, low interest rates and repeated liquidity injections by industrial nations battling recessionary tendencies, and rise in international commodity prices. High inflation and some of the measures to control liquidity have also had detrimental effect on growth in the short run. The priority, however, has been to contain price rise so that long-term growth prospects are not affected. With inflation projected to follow a downward trajectory and downside risks to growth increasing, the RBI in the Third Quarter Review of Monetary Policy 2011-12 on 24 January 2012, lowered the Cash Reserve Ratio (CRR) by 50 bps from 6.0 per cent to 5.5 per cent of net demand and time liabilities (NDTL) of scheduled banks to ease the liquidity situation in the banking system and revive growth.

The monetary policy stance during 2011-12 changed course during the year, from tightening driven by inflation concerns to gradual pause recognizing the risks to growth as inflation moderated, albeit marginally. The monetary policy stance during May-October 2011 was based on the premise that over the long run, high inflation is inimical to sustained growth as it affects investment by creating uncertainty. Bringing inflation down, even at the cost of sacrificing some growth in the short run, was therefore accorded precedence. Year-on-year headline WPI inflation remained stubbornly high, averaging around 9.6 per cent during May-September 2011. Inflation was driven by all the three major groups, namely primary articles; fuel and power; and manufactured products. Hence, the focus of monetary policy stance during May-October 2011 was on containing inflation and anchoring inflation expectations even as it entailed sacrificing some growth.

The period from December 2011 to January 2012 marked a reversal of the cycle as policy rates were kept unchanged. Growth started moderating in 2011-12, in part anticipated as a consequence of cumulative impact of past monetary policy action, but more importantly, on account of investment uncertainties, worsening global scenario and the large linkages of the manufacturing sector with global demand. GDP growth moderated for the sixth consecutive quarter to 6.9 per cent in Q2 of 2011-12. The growth rate of GDP during 2011-12 is estimated at 6.9 per cent. Since November 2011, however, inflation has broadly followed the projected trajectory and has shown moderation with headline WPI inflation moderating to 7.5 per cent in December 2011. The decline in inflation was driven largely by a decline in primary food and non-food articles inflation. The momentum indicator of the WPI, as measured by the seasonally adjusted three-month moving average inflation rate, also showed a decline.

High interest rate policy has told upon industrial growth. The IIP data has been showing a declining growth in many sectors. Thus, industrial production and economic growth have been compromised with to control inflation. India is one of the few nations that did well during the economic slowdown of 2008-09. Its GDP growth picked up in 2010-11 and was 8.4 per cent. But it has reversed to below 7 per cent in 2011-12 for which tight money policy is also responsible though not entirely.

RBI has tried to bring down inflation through monetary measures, i.e. controlling money supply by keeping interest rates high. It has totally overlooked the fact that low supply of various types of goods leads to high inflation, and the best way to keep inflation in check is to boost supply. In keeping interest rates high it has let the economic growth slide down from a healthy 8.4 per cent in 2010-11 to moderate 6.69 per cent in 2011-12. Industrial production in various segments has gone down and businesses in general have suffered due to high interest rate policy. Food prices which fell sharply for a short period of December 2011 to February 2012, because of seasoned supply, rose again to their previous levels in March 2012. Non-food sector too is expected to see higher prices because of increase in taxes in some items in Budget 2012-13, as also due to the fact that oil prices are likely to remain high in international market and will necessitate further increases in the domestic prices of petrol and petroleum products sooner or later. If prices are not increased and oil subsidies continue like before, fiscal deficit will go on increasing affecting growth, leading to low production and unemployment.

In its attempts to control high inflation, RBI persisted with its high interest rate policy for long. There was a series of repo rate and reverse repo rate hikes from March 2010 to September 2011. CRR and SLR were also kept high. This affected credit growth and adversely impacted economic growth. While industry experts were expecting rate cuts and economists were recommending the same, there was a pause of six months from October 2011 to March 2012 when policy rates were kept unchanged. It may well be called a period of uncertainty as no one knew which way the policy will go. Some expected a rate cut just after the Budget 2012-13, others thought it will be after the close of the financial year 2012-13. Meanwhile RBI reduced CRR by 50 basis points and 75 basis points in January 2012 and March 2012 respectively, but this was a step which many considered taken only to improve a tight liquidity position. RBI admitted the same by saying that "in December 2011, the liquidity deficit escalated partly on account of third quarterly advance tax outflow. Keeping in view the prevailing overall liquidity conditions, OMO purchases continued. In order to provide flexibility to scheduled commercial banks (SCBs) in their liquidity management, the RBI conducted additional repo operations under the LAF on 16 December 2011 (over and above the existing LAF and MSF arrangements) to permit banks to avail of funds on overnight basis against their excess SLR holdings, in addition to the existing facility...."[9]

But when this did not work as banks have to keep large sums in cash to maintain CRR, RBI thought of reducing the CRR. Some people called it a shift from tight money policy. But it was more of a compulsion than a policy decision. Moreover, the fact that key interest, i.e. repo rate was left untouched, was an indication that RBI was not ready to change its policy stance.

The two major developments during the period of so-called pause were: (i) an overall decrease in prices; and (ii) fall in the growth of production across various sectors of the economy. The rate of inflation which hovered around 10 per cent for most part of the year, came down to around 7 per cent. But RBI, ignoring this development, decided not to respond by reducing interest rates during this period. This defied its own logic that interest rates have been kept high to control prices, because when prices came down, interest rates were still kept high. Secondly, there was a deceleration in growth as IIP data showed during the period, but RBI was not prepared to take any prompt measure during that period. Regarding the fall in prices, the RBI argued that they were still at an uncomfortable level. "Though inflation has moderated in recent months it remains sticking and above the tolerance level", stated

D. Subbarao, adding that it may rise again. If that is the case, then what is the efficacy of RBI's high interest rate policy?

RBI has admitted all along that its tight money policy will affect economic growth in the short run, and that we should not worry unless it is affected in the long run. Now, GDP growth rate has come down from 8.4 per cent in 2010-11 to 6.69 per cent in 2011-12. For the current financial year 2012-13, it is projected to only marginally increase to 7.3 per cent. This too may be revised downwards as was done for the year 2011-12. As a matter of fact there were two downward revisions in 2011-12. This in clear that India's long-term growth is being adversely impacted.

Some realization of the above facts was visible in RBI's Monetary Policy Statement 2012-13 (17 April 2012) in which RBI Governor D. Subbarao admitted that "the state of the economy is a matter of great concern". RBI said it was looking for a "rate that can be sustained over longer periods without endangering demand-side inflationary pressures."[10] RBI further said even though "growth has fallen significantly...our projections suggest that the economy will revert close to its post-crisis trend growth in 2012-13, which does not leave much room for monetary policy easing without aggravating inflation risks."[11]

RBI decided to effect a 50 basis point cut each in repo rate and reverse repo rate on 17 April 2012 with a view to reviving the flagging economic growth. Although the reduction was widely welcomed by businessmen, "many expressed doubts on whether the corporate sector and individuals will benefit immediately as banks are reluctant to commit to lower borrowing costs immediately".[12] Thus, businesses which are reeling under high interest rates may have to wait longer before lending rates are actually brought down by banks. This does not angur well for industry. *The Economic Times* called this reduction "a gamble" and suggested that there is "a faint possibility of kickstarting growth in a scenario where government failure, rather than high interest rates, is the drag on investment", while "probability of reigniting lurking inflation is distinct".[13] It said that a situation called for a nominal 25 basis points reduction in policy rates. But one may argue that a mere 25 basis point cut after a series of hikes would have made little difference, if at all.

According to *The Economic Times*, "abundant global liquidity, sharp increase in private final consumption, rising oil prices without a corresponding pass-through to domestic prices, high current account deficit and government's fiscal profligacy have limited the space for reduction in policy rates". But the question is how long can we keep interest rates high without sacrificing economic growth and inviting other serious troubles including low investment, increasing unemployment, looming slowdown which may become a reality, and eventually a downgrade? And how can we tame inflation without attending to supply side constraints, for which a boost to manufacturing, trade and agriculture sector is necessary? Clearly, high interest policy is not the answer to the problems India is facing at present. On the contrary, it is aggravating the problems further. What we need is right policy decisions and a balanced approach where inflation is targeted through a combination of demand side as well as supply side measures, fiscal deficit is reduced and growth momentum of the economy is maintained.

Notes

1. *Economic Survey 2011-12.*
2. *Ibid.*
3. *Ibid.*
4. *Ibid.*
5. D. Subbarao (RBI Governor). "Reserve Bank of India Monetary Policy Statement 2012-13", 17 April 2012.
6. *Ibid.*
7. *Ibid.*
8. *Ibid.*
9. *Economic Survey 2011-12.*
10. D. Subbarao (RBI Governor). "Monetary Policy Statement 2012-13", 17 April 2012.
11. *Ibid.*
12. *The Economic Times*, 18 April 2012.
13. *Ibid.*

5

The Challenge of Food Inflation

Duvvuri Subbarao, Governor, RBI

22 Nov. 2011

...

I. THE CONTEXT

2. Persistent and elevated food inflation over the last few years has emerged as a major policy concern, especially as it can potentially threaten our collective aspiration for a 'higher, inclusive and sustainable' growth. Intriguingly, we are experiencing high food inflation in the face of record production of food grains, robust buffer stocks and growing resilience of agriculture to monsoon uncertainties. Evidently, the dynamics of food inflation have changed significantly, and understanding them is obviously important for a policy response.

3. A related question that has engaged economists has been the role, if any, of the central bank in combating food inflation. Opinion on this has spanned the entire spectrum. At one end is the view that monetary policy should be the 'first line of defence' no matter what the drivers of inflation. At the other end is the view that monetary policy is an inappropriate instrumentality to address supply pressures, and that the central bank should adopt a 'hands off' approach. Real world, as we know, is too complex for such binary textbook prescriptions; management of food inflation has always been a complex challenge for the Reserve Bank, both by way of policy action and its communication.

4. What I propose to do in this address is to first highlight the trends in food inflation over the past 60 years. Having thus set the context, I will turn to factors driving structural food inflation, which should give us a perspective of the underlying dynamics and the nature of the challenge. I will then move on to indicating the policy measures for addressing the challenge of food inflation on a durable basis. I will, in the end, address an issue more directly relevant to the Reserve Bank—the role of monetary policy in the face of supply shocks.

II. TRENDS IN FOOD INFLATION OVER LAST SIX DECADES

5. An assessment of the inflation trends over last six decades indicates that India has encountered successive bouts of high food inflation, but the underlying drivers have changed over time; the influence of monsoon has declined and some new sources of price pressures have emerged. What is particularly notable is that during the 2000s, average food inflation fell significantly (Fig. 5.1). In contrast, since 2008-09 (i.e. about last three and half years), average food inflation has been higher than the average food inflation in each of the past six decades. This cannot all be attributed to poor monsoon. Sure, rainfall was deficient in 2009, but so was it in 2002 and 2004. But, in the earlier years, food inflation remained modest, at less than three per cent over three successive years during 2002-05, whereas it shot up to double digits in 2009. What has changed in recent years to cause sustained price pressures? This is the big question we need to answer to find a durable solution to food inflation.

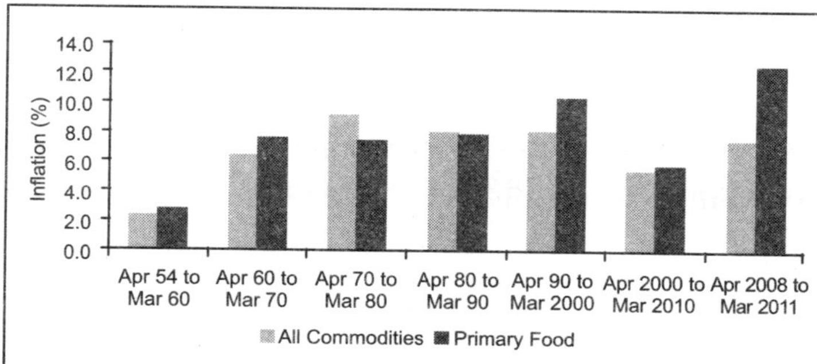

Fig. 5.1: Decade-wise Average Inflation

III. FACTORS DRIVING FOOD PRICE PRESSURES

6. What are the factors driving food inflation? I would emphasize the following: (i) shift in dietary habits towards protein foods; (ii) pressure stemming from inclusive growth policies; (iii) large increases in MSPs of food grains; (iv) shocks from global food inflation; and (v) financialisation of commodities. Let me take them up one by one.

(i) Shift in Dietary Habits Towards Protein Foods

7. A distinct feature of recent food price inflation has been the sustained price pressure in protein rich items (pulses, milk, fish, meat and eggs). Inflation in protein rich items has generally exceeded both headline (WPI) inflation and inflation in primary food articles (Fig. 5.2).

8. As one would expect, the share of food in total expenditure has declined over successive rounds of NSSO surveys alongside

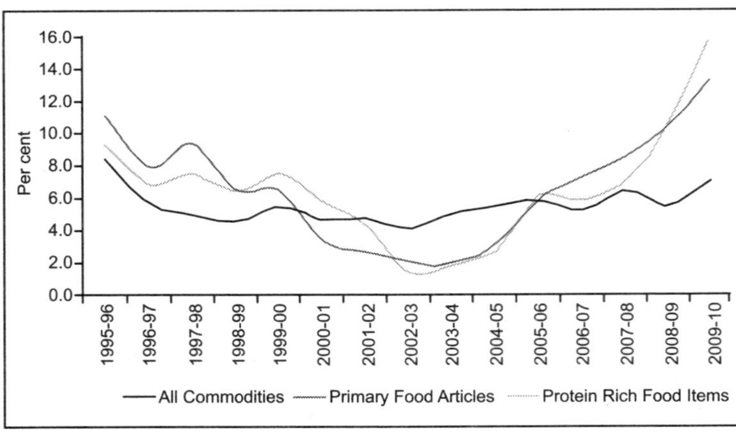

Fig. 5.2: Inflation in Food Articles and Overall Inflation*

* year moving averate to smoothen the volatility in Annual Data

increases in per capita income, consistent with Engel's Law (Fig. 5.3).

9. We need to turn to the lesser known Bennet's Law for an explanation of food inflation. Bennet's Law suggests that as incomes increase, the proportion of starchy staples in the food basket declines relative to the share of more expensive sources

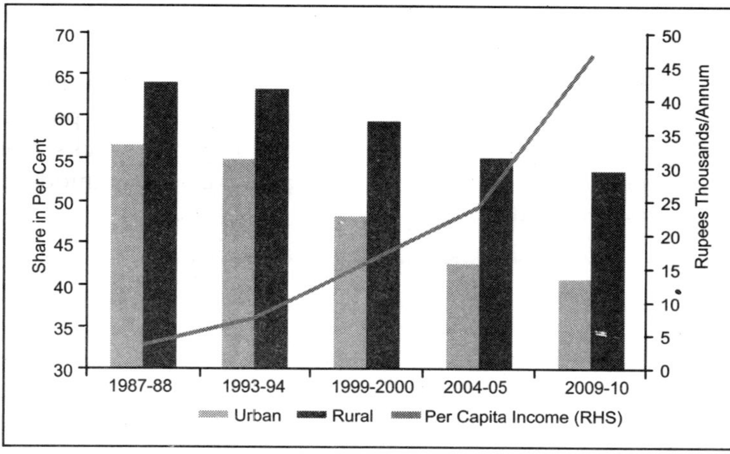

Fig. 5.3: Declining Share of Food in Total Consumption

of calories. Recent NSSO data showing a significant increase in the share of protein rich items in total food expenditure, both in rural and urban areas, confirm this hypothesis (Fig. 5.4). Though protein inflation, reflecting changing dietary habits, was evident earlier as well, the pace of increase has been sharper in recent years reflecting, in part, accelerated increases in nominal wages.

10. Even in the face of such structural changes in dietary habits, inflation is not inevitable. The reason structural changes have triggered inflation in India is that the supply response in respect of most protein items has not been adequate. With the exception of pulses, other protein rich items are not crop products. This is an important point since it explains the growing disconnect between the performance of agriculture and the trajectory of food inflation.

(ii) Pressure on Food Inflation Stemming from Inclusive Growth

11. Unlike the growth-inflation tradeoff, the possible tradeoff between inclusive growth and inflation has not received much attention. The need for making growth inclusive is incontestable, but it is important to recognize that policies aimed at inclusion can stoke inflationary pressures, at any rate in the short-term. I could mention two examples here: first, the significant increase

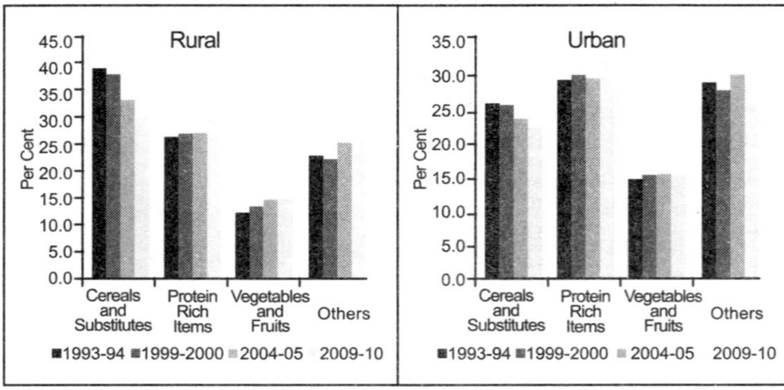

Fig. 5.4: Shares of Various Components in Total Food Expenditure

in rural wages triggered by the Mahatma Gandhi National Rural Employment Guarantee Scheme (MGNREGS), and second, inflationary implications of the proposed Food Security Bill.

12. The MGNREGS, guaranteeing at least one hundred days of wage employment to rural labour, in implementation since February 2006, has pushed up rural wages, in line with the expected outcomes of the scheme. The indexation of the wage rate to CPI-AL since the beginning of 2011 has exacerbated the wage-price inflation spiral. National Sample Survey Organisation (NSSO) survey data (61st Round and 66th Round) suggest that nominal wages of workers, in both rural and urban areas, increased much faster in the second half of the 2000s than in

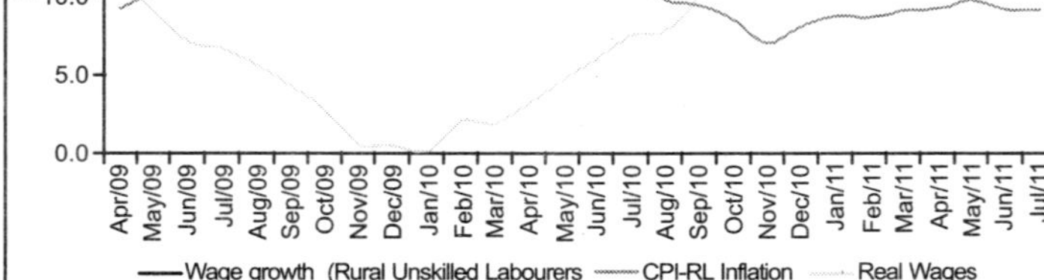

Fig. 5.5: Increase in Rural Wages Relative to Inflation*

*Y-O-Y Growth in Rural Unskilled Labourer (Male) wages and CPI-Rural Laboureres Inflation Y-O-Y.
Source: Labour Bureau, Ministry of Labour

the first half. In most states, wages have increased faster than CPI-RL inflation, pushing up real wages (Fig. 5.5).

13. Consistent with the characteristic of a low income country, increase in wages in India has quickly translated to increase in per capita expenditure. Average nominal per capita expenditure increased sharply in the second half of the decade (2005-10) compared to the first half (2000-05), rising from 3.6 per cent per annum to 10.5 per cent in rural areas, and 5.3 per cent per annum to 10.9 per cent in urban areas. The MGNREGS has evidently set the floor for the rural wage level, making wage push inflation more visible and prominent. Admittedly, increase in wages need not be inflationary provided it reflects higher productivity, but that is not currently the case, a point to which I will return later.

14. The National Food Security Bill, 2011 is another potential source of pressure on inflation, and its inflationary impact will depend on the extent to which it will raise demand for food grains relative to the normal increase in supply. The proposed billtargets two categories of households—priority households and general households—under which 75 per cent of the rural population (with at least 46 per cent of the population belonging to priority households) and 50 per cent of the urban population (with at least 28 per cent of the population belonging to priority households) will become entitled to subsidized food grains. The price restrictions are quite exacting and failure by the government to meet the obligations entails payment of a food security allowance to the beneficiary.

15. Estimates suggest that 68 per cent of the country's 1.2 billion population will get a legal entitlement for food grains after the bill is enacted, significantly raising the annual grain procurement demand even as the available marketed surplus would not increase correspondingly. This will create demand pressures, which will inevitably spillover to market prices of food grains. Furthermore, the higher food subsidy burden on the budget will raise the fiscal deficit, exacerbating macro level inflationary pressures.

(iii) Large Increases in MSPs of Food Grains

16. Recent years have witnessed a significant increase in minimum support prices (MSP) of several agricultural commodities, pushing up food inflation. This is particularly evident from the neatly anchored co-movement of market prices and MSPs for rice and wheat (Fig. 5.6). The Commission for Agricultural Costs and Prices (CACP) has typically followed a cost plus pricing formula for determining the MSP, and in an environment of rising wages and increasing input costs, rising MSPs have accentuated inflation pressures.

17. Compared with the past, hikes in MSPs for wheat and rice have been more substantial in recent years, as the following table shows.

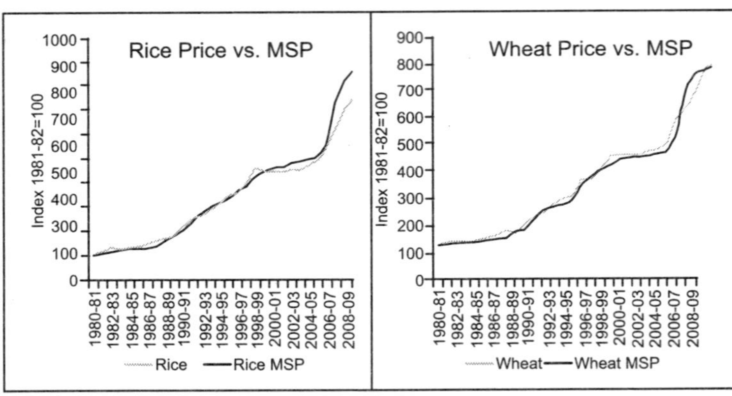

Fig. 5.6: Higher Minimum Support Prices (MSPs) Drag Market Price Up

Annual Average Percentage Increase in MSP

	2002-07	2007-12
Rice	1.8	13.6
Wheat	4.0	11.9

18. Given the cost plus formula for the determination of MSPs, the increase in MSPs as above is consistent with the rising input costs as evidenced by figures below.

Percentage Increase in Agricultural Input Prices

	2008/09	2009/10	2010/11
Inputs	3%-19%	18%-28%	3%-19%
Wages	9%-36%	5%-30%	18%-43%

Inputs: Fodder, diesel oil, lubricants, fertilizer and pesticides

19. It is a fair presumption that MGNREGS has considerably affected labour costs while also tightening availability of agricultural labour during peak seasons. Given that Indian agriculture is labour intensive, sustained wage pressures can keep food price inflation high even in years of record food production as was the case in 2010-11.

(iv) Shocks from Global Food Inflation

20. Given India's growing integration with the world economy, global food prices affect our domestic prices even if there is no trade. Global food price pressures have been quite acute in recent years reflecting growing demand and a weak supply response. Demand side pressures have stemmed from growing population and rising incomes. Supply side pressure have been triggered by a host of factors—increasing urbanization, diversion of land for bio-fuel production, inadequate investment in research and technology, spikes in costs of inputs such as diesel and fertilizer and disturbances arising from climate change. The impact of these factors underpinning high food prices was amplified further by country specific policy interventions, particularly export bans on specific commodities by certain countries. Import barriers in some countries to protect domestic producers and large subsidies to farm production in several advanced economies have also influenced the supply response of farm output to distorted price signals.

21. According to an assessment by OECD-FAO, global food inflation situation will remain grim over the next ten years. It is important to note that prices of food items actually declined in real terms over several decades from early 1960s to early 2000 (Fig. 5.7). This trend began to be reversed, gradually during 2003-06, and rapidly thereafter up until the 2008 global financial crisis. After some moderation in 2009, food prices have again edged up, tending closer to pre-crisis peaks. The OECD-FAO

Agricultural Outlook 2011-20 indicates that prices may be higher in real terms over the five years 2015-20, relative to the levels prevailing during the five year period 1998-2003 by 40 per cent in case of rice, 27 per cent for wheat, 48 per cent for maize and 36 per cent for oil seeds. What the above global outlook clearly suggests is that we will not get any comfort from the global situation in managing our food inflation.

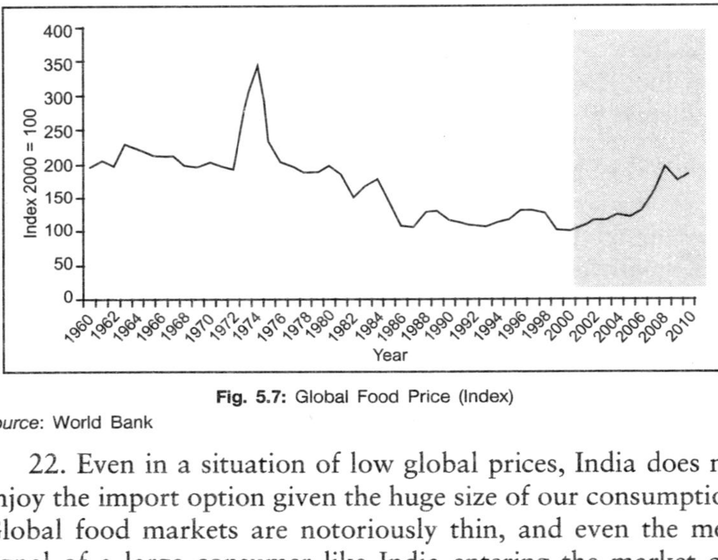

Fig. 5.7: Global Food Price (Index)

Source: World Bank

22. Even in a situation of low global prices, India does not enjoy the import option given the huge size of our consumption. Global food markets are notoriously thin, and even the mere signal of a large consumer like India entering the market can spike up prices. Moreover, in some commodities such as wheat and sugar, Indian prices have been higher than global prices (Fig. 5.8) suggesting that even if imports could improve domestic supply, they would not soften inflationary pressures.

(v) Financialisation of Commodities—A New Source of Price Pressure

23. Some analysts contend that speculation in commodity futures has been a key driver of global food inflation in recent years. In general, there has been a marked increase in financial investment in commodity markets, relative to both global GDP and physical commodity production. Do activities in commodity futures market reflect genuine needs of hedging? Does speculation systematically influence the commodity prices and lead to

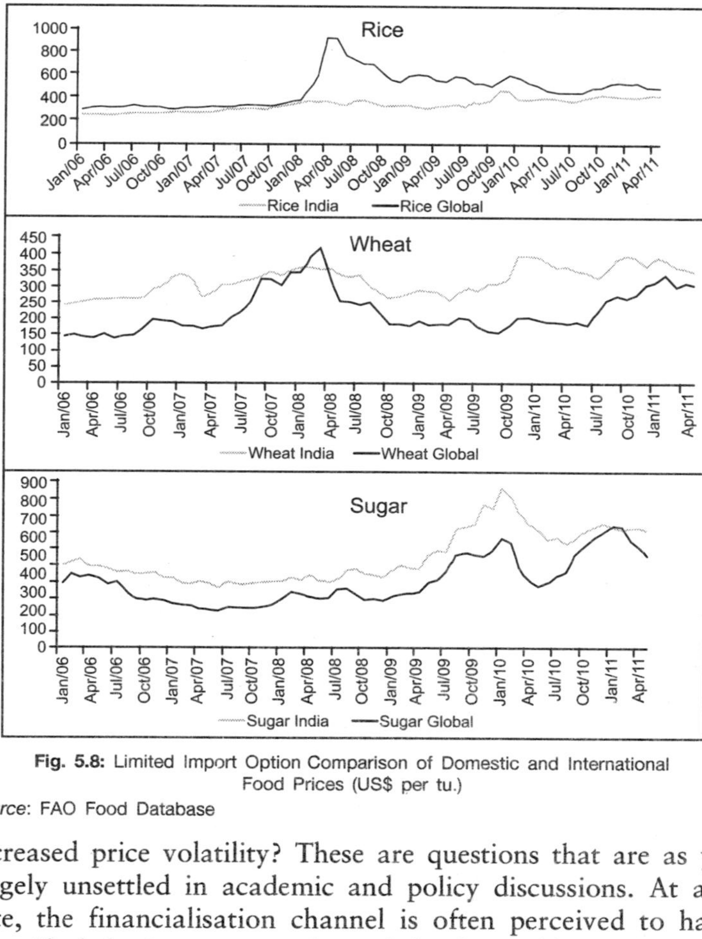

Fig. 5.8: Limited Import Option Comparison of Domestic and International Food Prices (US$ per tu.)

Source: FAO Food Database

increased price volatility? These are questions that are as yet largely unsettled in academic and policy discussions. At any rate, the financialisation channel is often perceived to have magnified the impact on prices of the disequilibrium between demand and supply, thereby weakening the role of fundamentals in the price formation process.

24. In India, prices of several commodities which are not traded on the commodities exchange such as fruit and milk, have significantly increased in the recent period. Moreover, certain commodities that were banned for trading in 2007 such as rice, wheat, tur and urad also exhibited price increases subsequently. Even after the ban imposed on trading of sugar in 2009, sugar prices had increased considerably. Evidence of any

relationship between futures market activities in commodities and their spot prices is ambiguous. Nonetheless, this needs close monitoring and certainly further research.

IV. ADDRESSING THE CHALLENGE OF FOOD INFLATION

25. Having discussed the sources of food price pressures, let me now turn to how we may respond to the challenge of food inflation.

(i) Raise Agricultural Productivity

26. The Green Revolution, entailing adoption of high yielding variety (HYV) seeds in the mid-1960s and the use of the fertilizer-pesticides-irrigation package, resulted in quantum jumps in productivity (i.e. output per acre), especially of rice and wheat. By the early 1980s, productivity across all major crops had peaked, but the momentum had slowed thereafter. Consequently, per capita availability of food grains, especially of rice and wheat, has started declining (Fig. 5.9). A comparison of crop yields across G-20 countries shows the extent to which India has lagged behind others (Fig. 5.10).

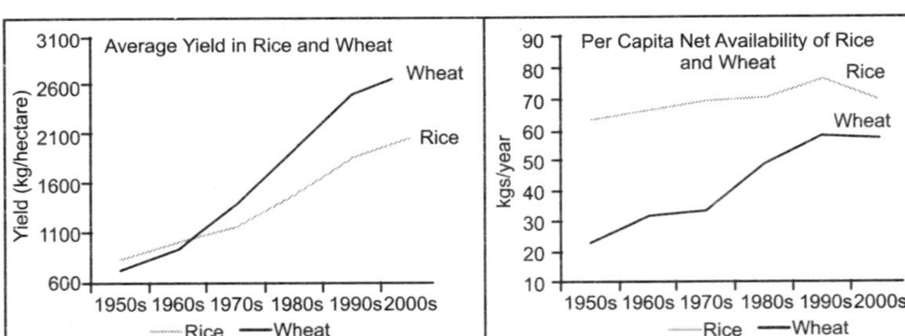

Fig. 5.9: Moderating Yield and Per Capita Availability of Food Grains

27. Even our best productivity achievements in terms of yields of major crops are way behind world numbers. During 2010-11, Punjab, with the highest yield in rice, produced 3.8 tonnes per hectare as against the world average of 4.3 tonnes per hectare. Yield of oilseeds in Tamil Nadu, the highest in India, at 2.1 tonnes per hectare is lower than the US average of 2.7 tonnes per hectare. There are wide variations in productivity levels of crops across states. Unlike food grains where the Green

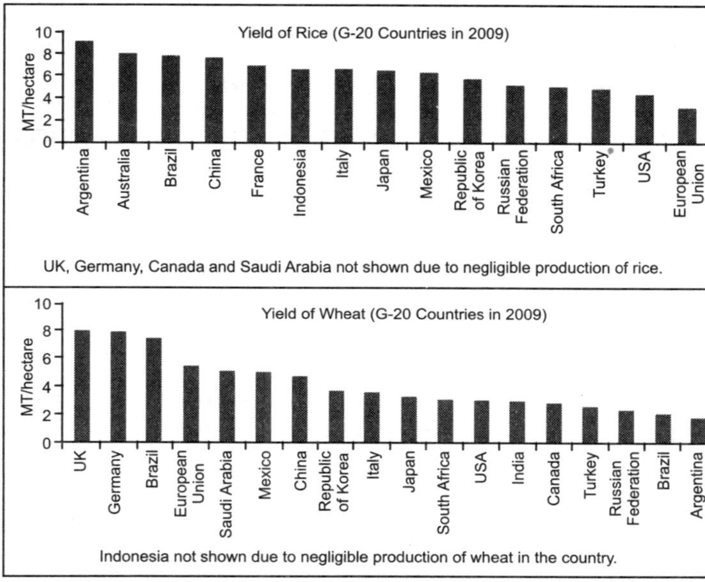

Fig. 5.10: India's Lagging Yield in Food Production Relative to G-20 Countries

Revolution improved the food security situation, we are still not self-sufficient in pulses and edible oilseeds. The demand for other farm products like fruits and vegetables has also been rising significantly faster than supply, putting pressure on food inflation.

28. The growth of agriculture and allied sector was most impressive during the 6th Five Year Plan period (1980 to 1985) when it peaked at 5.8 per cent. The annual average agricultural growth rate moderated thereafter as shown in the following table.

Annual Average Agricultural Growth Rate

Plan Period	Growth Rate (percentage)
6th Plan (1980 - 1985)	5.8
7th Plan (1985 - 1990)	3.0
8th Plan (1992 - 1997)	4.8
9th Plan (1997 - 2002)	2.5
10th Plan (2002 - 2007)	2.4
11th Plan (2007 - 2012) (in first 4 years)	3.2

29. How do we respond to declining growth and moderating productivity improvements? The overall policy framework for agriculture, driven primarily by remunerative prices and subsidized provision of inputs, needs to change; the focus would have to shift to productivity and selective policy stimulus to items where the supply response has been weak. Public expenditure needs to reorient towards building capital infrastructure for agriculture which in turn would 'crowd-in' private investment and help realize the full potential of agriculture growth. There has been no major technological breakthrough in agriculture since the Green Revolution of the mid-60s. There have been achievements in some specific crops such as cotton, basmati rice and maize, but that needs to be broad based. The Green Revolution also needs to penetrate the eastern region, where the yields have generally remained low.

30. Management of climatic concerns is becoming increasingly important given the continuing dependence on rainfed farming, frequent floods in eastern India, frost, particularly in north-western India, and heat waves and cyclones on the east coast. These climatic changes are likely to significantly increase volatility in agricultural production. Recent large increases in prices of some items like onion, sugar, vegetables and cotton are, at least in part, a result of seasonal weather related factors, both domestic and external.

(ii) Rethink Price Policy Interventions

31. Paradoxically, in India, we subsidize both agricultural inputs and outputs, and we subsidize both producers and consumers. There is a case for revisiting the subsidy regime for a number of reasons, including the pressure it exerts on food inflation. Subsidies on inputs (fertilizer, electricity, irrigation) to incentivize production and subsidies on output for the public distribution system (PDS), entail a large fiscal burden (Fig. 5.11). Over and above the input subsidies, remunerative MSPs and procurement for the PDS at prices linked to MSP further distort the price situation. There is a moral hazard here like in any subsidy. A farming sector that depends excessively on input subsidies and cost plus MSPs to raise production does not have much of an incentive to raise productivity. If the amount spent

on subsidies could be diverted to augment capital formation in agriculture and creation of rural infrastructure, higher productivity would raise the income of farmers while lowering the prices for the consumers.

32. MSPs pose a major policy dilemma. Remunerative prices are necessary to engineer the desired supply response, but higher MSPs also lead to higher inflation. A segment of the population

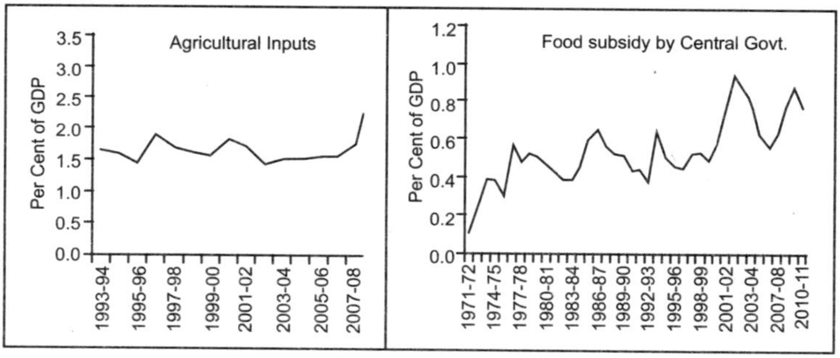

Fig. 5.11: Subsidies on Inputs and Output (at Percentage of GDP)

could be protected against inflation through the subsidized PDS, but depending on the difference between the PDS price and the MSPs at which procurement is made, and the quantity supplied through PDS, food subsidies could swell.

33. The share of agriculture in GDP has declined significantly (to about 15 per cent), but a large section of the labour force (about 53 per cent) still depends on agriculture for its livelihood. If the per capita income of those who depend on agriculture has to increase, productivity of agriculture has to increase (so that even without higher food prices, per capita income could increase) and the percentage of labour force depending on agriculture has to decline (which would require creation of employment opportunities in non-farm activities).

(iii) Improve Supply Chain Management

34. The supply chain through which farm products move to reach the final consumers is a major source of price pressures. Two initiatives, currently under debate, that could potentially improve the situation are: (a) revamping the PDS to check leakage

of food subsidies, and (b) allowing entry of FDI into multi-brand retailing.

35. Let us take the PDS first. The government's food management policy has been largely driven by two goals: (a) maintaining buffer stocks to deal with food shortages and thereby ensuring food security; and (b) providing food at subsidized prices to the poor through the PDS. The food stocks at any point of time, thus, reflect the end result of additions through procurement and depletions through release for PDS.

36. Management of food stocks is riven by a debate between two opposing points of view. One view is that food stocks should play a market stabilization role such that whenever market prices rise significantly, reflecting particularly supply chain manipulation, stocks should be released into the market to soften prices. The opposing view is that use of food stocks to intervene in the market dilutes the role of competitive market forces, and that the government should instead focus on easing supply chain rigidities.

37. Given the enormous administrative costs of the PDS and its perceived leakages, several alternatives have been suggested, although none of them is without its specific problems. By far the most straightforward is direct cash transfers, but its implementation is conditional on universal financial inclusion. Besides, since cash is fungible, the objective of distributing food at subsidized prices can potentially be compromised. Distribution of food grains with utilization linked to UID is another option, but that again is conditional on universal UID coverage. In the event of a switch over to cash transfers, the supply chain could become even more important in rural areas, since by manipulating supply and prices, food dealers could extract a share of the cash transferred to the beneficiaries.

38. There are also several proposals on the table for improving supply chain management. Given that protein food inflation stems especially from perishable items such as milk, eggs, meat, fish, vegetables and fruits, the case for a better supply chain management becomes stronger. The most actively discussed option is allowing FDI into multi-brand retail. The government's discussion paper on the subject argues that super market-chains

could lower costs and increase efficiency because of scale economics. They will also lead to better safety and quality standards.

39. Evidence from cross-country experience on the benefits of multi-brand FDI on inflation is ambiguous. Several questions persist. Will the supermarket chains, focusing as they do on urban consumption centres for scale of economy reasons, leave the rural population behind? Also, if there are such clear scale economies and cost advantages, why aren't domestic investors jumping in to exploit the potential?

40. Another issue in supply chain management is reform of some restrictive statutes and regulations. Even as production of vegetables and fruits has increased in recent years, around 40 per cent of it goes waste between the farm gate and the market for want of cold chain and transport infrastructure. Implementation of the model Agriculture Produce Marketing Committee (APMC) Act 2003, which provides for direct marketing, contract farming and setting up of markets in private and cooperative sectors is a possible option to address this problem.

(iv) Manage Competition for Land from Non-farm Activities

41. Land is the single most important input for agriculture. Besides being a key determinant of socio-economic status, it provides collateral for credit and for security in the event of natural hazard or contingencies. The supply of land, as we know, is fixed. Over the years, there has been a significant change in the pattern of land use. Net sown area, which increased at a rate of 18 per cent during 1951-71, has either declined or remained stagnant since then. Increased cropping intensity over the years, however, has led to an increase in gross cropped area, though at a slowing pace in recent decades. As a result, there has been no significant increase in the share of net cropped area in total geographical area since the 1970s.

42. A notable aspect of the changing land use pattern is that the share of cultivable land not used for agricultural purposes has increased from a low of 2.8 per cent of the total geographical areas in 1950-51 to 7.5 per cent in 2004-05. This may be

indicative of increased diversion of agricultural land for non-agricultural purposes such as urbanization, housing, industrialization, and infrastructure. It is a fair presumption that such diversion would have further gained pace since 2004-05. Land acquisition for industrial and other commercial uses is an issue that has been headline news in recent years; clearly, it is an emotive issue involving difficult tradeoffs. No matter how the tradeoffs are resolved, the reality of increasing demand for land from fast growing and more productive sectors cannot be ignored. The possibility of declining arable land available for cultivation underscores the importance of increasing productivity if we are to contain food inflationary pressures.

43. There are several other problems. First, land holding in India is highly fragmented, with marginal holdings (of one hectare or less) accounting for as high as 62 per cent of all operational holdings. The small farm size in a labour surplus agrarian sector leads to intensive use of land, but in the absence of supporting infrastructure and capacity to access modern technology and inputs, productivity remains low. Second, rainfed agriculture constitutes as much as 55 per cent of the cropped area and 45 per cent of the total agricultural output. More than 70 per cent of pulses and oilseeds production as well as a substantial part of horticulture and animal husbandry produce is from rainfed farming, underscoring significant continuing monsoon dependence. Third, water is going to be as precious as land in the long-run, and costs of irrigation will increase significantly, not only in terms of the actual cost of access to the irrigation facility, but also by way of costs arising from competing demand from non-agriculture sectors for the limited supply of water. Fourth, dry land farming would have to receive greater attention, but there will be greater competition even for dry lands from urbanization and infrastructure.

V. MONETARY POLICY AND INFLATION

44. Now let me turn to a question that is more directly relevant to the Reserve Bank—what is the role of a central bank in combating food inflation? As I said earlier, the answer to this question spans the entire spectrum.

45. That monetary policy should respond if there is inflation, meaning there is sustained increase in the general price level, is beyond question. But high food prices often result from adverse supply shocks or large increases in input costs. The conventional wisdom is that if inflation expectations are well anchored, monetary policy need not react to supply shocks. This premise is based on the assumption that the supply shocks are purely temporary. This assumption does not always hold. In the real world, oftentimes supply shocks are structural and lead to a permanent trend upward shift in prices.

46. So, the challenge for a central bank is to determine if the supply shock is temporary or permanent. If it is permanent, then the change in relative prices caused by it can result in higher general inflation, in the first round by the higher input costs, and in the second round through the impact on inflation expectation and wage bargaining. In other words, when supply shocks impact the trend or the core component of inflation, monetary policy should respond.

47. The question of responding to a supply shock gets more complex in the context of the growth inflation tradeoff. Unlike demand shocks, supply shocks have asymmetric implications for inflation and growth. In the case of a negative demand shock such as wealth loss caused by say, a crash in asset prices, the impact on output and prices is generally in the same direction. The policy response in such a situation is unambiguous. In the event of a negative supply shock such as lower farm output resulting from monsoon failure, however, while headline inflation goes up, output may come down. Thus, in the case of a negative supply shock, monetary policy confronts the dilemma of stabilising output versus containing inflation.

48. Oftentimes, this is a delicate balancing act. If the supply shock is transitory, then the preferred policy response could be to accommodate the price pressures, recognizing the limitations of monetary policy in directly dealing with supply induced price pressures. If on the other hand, the supply shock persists, or due to strong demand conditions, the supply shock transmits to other components of general inflation, then monetary policy has to respond. Thus, in case of the former, monetary

accommodation prevents further disruption to the growth momentum. In the latter case, however, ant-inflationary monetary response may involve some sacrifice of growth.

Conclusion

49. Let me now conclude. The thrust of my address has been to emphasize the several factors that are driving food inflation: (i) shift in dietary habits towards protein foods; (ii) pressure stemming from inclusive growth policies; (iii) large increases in the minimum support prices (MSP) of food grains; (iv) shocks from global food inflation; and (v) financialization of commodities.

50. Inflation is a regressive tax and hurts the poor the most. The impact can be particularly severe in a country like India with a population of 1.2 billion, a per capita income of less than $1500 and a large share of food in the total consumption basket.

51. As discussed earlier, the direct role of monetary policy in combating food price pressures is limited, but in the face of sustained high food inflation, monetary action may still be warranted to anchor inflation expectations. A lasting solution to food price pressures lies in a supply response that raises agricultural production and productivity, improves supply chain management and sets the right incentive framework for both producers and consumers. The outlook on food inflation in the short to medium-term will be determined by the speed and quality of such a supply response by the government.

(Presidential Address delivered by Dr. Duvvuri Subbarao, Governor, Reserve Bank of India at the 25th Annual Conference of the Indian Society of Agricultural Marketing at Hyderabad on November 22, 2011) • *Courtesy*: www.rbi.org.in

6

Striking the Balance between Growth and Inflation in India

Subir Gokarn, Deputy Governor, RBI

07 Jul. 2011

STRIKING THE BALANCE BETWEEN GROWTH AND INFLATION IN INDIA*

I. Introduction

The Indian economy recovered relatively quickly from the financial crisis of 2008, but inflationary pressures emerged even in the early stages of the recovery in late 2009. Over the past year and a half, the challenge for monetary policy has been to contain these inflationary pressures without disrupting the recovery. The economy grew by 8.5 per cent in the fiscal year 2010-11, which is close to the five-year average pre-crisis, but year-end headline inflation was over 9 per cent, well above tolerance limits. Meanwhile, global developments have implications for both growth and inflation trajectories in India over the coming months. In this presentation, I propose to talk about the key global and domestic factors that are shaping our growth and inflation outlook, as a backdrop to discussing monetary policy actions and their impact. I will then briefly talk about challenges to communication.

II. Global Forces

There are widespread perceptions and increasing concerns about the recovery in the advanced economies losing momentum. High energy prices appear to be feeding into a negative cycle of persistent unemployment and depressed housing prices in the

US and UK, while the prospect of sovereign default and its real and financial consequences dominates the European policy discussion. In contrast, emerging market economies (EMEs) are showing symptoms of demand-driven inflationary pressures, which have, over the past several months, been exacerbated by rising global commodity prices. Apart from all the other things that are going on in the global environment, commodity prices have played a key role in India's inflation over this period. Consequently, their likely trajectory is going to be an important factor in influencing India's inflation path.

Figures 6.1 and 6.2 provide some perspective on this. They display the correlations between the build-up of non-commercial long positions in four commodities—crude oil, copper, cotton and soya beans—and price movements. It appears that trading positions, possibly driven by abundant liquidity, are contributing

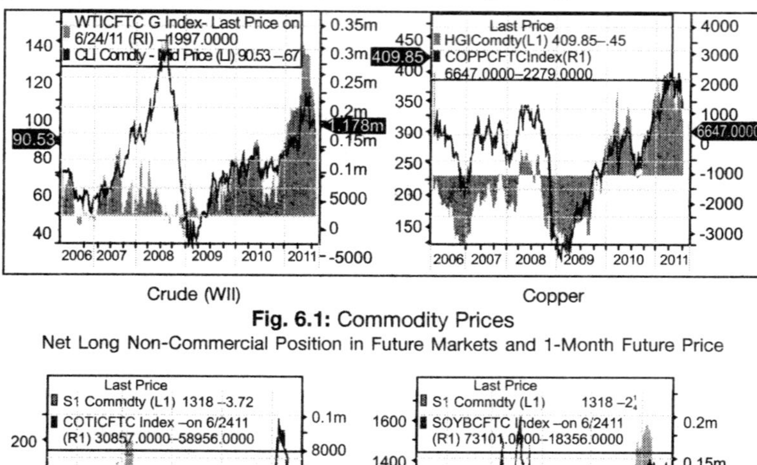

Crude (WII) Copper

Fig. 6.1: Commodity Prices

Net Long Non-Commercial Position in Future Markets and 1-Month Future Price

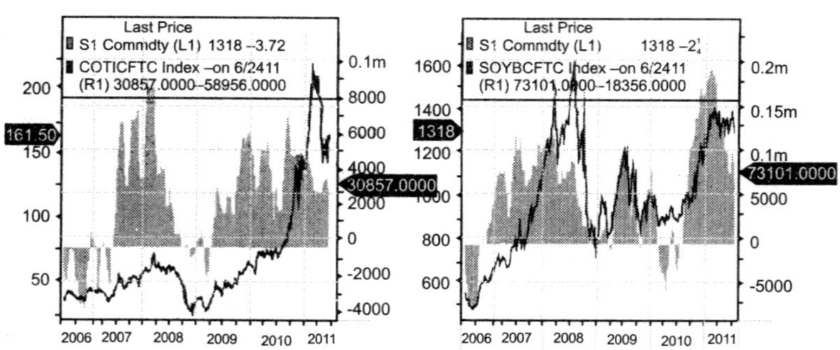

Cotton Soya beans

Fig. 6.2: Commodity Prices

Net Long Non-Commercial Position in Future Markets and 1-Month Future Price to recent price escalations, except in cotton, where temporary supply disruptions have been the main factor. Significantly, in recent weeks, there has been a reversal in long positions, which in turn is associated with softening of prices. If this trend persists, it will provide substantial relief for global inflation management, particularly for large commodity importers, including India. Further, although hardly a desirable way to control inflation, slowing global growth, in addition to reinforcing these favourable commodity price trends, will also help to moderate demand and keep capacity utilization low. This will contribute to moderating inflationary pressures coming from traded or tradable goods.

III. Domestic Growth Prospects

2010-11 was a year in which the economy continued its recovery from the impact of the financial crisis. Growth bottomed out at 6.8 per cent in 2008-09, the crisis year, picked up to 8 per cent in 2009-10 and further to 8.5 per cent in 2010-11. Figure 6.3 shows two pictures of the growth trajectory. With reference to aggregate and sectoral Gross Domestic Product (GDP) estimates, the trajectory in the graph suggests that the momentum is moderating somewhat, as the most recent quarters show decelerating year-on-year growth rates. The main contributor to this tendency is the industrial sector, which has shown relatively high volatility over the period displayed. It

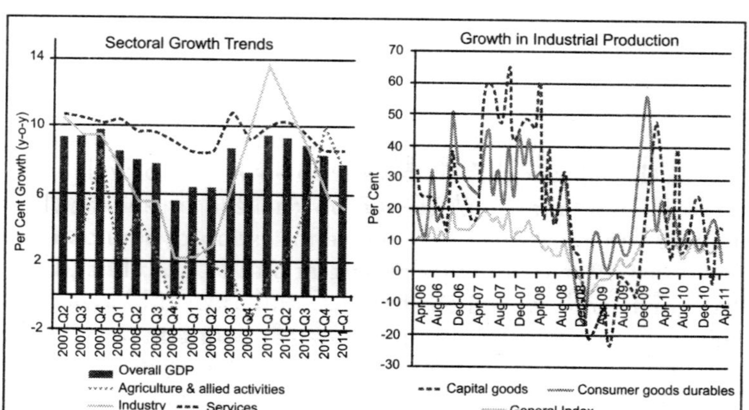

Fig. 6.3: Domestic Growth Scenario

slowed significantly during the crisis, recovered sharply subsequently and has recently begun to slow down.

Looking at the industrial sector a little more closely, the graph displaying trends in industrial production provide some clues to its dynamics. The most volatile segments of the index, both of which are displayed on the graph, are capital goods and consumer durables. These are generally seen as being the most interest-sensitive components of the index and their recent trends suggest that the impact of contractionary monetary policy is having an impact. Along with softening commodity prices, this trend will contribute to bringing inflation under control, by helping moderate demand pressures. Of course, industry associations, including Confederation of Indian Industry (CII), have been consistent critics of the monetary policy stance, arguing that it is slowing growth without really impacting inflation, which is being driven by supply side pressures. I will address this critique both in the discussion on inflation and the one on communication.

In short, the domestic growth scenario suggests that the growth rate will moderate somewhat in the coming year. The Reserve Bank of India projects growth during 2011-12 to be 8 per cent in its baseline scenario. From the inflation management perspective, this is not an entirely undesirable outcome. If it results in a significant reduction in the inflation rate, it will represent a soft landing, which in turn opens up the opportunity for a reversal in the interest rate cycle. However, many unknowns stand in the way and ultimately, inflation outcomes will determine the monetary stance.

IV. Domestic Inflation Dynamics

Over the past year, the nature of inflation has changed in significant ways. Figure 6.4 provides a broad picture of the dynamics. Headline inflation began to accelerate in the second half of 2009-10, at a time when growth was still relatively sluggish. It stayed high through 2010-11, actually accelerating in the last quarter of the year. In the first two months of 2011-12, that pattern has persisted. However, the relative importance of the drivers of inflation clearly changed over the period

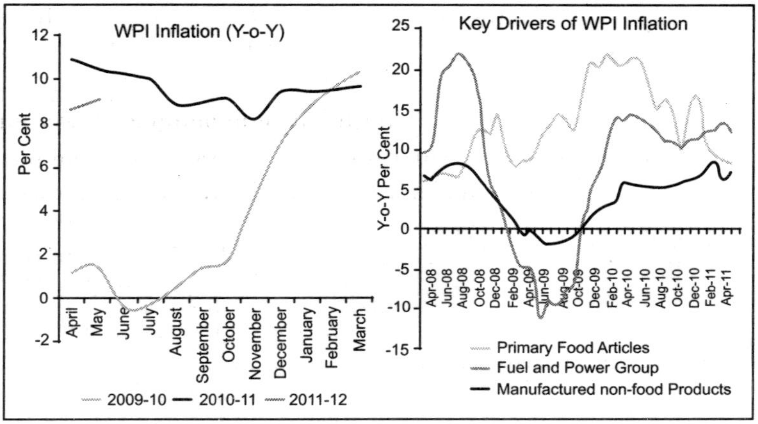

Fig. 6.4: Domestic Inflation Scenario

displayed. Food inflation was the predominant contributor in the early phase, but a resurgence of energy prices in the post-crisis environment began to play an increasingly important role. The prices of non-food manufactured products, which the RBI views as a reflection of demand pressures, began to rise noticeably in early 2010, but saw their rate of increase stabilize and even moderate somewhat in the third quarter of 2010-11. However, that pattern was short-lived and the rate of inflation for this category surged in the fourth quarter, a momentum that has clearly persisted into the current year.

The changing contributions of different drivers are very sharply brought out in the decomposition exercise displayed in Fig. 6.5. The analysis looked at recent patterns in terms of three periods of roughly equal lengths over the past 14 months, beginning April 2010. In the first period, food and energy, reflecting classic supply-side forces, were the primary contributors to inflation. Non-food manufacturing inflation, which, to the extent that it represents demand pressures, was not insignificant, suggesting that pricing power was present. In the second period, the weight of the contribution shifted dramatically towards commodities other than energy. The contribution from food moderated a bit, as did that from non-food manufacturing, suggesting that the pass-through or "generalization" risk was moderating. However, this pattern was short-lived. In the last

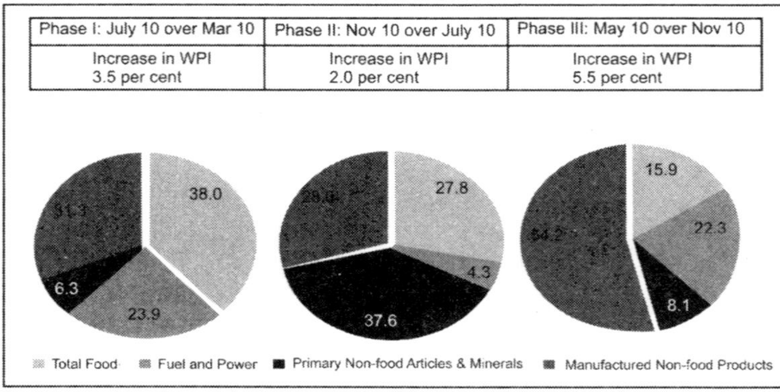

Fig. 6.5: Changing Drivers of Inflation

period, energy returned as a major contributor and the sharp increase in the contribution of non-food manufacturing indicated that producers were able to pass on higher input costs without too much difficulty. The strength of the pass-through in this period indicated that demand conditions remained quite robust, even as some early signs of moderation were coming through the production estimates and feedback from industry.

I want to put particular emphasis on food price dynamics, as I believe that this is likely to be a significant factor in the medium term. Although the overall contribution of food to inflation moderated over the past year, there are structural demand-supply imbalances at work, which will keep the pressure up in the absence of large and sustainable increases in supply. This phenomenon is demonstrated in the graph in Fig. 6.6. The main point that the graph makes is that the prices of protein sources have deviated sharply from their trend in recent years and show no signs of reverting to it. By contrast, the prices of other foods have also shown periodic deviations from trend, but have generally reverted. This pattern has, of course, contributed to high volatility, as the figure also demonstrates.

Volatility in food prices does have a welfare-reducing impact, but in the current Indian context, the much greater concern is the long-term nutritional impact of elevated protein prices. At a time when the combined impact of demographic transition and income increases is generating enormous demand for proteins, the supply chain is clearly struggling to meet this demand.

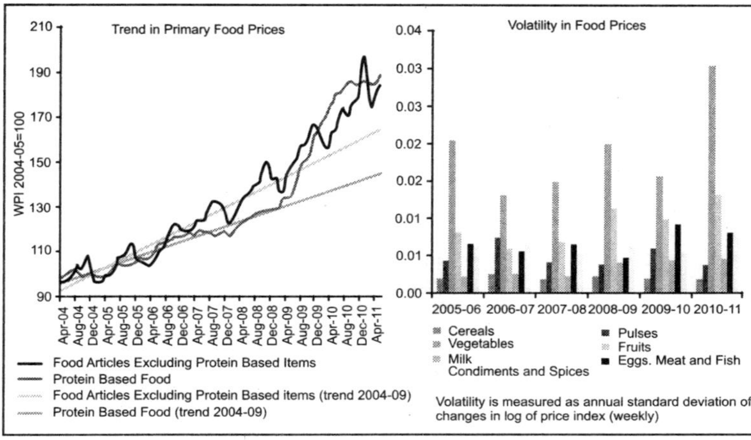

Fig. 6.6: Food Inflation: Trends and Cycles

To conclude this part of the discussion, let me bring in the issue of inflationary expectations. The persistence and recent acceleration of inflation has clearly increased the risk of expectations becoming unanchored. The RBI monitors short-term expectations through household surveys. Recent surveys have reinforced the perception that household expectations are moving up. Food prices play an important role in this process, but whatever the causes, the impact on wage-setting in both explicit and implicit contracts cannot be dismissed. However, the relative stability of long-term (10-year) yields on government securities suggest that expectations over this horizon remain anchored. This is reinforced by our regular surveys of professional forecasters, which also indicate no loss of confidence in a moderate inflation scenario over the medium and long run.

V. Monetary Policy : Actions and Transmission

The current cycle of contractionary monetary policy was initiated in the context of two important factors. First, there was an enormous volume of liquidity in the domestic financial system, as a result of policy responses to the crisis, which also took policy rates to very low levels. Second, even as the early signs of recovery were visible, inflationary tendencies had also begun to show. All this was happening in a global environment which was still quite turbulent and uncertain in late 2009 and early 2010. Figure 6.7 shows the trajectory of policy instruments —the Repo, the Reverse Repo and the Cash Reserve Ratio (CRR) in the pre-crisis, crisis and recovery periods.

In contrast to the very sharp and quick actions on rates and liquidity that were taken in responding to the crisis, the recovery

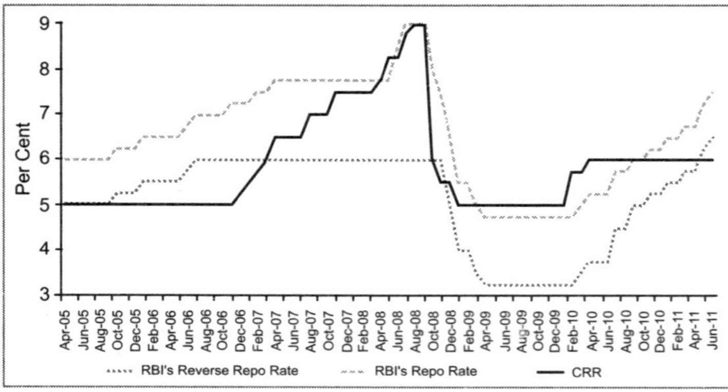

Fig. 6.7: Monetary Policy Trajectory

has been characterized by a much more calibrated approach. This was motivated by considerations related to the factors that I mentioned earlier. A more aggressive response to the incipient inflationary pressures may have been warranted under somewhat more predictable domestic growth and global scenarios, but in both these respects the situation in early 2010 was nowhere near stable or predictable. A calibrated approach, which was essentially a relatively frequent series of small rate hikes, was seen as the best way to balance the potentially conflicting objectives.

In the early phase of the cycle, surplus liquidity conditions persisted, which, clearly made transmission of policy rates through to transaction rates very sluggish. From this perspective, the early actions were essentially a signaling effort, accompanied by steady moves to eliminate the liquidity surplus through CRR increases. By the middle of the 2010, the liquidity scenario had moved to a deficit and transmission became much stronger. Figure 6.8 shows the immediate impact on the call rate, which is effectively the operating target of monetary policy, of a change

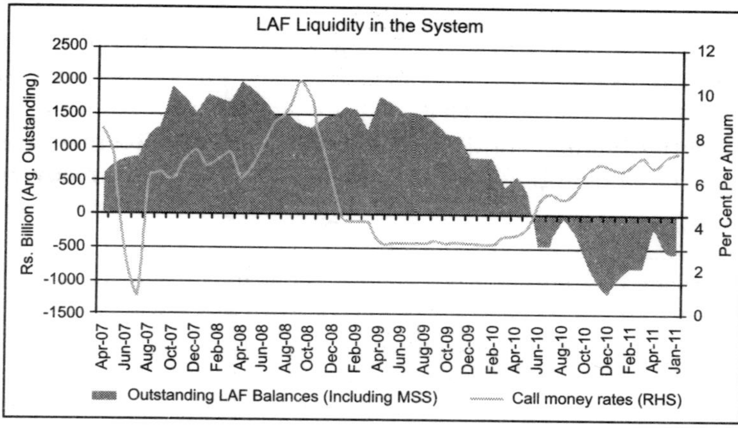

Fig. 6.8: Liquidity and Transmission

in the liquidity situation. The strengthening of transmission was visible across a variety of financial market segments. Figures 6.9 and 6.10 provide some illustrative evidence of this.

In Fig. 6.9, the call and Collateralized Borrowing and Lending Operations (CBLO) rates, a secured short-term channel

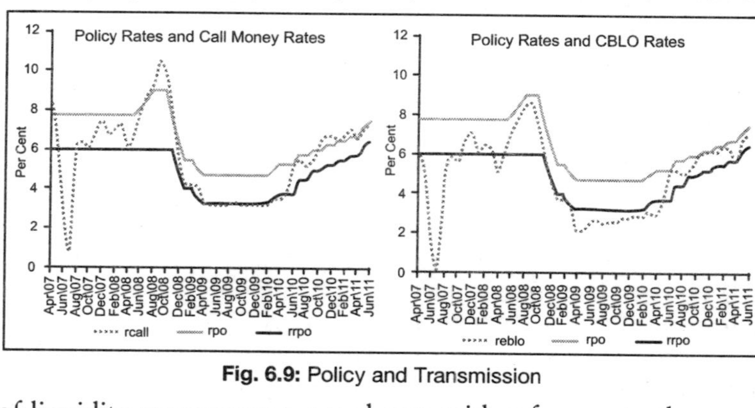

Fig. 6.9: Policy and Transmission

of liquidity management, are shown with reference to the repo-reverse repo corridor. The transmission intensity is quite clear, with the added dimension of movement from the lower bound of the corridor to the upper bound, as liquidity conditions tightened. Figure 6.10 shows the yield on 10-year government securities and that on 5-year AAA corporate bonds from the same perspective. Transmission is visible here as well.

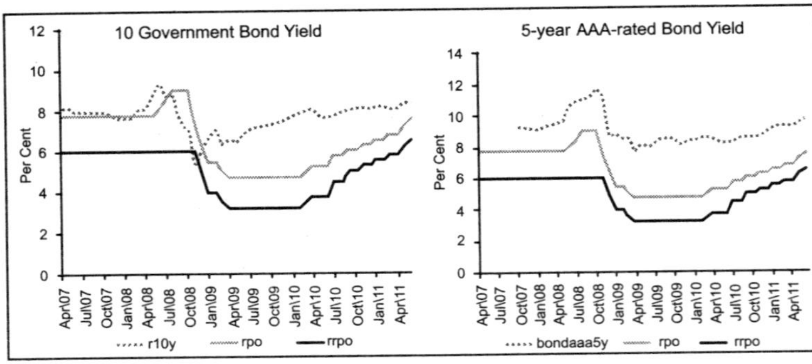

Fig. 6.10: Policy and Transmission

Of course, the banking system is by far the more important intermediary in the Indian financial context and what banks do matters a great deal. Significantly, a similar analysis of transmission through bank lending rates does not suggest that it is as strong as that in markets. Figure 6.11 displays the dynamics of bank lending rates in response to policy rate changes in both the expansionary and contractionary cycles. The sensitivities do not appear to be very strong. Rates did not come down very sharply in the expansionary phase and, while they are increasing in the contractionary phase, the magnitudes appear to be small. Aggregation problems may be masking some of the impact. In the RBI's consultations with industry, the fact that banks are aggressively passing on rate increases is often alluded to, which is undoubtedly intended as a complaint, but is entirely consistent with monetary policy objectives.

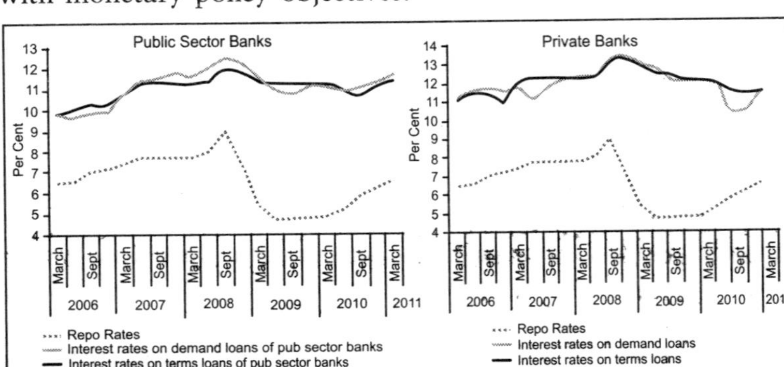

Fig. 6.11: Policy and Transmission to Bank Lending Rates

Finally, in the context of monetary actions and transmission, let me address the issue of real rates. One consistent critique of the monetary stance, that it has been behind the curve, is based on the criterion that real rates have been and still are negative. Of course, this leads to a usually inconclusive debate on what the deflator should be, but widespread perceptions that real rates are negative are likely to impact both spending behaviour and expectations. This then leads to the more operational issue of whether rates are to be brought into positive territory relatively rapidly or gradually.

Figures 6.12 and 6.13 provide some perspective on the real rate issue. As Fig. 6.12 shows, with the recent acceleration in inflation, many real rates, measured in the simplest way of subtracting either current headline inflation or core inflation from the nominal rate, are negative when the headline rate is used to deflate. The picture changes, but hardly decisively, if

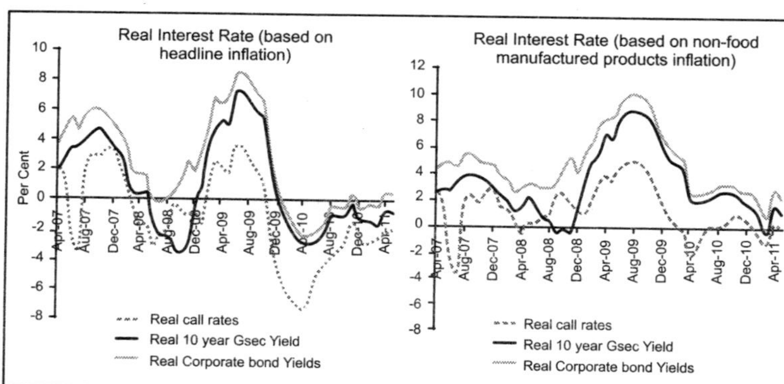

Fig. 6.12: Real Interest Rates

the core (non-food manufacturing) inflation is used. So, going by some of these indicators, it may appear that the policy stance is not contractionary enough. However, when we look at some other measures of real rates, specifically bank lending rates as shown in Fig. 6.13, the picture is a little different. Allowing for differences in risk and other differentiating prices, real rates are significantly positive. As I said, this is a criterion on which the debate in the Indian context is yet unresolved and is keeping some of my colleagues in the research departments engaged.

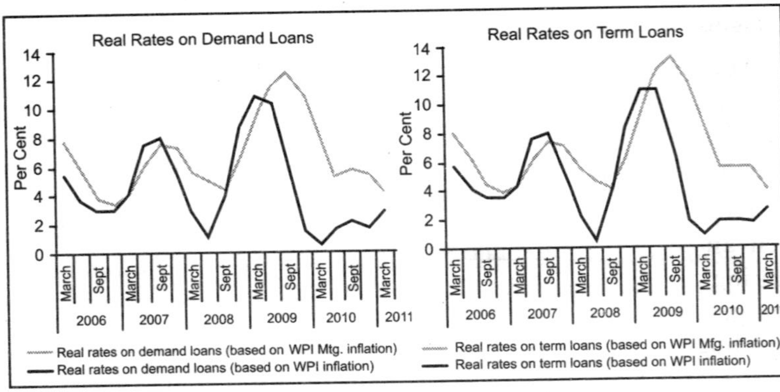

Fig. 6.13: Real Interest Rates on Bank Loans

The point I would like to make is that, at least in terms of a large proportion of financial transactions, real rates are positive. It remains a matter of judgment whether they are lower than they should be and, if so, how quickly the necessary adjustment should be made.

This judgment is partly related to the issue of expectations. Looking back over the past year and a half, the balancing act between growth and inflation can also be seen in a slightly different way. There is also a trade-off between minimizing the sacrifice of growth and not letting expectations run out of control as a result of inflation persistence, exacerbated by new shocks.

In the run-up to its recent Annual Policy statement, the RBI made an assessment that this had indeed emerged as a risk. Against a backdrop of firm and possibly rising commodity prices, the prospects of inflation going down soon were seen as not being very high. This supported the decision to send a stronger signal of commitment to bringing inflation under control. However, in our baseline projections, the cumulative impact of the tightening that has been done over the past few quarters—the call rate has moved up by about 450 basis points over a little more than a year—is likely to soften both growth and inflation in the second half of 2011-12. If this trajectory materialized as anticipated, the monetary stance could then respond accordingly. But, ultimately, as I indicated earlier, the stance is going to be predominantly determined by the actual and prospective inflation outcomes.

VI. Issues of Communication

This is an enormous challenge at the best of times, which becomes even more complex in circumstances like the current ones. Let me briefly address two sets of issues, to which a lot of thought is being given.

First, there is the concern with forecasts going wrong. Having been an analyst in my previous position, I am quite used to making frequent changes in forecasts, as new information emerges. The difference in this position is that actual decisions, with huge national consequences have to be made on the basis of forecasts that might be very short-lived. This poses risks to credibility, because actions consistent with one forecast may not be equally so with the revised one. Apart from improvements in forecasting methodology, which is really a long-term process, there are immediate implications of this problem. One is to make better and more explicit assessments of alternative scenarios and then make policy decisions, taking into account the risks associated with different scenarios materializing. In effect, this is being done, but perhaps the communication strategy around it perhaps needs to be fine-tuned.

Second, there is the issue of communicating the goals of monetary policy. For a variety of reasons, we have chosen not to commit to a formal and explicit inflation target, which has many advocates in the country. There is a credibility risk to not being held accountable to a single target, but there is also a risk to regularly missing that target, even if it is due to factors outside the control of monetary policy. But that does not mean that some clear and, most importantly, achievable, goals should not be articulated. We attempt to do this with every policy statement and look very carefully at feedback and public comments and debate that appear to have read messages different from what we intended and how we can sharpen it.

In this connection, the growth-inflation trade-off and sometimes conflicting perceptions of it is a significant issue. Going by theory and empirics, the trade-off is essentially a short-term one, with monetary policy aiming to keep growth at close to its long-term, structural trend as possible. Contractionary policy will slow growth down only to the extent that the economy is growing beyond its capacity, provoking inflation. It cannot, in terms of this framework, have any significant impact on the trend rate of growth. In fact, long-term growth can only be helped, not hurt, by low and stable inflation. However, much of the debate tends to view any slowdown in growth resulting from an anti-inflationary monetary stance as a long-term sacrifice, i.e. a downshift in trend. We need to articulate the distinctions involved more strongly, which has been done rather consciously in recent statements, but again perhaps needs to be sharpened.

VII. Concluding Remarks

The inflationary situation is India's most significant near-term macroeconomic challenge. There are some factors, global and domestic, that are clearly outside the purview of monetary influence. But that does not mean that monetary policy does not have a role in addressing factors that it does influence—demand pressures and the risks of inflation becoming generalized through expectations and price-setting actions. To the extent that growth may be impacted, it must be understood as a short-term trade-off, with positive consequences for long-term performance. Finally, the contribution of supply forces, which I have highlighted with the example of proteins, but which also exert pressure elsewhere, can only be addressed by increasing supply. Measures to do this are an integral part of a long-term inflation management strategy.

(Presentation by Dr. Subir Gokarn, Deputy Governor, Reserve Bank of India at the US-India Economic and Financial Partnership: CII and Brookings Institution, Washington DC, 27 June 2011), • *Courtesy*: www.rbi.org.in

7

Inflation: Decoding the Dynamics

Deepak Mohanty, Executive Director, RBI

19 Oct. 2011

In India, we have multiple price gauges—six Consumer Price Indices (CPIs) and a Wholesale Price Index (WPI). While the Reserve Bank of India (RBI) examines all the price indices, both at aggregate and disaggregated levels, changes in WPI are taken as the headline inflation for policy articulation. Within WPI, non-food manufactured products inflation is considered the core inflation—an indicator of demand condition.

Going by any measure of inflation, India comes out as a moderate inflation country, though occasionally inflation crossed into the double-digit territory. The historical average long-term inflation rate was around 7.5 per cent.

But, significantly, inflation moderated sharply in the last decade. The annual average inflation rate was around 5.5 per cent in the 2000s, irrespective of the inflation indices taken, whether WPI or CPI.

However, WPI inflation rose to an average of 9.6 per cent in 2010-11 and continues to be over 9 per cent in the current fiscal so far. The various measures of CPIs are also currently around 9 per cent.

The persistence of inflation over a year-and-a-half raises three key questions:

How did the inflation dynamics change? How will inflation evolve in future? Why do we need to contain inflation?

Inflation Dynamics

While a number of domestic and international supply shocks, coupled with firm demand conditions, exacerbated inflationary pressures over the past 18 months, structural changes in the inflation process were evident earlier.

Monthly WPI inflation data suggested there was a structural break around the mid-2000s, with the inflation rate during the latter half of the 2000s being higher. Higher levels of food prices seemed to have caused this break.

Food inflation, being subject to supply shocks, tends to be volatile. For example, the performance of monsoon has a significant bearing on the trend of domestic food grain prices. Spikes in food prices normally subside as they are transitory.

However, empirical analysis indicates that within the food group, inflation in protein items has become persistent. This suggests that protein inflation has assumed a structural character, adding rigidity to the overall level of food inflation.

The increase in protein prices is supported by the changes in consumer preference. For example, the 66th round of National Sample Survey Organisation survey shows that while the share of per capita expenditure on food has gone down—both in rural and urban centres—the dietary pattern has shifted in favour of protein items, whose share has gone up.

As the supply response has not been adequate, prices have increased and remained elevated. The rural consumption of protein is sustained by increase in wage rates.

There was another structural break in the core non-food manufactured products inflation towards the middle of 2009-10, around the time global commodity prices rebounded. The pass-through from non-food international commodity prices to domestic raw material prices has increased, particularly in recent years, reflecting growing interconnectedness of domestic and global commodity markets.

A sharp increase in non-food manufactured products inflation suggests producers are able to pass on the cost increases, given higher demand. In addition, reflecting the sharp rise in international crude oil prices, domestic fuel prices have also increased, as over 70 per cent of our requirement for petroleum is met through imports.

To the extent the government has tried to cushion the impact of high international prices of oil by not passing on the increase fully to the consumers, it has increased the subsidy burden. Higher subsidy translates into higher fiscal deficit, which has inflationary implications.

On the demand side, there has been a significant increase in wages—both in the formal and informal sectors—in recent years. Even after accounting for high inflation, the increase in real wages has been positive both in urban and rural areas.

In addition, there has also been a significant demand stimulus from the crisis-driven fiscal and monetary policies. The current inflation process, therefore, is an amalgam of both supply constraints and demand pressures.

Shaping Inflation's Path

Five factors will shape the inflation trajectory. The first is the trend in domestic food prices. Given the current stage of our economic development, the demand for food items, particularly animal protein, will increase with economic growth and a rise in income levels.

The demographic dividend, which has been contributing to our growth and productivity, has also raised consumption demand, particularly food.

As per a United Nations projection, a high consumption cohort in India's total population will continue to dominate demand till 2040.

On the other hand, current per capita availability of cereals and pulses has been lower than that in the previous five decades. Oilseed production falls far short of demand.

Food prices in India are primarily determined by domestic demand and supply factors, and domestic price policy. With India's domestic food prices being higher, import is not an option for reducing the prices. Hence, increasing agricultural productivity and expanding livestock production will be important for moderation of food inflation.

Second, global commodity prices and, particularly, crude oil prices will have an impact on overall inflation. This requires policy initiatives towards energy conservation, efficiency in energy usage, recourse to alternative sources of energy, and step up in domestic exploration of oil and gas. For a fast growing economy such as ours, energy supplies will tend to lag demand.

It is, therefore, important to contain demand by letting the pricing mechanism play its allocative role. For this, it will be desirable to make further progress towards deregulation of petroleum prices, particularly diesel. This will not only allow the price signals to operate, but also balance the demand for petroleum products.

Third, on the demand side, there is a need to shift aggregate demand away from consumption towards investment, to augment the potential output of the economy. The demographic dividend that we have in terms of addition of younger people to the labour force could be better harnessed when combined with increasing capital accumulation.

If the potential output does not expand, and the economy tends to grow faster than potential, it will result in overheating. The resultant inflationary pressures, by itself, will impact growth adversely. It is, therefore, important to enhance the potential output to dampen the inflationary impulses.

Fourth, the level of the fiscal deficit and the quality of government expenditure have significant influence on inflation. Under normal circumstances, when private demand is buoyant, expansion in the fiscal deficit could be inflationary. Since private borrowing competes with government borrowing, it could exert upward pressure on interest rates. This could crowd out private investment, which would have an adverse impact on the overall economic growth.

Further, it also matters whether the government borrowing is for financing consumption or investment. The fiscal multiplier works better with investment, but a rise in government consumption expenditure could be potentially inflationary. There is, therefore, a need to move towards credible fiscal consolidation to contain demand-side pressures on inflation.

Fifth, the stance of monetary policy and its ability to anchor inflationary expectations will affect how inflation evolves in future. The level of the policy interest rate should be such that it is neither too stimulative nor too tight.

This requires active liquidity management by RBI so that the systemic liquidity mostly remains in deficit in order to strengthen monetary transmission.

For an economy such as ours, with a large informal sector, there is also a need to foster financial deepening through financial inclusion to enhance our potential output.

Containing Inflation

Prolonged high inflation, even if originating from the supply side, could give rise to increased inflation expectations and cause general prices to rise. Poorly anchored inflation expectations make long-term financial planning more complex, with potential adverse effects on investment and growth.

High inflation deters financial saving and increases lending rates, which discourage investment.

Moreover, high inflation is the most regressive form of taxation, particularly on the poor. It is, therefore, important to contain inflation and keep inflation expectations anchored so that consumers do not mark up their long-run inflation expectations by reacting to short periods of higher-than-expected inflation.

Keeping in view the costs of inflation and the fact that high inflation is inimical to sustained growth, the medium-term objective of RBI is to bring down inflation to 3 per cent, consistent with India's broader integration with the global economy.

In this direction, monetary policy aims to contain perceptions of inflation in the range of 4-4.5 per cent with a particular focus on the behaviour of the non-food manufacturing component, which is considered as core inflation given its high degree of persistence.

This objective is consistent with the estimated threshold level of inflation of 4-6 per cent, suggesting the absence of a so-called new normal for inflation in India.

Both global and domestic factors will shape the inflation outlook in the future. RBI signalled the reversal from its crisis-driven expansionary monetary policy stance in October 2009. Since then, the cash reserve ratio has been raised by 100 basis points (bps).

One basis point is one-hundredth of a percentage point.

The policy repo rate has been raised by a cumulative 325 bps. As the liquidity in the system went from surplus to deficit, the effective policy rate tightening has been of the order of 475 bps. Thus, the cumulative monetary policy action would have the desired impact on inflation going forward.

Conclusion

While inflation is expected to moderate towards the later part of the year, reflecting monetary tightening and likely softening of global commodity prices, fiscal policy needs to be supportive in containing aggregate demand.

In addition, there is an urgent need to address the issue of structural supply constraints, particularly in agriculture, so that these do not become binding constraints in the long run, hampering the task of inflation management.

(Article by Shri Deepak Mohanty, Executive Director, Reserve Bank of India, published in www.livemint.com) • *Courtesy*: www.rbi.org.in

8

Monetary Policy Response to Recent Inflation in India

Deepak Mohanty, Executive Director, RBI

03 Sep. 2011

...It has been about two years since October 2009 that the Reserve Bank of India announced its exit from the crisis-driven accommodative monetary policy stance. However, inflation continues to remain elevated, despite sustained monetary policy action. Headline inflation, measured by year-on-year changes in the wholesale price index (WPI), averaged 9.6 per cent in 2010-11 and it has continued to be over 9 per cent in the current financial year so far. This spell of high inflation has been the longest since the mid-1990s. It has, therefore, posed a major challenge for policymakers, especially for the Reserve Bank as the key objective of monetary policy is price stability.

Why do we need to worry about inflation? How did the inflation dynamics evolve over the past two years? What was the monetary policy response? These are primarily the questions that I will address.

Why do We Need to Worry about Inflation?

We need to be concerned about inflation as it has adverse impact on the real economy. First, high and persistent inflation imposes significant socio-economic costs. Given that the burden of inflation is disproportionately large on the poor, high inflation by itself can lead to distributional inequality. Therefore, for a welfare-oriented public policy, low inflation becomes a critical element for ensuring balanced progress. Second, high inflation distorts economic incentives by diverting resources away from productive investment to speculative activities. Third, inflation reduces households saving as they try to maintain the real value of their consumption. Consequent fall in overall investment in the economy reduces its potential growth. Fourth, as inflation rises and turns volatile, it raises the inflation risk premia in financial transactions. Hence, nominal interest rates tend to be higher than they would have been under low and stable inflation. Fifth, if domestic inflation remains persistently higher than those of the trading partners, it affects external competitiveness through appreciation of the real exchange rate. Sixth, as inflation rises beyond a threshold, it has an adverse impact on overall growth. The Reserve Bank's current assessment suggests that the threshold level of inflation for India is in the range of 4-6 per cent.[1] If inflation persists beyond this level, it could lower economic growth over the medium-term. These costs, therefore, necessitate monetary policy response to control inflation.

How did the Inflation Dynamics Change?

It is important to appreciate the background in which the inflation surge has occurred. The current phase of high inflation followed the global financial crisis, which affected the India's economy, though not with the same intensity as advanced countries. Managing inflation in an economy which is recovering from a downturn is much more complex because of associated uncertainties than managing inflation under normal conditions.

Prelude to Current Inflation Surge

In the initial phase of the crisis, it appeared that emerging market economies (EMEs) were better positioned to weather the storm created by the global financial meltdown on the back of their substantial foreign exchange reserve cushion, improved policy frameworks and generally robust banking sector and corporate balance sheets. However, any hope about EMEs escaping unscathed could not be sustained after the failure of Lehman Brothers in September 2008 which triggered global deleveraging and heightened risk aversion. Eventually, EMEs were also adversely affected by the spillover effects: first through contraction in world trade and then from reversal in capital flows.

India, though initially somewhat insulated from the global developments, was eventually impacted significantly by the global shocks through all the channels—trade, finance and expectations channels. In response, the Reserve Bank swiftly introduced a comprehensive range of measures to limit the impact of the adverse global developments on the domestic financial system and the economy. The Reserve Bank, like most central banks, took a number of conventional and unconventional measures to augment domestic and foreign currency liquidity, and sharply reduced the policy rates. In a span of seven months between October 2008 and April 2009, there was unprecedented policy activism. For example: (i) the repo rate was reduced by 425 basis points to 4.75 per cent, (ii) the reverse repo rate was reduced by 275 basis points to 3.25 per cent, (iii) the cash reserve ratio (CRR) of banks was reduced by a cumulative 400 basis points of their net demand and time liabilities (NDTL) to 5.0 per cent, and (iv) the total amount of primary liquidity potentially made available to the financial system was over ₹ 5.6 trillion or over 10 per cent of GDP. The government also come up with various fiscal stimulus measures.

In October 2009, it was not easy to exit from the excessively accommodative monetary policy stance for two main reasons. First, the year-on-year headline WPI inflation had just barely turned positive and was entirely driven by food inflation. Industrial production had started to pick up but exports were still declining. Hence, recovery was not assured. Second, globally, most central banks were in favour of continuing stimulus. On the other hand, domestically, consumer price inflation was high, households' inflation expectations were rising and surplus liquidity was substantial as reflected in the Reserve Bank's Liquidity Adjustment Facility (LAF) window. These developments had inflationary consequences.

In its Second Quarter Review of Monetary Policy for 2009-10, the Reserve Bank after wider consultations provided the arguments for and against beginning reversal of monetary easing. On balance of considerations, the Reserve Bank judged that the time was appropriate to sequence the exit in a calibrated way so that while the recovery process was not hampered, inflation expectations remained anchored. The exit process thus began with the closure of the special liquidity facilities instituted during the crisis. This amounted to withdrawal of potential liquidity to the tune of ₹ 1.7 trillion.

Phases of Inflation

The evolution of the inflation process since the beginning of the exit in October 2009 can be characterised into four different phases: Phase I—October 2009-March 2010; Phase II—April-July 2010; Phase III—August-November 2010; and Phase IV—December 2010 onwards. As the drivers of inflation changed over the phases, the response of monetary policy was calibrated on the basis of changing dynamics of inflation as also the growth-inflation balance and the evolving global economic conditions.

Phase I. October 2009-March 2010

The year-on-year headline WPI inflation accelerated from under 2 per cent in October 2009 to above 10 per cent by March 2010 (Fig. 8.1).

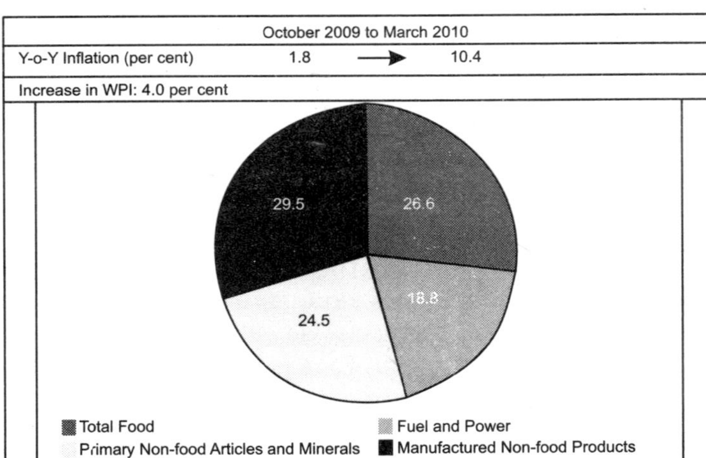

Fig. 8.1: Weighted Contribution to Increase in WPI (Phase I)

A major part of this increase in inflation was attributed to the waning of base effect. In addition, the price pressures largely emanated from food. There was severe deficiency in rainfall during 2009-10, which adversely affected the food prices. Moreover, global commodity prices rebounded from the trough reached during the crisis. Fuel prices rose significantly during this period. Manufactured non-food products inflation also reverted to its medium-term trend (Fig. 8.2).

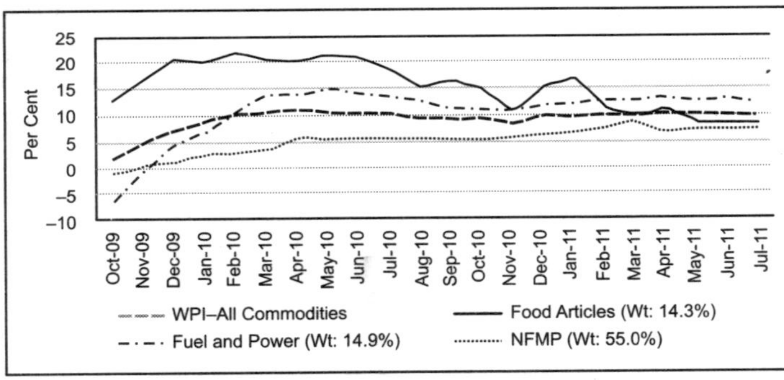

Fig. 8.2: WPI Inflation by Major Categories

The Reserve Bank, in its Second Quarter Review of monetary policy in October 2009, highlighted the need for exit from crisis-time monetary policy stimulus and withdrew the unconventional liquidity support measures and restored the statutory liquidity ratio (SLR) of banks to the pre-crisis level. At the same time, monetary policy had to recognise that the economic growth was recovering from the crisis time slowdown and any aggressive monetary tightening at that point would have affected the recovery. Subsequently, in January 2010, the CRR was raised by 75 basis points of banks' net demand and time liabilities (NDTL), and policy rates were increased for the first time in March 2010 by 25 basis points. The transmission of rate-based monetary policy actions was weak during the periods of surplus liquidity in the financial system and, therefore, bringing down liquidity levels was the crucial challenge.

The Reserve Bank's policy action during this period was effective in terms of bringing down the overall surplus liquidity available within the system to the levels consistent with monetary policy stance. At the same time, the recovery in economic growth was not dented as was seen from the trend in growth in industrial output, which picked up during this period (Fig. 8.3).

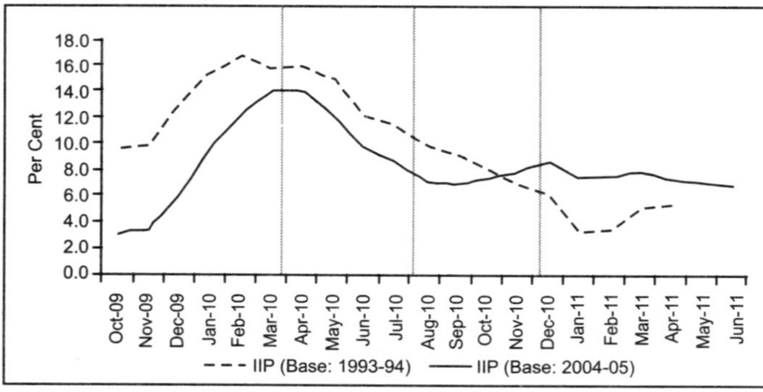

Fig. 8.3: Growth in Industrial Production (IIP) Old and New Base
(annual three months moving average growth rate)

Increase in headline inflation during this period, however, caught up with the households' inflation expectations (Fig. 8.4).

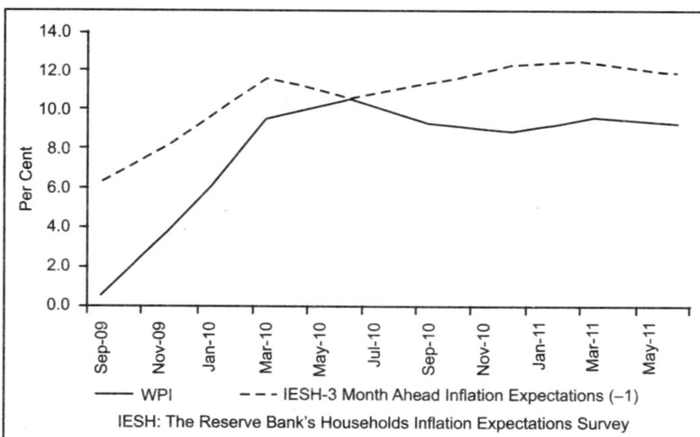

Fig. 8.4: Household Inflation Expectations and Headline WPI Inflation

During the initial months of this phase, the major challenge for monetary policy was, on the one hand, to remain supportive of recovery while on the other hand to keep a vigil on the build-up of inflationary pressures which were getting amplified by the deficit in monsoon rainfall. Subsequently, increases in global commodity prices, especially fuel, emerged as a key risk. At the same time, consolidating recovery necessitated a shift in the monetary policy stance from 'managing the crisis' to 'managing the recovery'.

Phase II. April-July 2010

During this phase, year-on-year WPI inflation remained stubborn around 10 per cent and the index advanced by 3.4 per cent (Fig. 8.5).

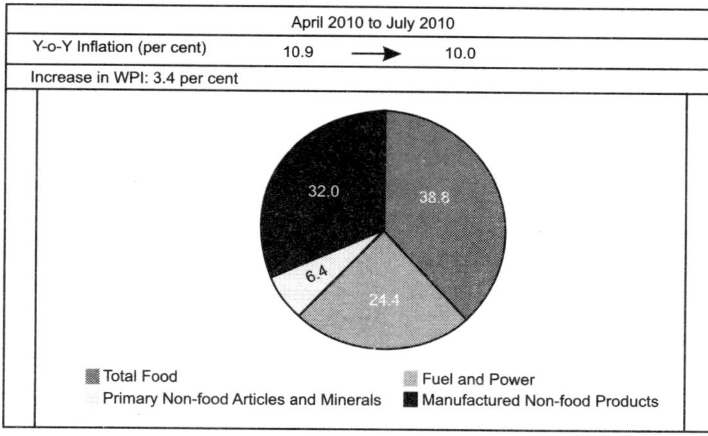

Fig. 8.5: Weighted Contribution to Increase in WPI (Phase II)

It was expected that with a normal monsoon during 2010-11, food inflation would moderate. But, contrary to expectations, the major driver of inflation in this period was food. In fact, inflation in cereals, pulses and vegetables was significantly lower in July 2010 as compared with the March 2010 levels indicating that the good monsoon indeed had a moderating impact on these items. However, food inflation did not decline as price pressures were emanating from the protein-rich items such as milk, egg, meat and fish, whose output was less responsive to monsoon (Fig. 8.6). The demand for these items has been growing with increasing per capita income and changing dietary patterns. In the absence of adequate supply response, price pressures were substantial. Another major contributor to increase in WPI during this period was the increase in administered prices of petroleum products and deregulation of petrol prices in June 2010. The major contribution to inflation thus emanated from food and fuel.

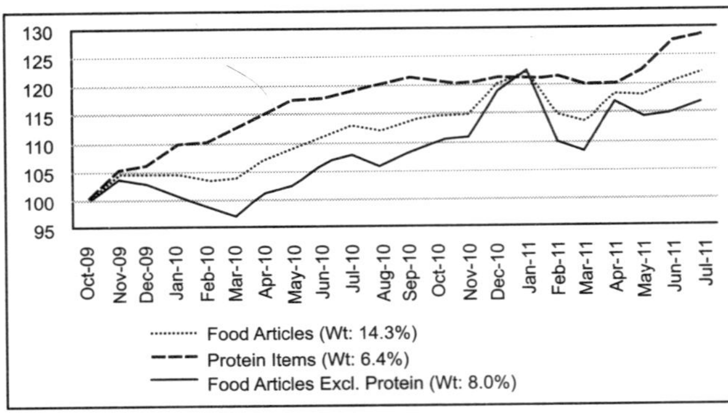

Fig. 8.6: Components of Food Price Index (October 2009=100)

During this period, the key policy rates were increased gradually with a narrowing of the LAF interest rate corridor in order to reduce volatility in the overnight interest rate. While the level of inflation had increased, industrial production was showing a declining trend (Fig. 8.3). On the global front, the weak US recovery and concerns over sovereign debt sustainability in euro area during this period raised fears of a double dip-recession and global commodity prices declined marginally. Moreover, the pressure on inflation during this period emerged largely from food and administered price revisions. Given the limitations of demand management policies to address supply shock induced inflation, monetary policy actions were geared towards normalisation of policy rates as well as anchoring inflation expectations. During this period, policy rates were raised thrice and the CRR was raised once (Table 8.1).

By the end of this period, the liquidity in the system turned into deficit as was evident from banks borrowing from the LAF of the Reserve Bank. Therefore, effective policy rate showed an additional increase by the width of LAF interest rate corridor, i.e. 100 basis points, as the repo rate became the policy rate.

Table 8.1: Changes in Key Policy Rates

Period	Repo Rate (%)		Reverse Repo Rate (%)		CRR (% of NDTL)		Systemic
	Magnitude	Frequency	Magnitude	Frequency	Magnitude	Frequency	Liquidity* (₹ billion)
I. Oct 09 to March 10	25	25 bps X 1	25	25 bps X 1	75	50 bps X 1 25 bps X 1	(+) 783
II. April to July 10	75	25 bps X 3	100	50 bps X 1 25 bps X 2	25	25 bps X 1	(-) 10
III. August to Nov 10	50	25 bps X 2	75	50 bps X 1 25 bps X 1	-	-	(-) 465
IV. Dec 10 to July 11	175	50 bps X 2 25 bps X 3	175	50 bps X 2 25 bps X 3	-	-	(-) 705
October 09 to July 11	325	50 bps X 2 25 bps X 9	375	50 bps X 4 25 bps X 7	100		

* Systemic liquidity measured by daily average liquidity in LAF; positive indicates surplus (reverse repo) and negative indicates deficit (repo). NDTL: Net Demand and Time Liabilities of Banks.

The transition of liquidity situation from surplus to deficit mode also set the stage for improved monetary transmission.

Phase III. August-November 2010

This phase was marked by slowing down of price pressures as headline inflation declined to 8.2 per cent by November 2010 from above 10 per cent in the preceding phase (Fig. 8.7). The increase in WPI during this phase by just 2.0 per cent was also moderate compared to the previous two phases. Of the increase in WPI, a major part emanated from the primary non-food articles, mostly raw cotton and minerals. The build-up in primary

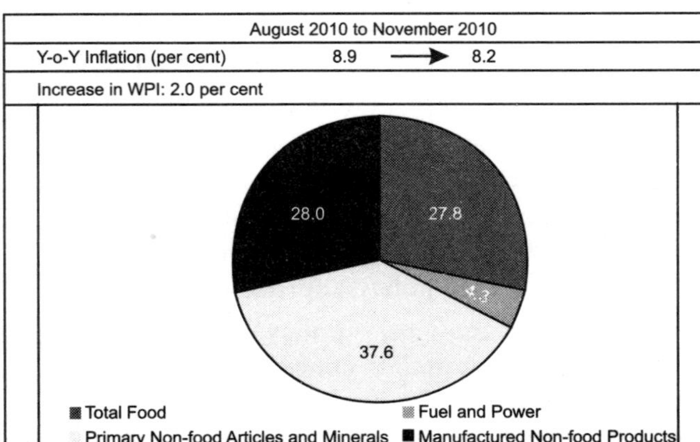

Fig. 8.7: Weighted Contribution to Increase in WPI (Phase III)

non-food articles prices, however, contained the risk in that they might pass-through to manufactured products inflation, depending on the prevailing demand conditions, the signs of which were first seen in November 2010.

Moderate softening of price pressures during this period also reflected that the calibrated approach of monetary policy was having an impact on demand in a non-disruptive manner. The available data then on industrial production from the old-base IIP series indicated that there was a slowdown in overall IIP growth. However, inflation expectations remained elevated. Global commodity price rebound in this period was largely driving the industrial raw material prices (Fig. 8.8). But monetary policy had to be cautious as mixed signs on growth sustainability

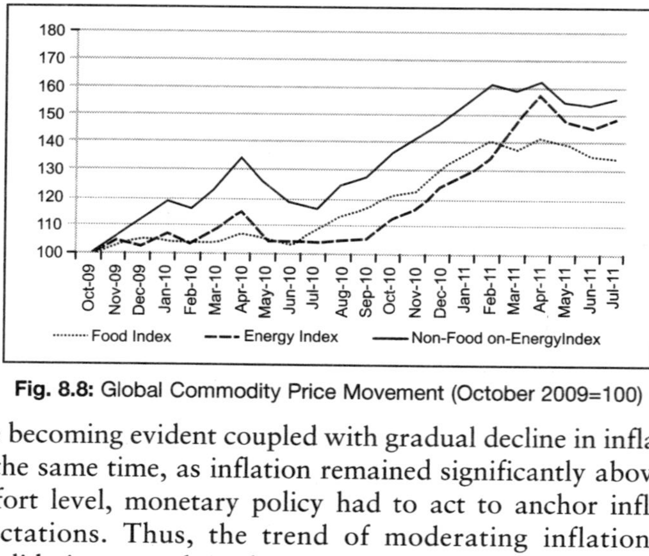

Fig. 8.8: Global Commodity Price Movement (October 2009=100)

were becoming evident coupled with gradual decline in inflation. sAt the same time, as inflation remained significantly above the comfort level, monetary policy had to act to anchor inflation expectations. Thus, the trend of moderating inflation and consolidating growth in the second and third quarters of 2010-11 justified the calibrated policy approach of the Reserve Bank.

Transmission of monetary policy improved significantly during this period as liquidity continued to remain in deficit with significant increase in banks borrowing from the repo window (Fig. 8.9). Rates in all the segments of the financial market increased during this period with more prominent increase in the call money rate.

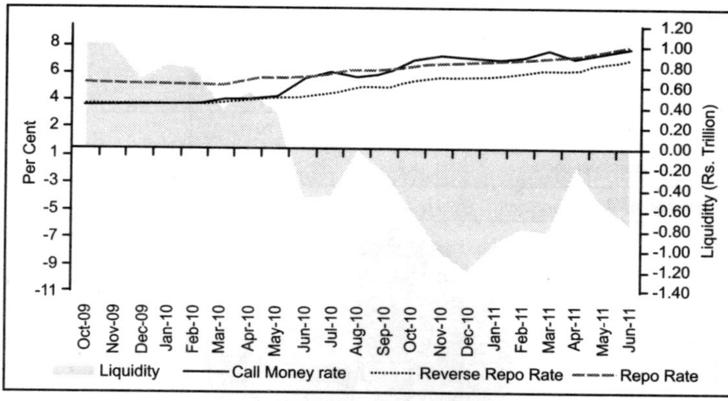

Fig. 8.9: Transmission Stronger Under Liquidity Deficit

Phase IV. December 2010 Onwards

The moderately declining trend in inflation changed course significantly during this period: first, on account of a spurt in food inflation as unseasonal rains in some parts of the country caused significant damage to output of vegetables and subsequently on account of stronger than expected pass-through of increase in input costs to output prices (Fig. 8.10).

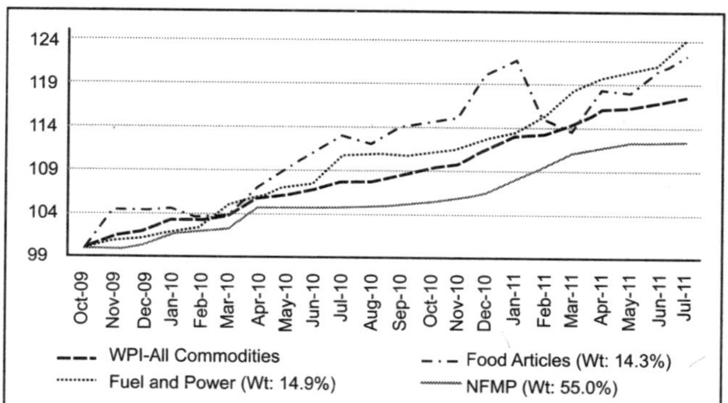

Fig. 8.10: Movement in WPI (October 2009 = 100) of Selected Items

The contribution of non-food manufactured products inflation to overall increase in WPI rose significantly during this period. The inflation in this group reached a high of 8.5 per cent in March 2011 and remained at or above 7 per cent thereafter indicating generalised price pressures. Consequently, the share of non-food manufactured product inflation rose sharply during this phase (Fig. 8.11).

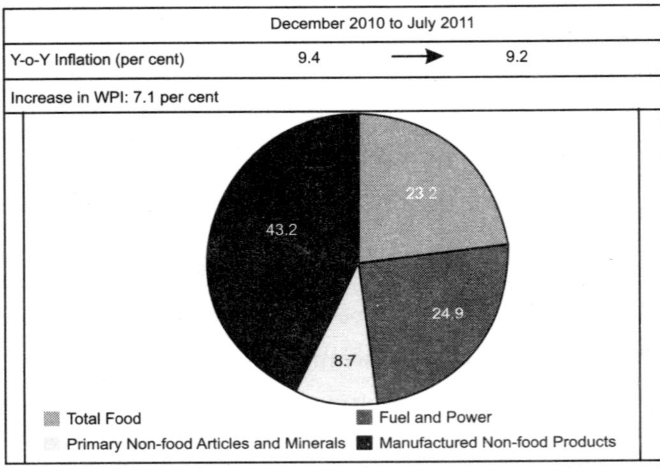

Fig. 8.11: Weighted Contribution to Increase in WPI (Phase IV)

Given the high global commodity prices and their likelihood to remain firm, the threat to price stability from global inflation continues to persist. The faster than expected increase in core inflation suggested that high inflation was becoming increasingly persistent. There was also evidence of demand pressure from increase in real wages besides high fiscal deficit. Monetary policy also had to recognise that over the long-run, high inflation is inimical to sustained growth. It slows investment by creating uncertainty and thus poses significant risks to future growth. It was indicated by the Reserve Bank that bringing down inflation, given its generalised nature, even at the cost of some growth in the short-run, should take precedence.[2]

Taking into account these emerging factors, monetary policy was continuously tightened during this period both in terms of the number of increases as well as in terms of the stepped up magnitude of increase in the policy rate Table 1. The increasing generalisation of inflation indicated that the supply shocks had morphed into a more generalised inflation process.

Conclusions

First, inflation in India has remained elevated and persistent over 18 months now. The inflation path was influenced by a number of domestic and international supply shocks. Monsoon failure in 2009-10 and sharp increase in international fuel and commodities prices accentuated domestic inflationary pressures.

Second, the evolution of inflation so far from its low level in October 2009 can be seen in four phases: first, driven by food prices and then by fuel and industrial raw material prices, and finally spilling over to a generalised inflation process. In fact, inflation was on a declining trajectory between August and November 2010 before reversing course in December and getting generalised.

Third, monetary policy response began early in October 2009 in anticipation of the likely path of the inflation trajectory as also on consideration of its source and composition. The background of calibrated monetary policy response is important as policy was reversed from its highly stimulative stance with policy interest rates at the historically lowest levels and liquidity was high. During this period, the global economy remained mired in uncertainties and domestic recovery was also not assured.

Fourth, the initial rounds of monetary policy response was in the nature of normalisation from an excessively stimulative stance in a non-disruptive manner. The policy response was calibrated to the domestic growth-inflation dynamics. As growth took hold and inflation became more generalised, monetary policy response was strengthened. Initially, monetary transmission was weak as systemic liquidity was in surplus. But once liquidity turned into deficit in July 2010, monetary transmission improved.

Fifth, since October 2009, the cash reserve ratio (CRR) has been raised by 100 basis points. The policy repo rate has been raised by a cumulative 325 basis points. As the liquidity in the system transited from surplus to deficit, the effective tightening has been of the order of 475 basis points. Thus, the cumulative monetary policy action would have the desired impact on inflation. It is expected that inflation would moderate towards the later part of 2011-12 and come down to around 7 per cent by the end of the year. The current monetary stance remains anti-inflationary.

Sixth, inflation imposes real costs which are borne disproportionately by the different segments of the economy. Prolonged high inflation, even if originating from the supply side, could give rise to increased inflation expectations and cause general prices to rise. As inflation is inimical to growth, it becomes necessary for monetary policy to respond to contain inflation and anchor inflationary expectations.

Seventh, the medium-term objective of the Reserve Bank is to bring down inflation to 3.0 per cent consistent with India's broader integration into the global economy. In this direction, monetary policy aims to contain perceptions of inflation in the range of 4.0-4.5 per cent with a particular focus on the behaviour of the non-food manufacturing component. This objective is consistent with the estimated threshold level of inflation of 4-6 per cent suggesting the absence of a 'new normal' for inflation in India.

Finally, at the end of my talk what advice can I give to this gathering of bright minds? I believe, innovation and enterprise coupled with the spirit of youth will rapidly propel India to its rightful place in the global economy in the coming years. So unless you dare the frontiers, we will not know what lies beyond.

Notes

1. Reserve Bank of India Annual Report 2010-11.
2. Monetary Policy Statement 2011-12, May 3, 2011, Reserve Bank of India.

(Article by Shri Deepak Mohanty, Executive Director, Reserve Bank of India, published in www.livemint.com) • *Courtesy*: www.rbi.org.in

9

Changing Inflation Dynamics in India

Deepak Mohanty, Executive Director, RBI

13 Aug. 2011

...What is inflation? Simply put, inflation is the sustained increase in the overall price level. Relative change in prices of goods and services is a desirable attribute of market economy as it reflects productivity changes as well as demand and supply conditions. However, when this process transforms into an acceleration of the overall price level, we need to worry as inflation imposes many socio-economic costs.

The headline wholesale price index (WPI) inflation averaged 9.6 per cent in 2010-11 as compared with 5.3 per cent per annum in the previous decade. Similarly, the average consumer price inflation, measured by the consumer price index for industrial workers (CPI-IW), was even higher at 10.5 per cent in 2010-11 as compared with 5.9 per cent per annum in the previous decade. Moreover, this elevated level of inflation also persisted through the first quarter of 2011-12. In response to inflationary pressures, the Reserve Bank has raised the policy repo rate 11 times bringing it up from a low of 4.75 per cent in March 2010 to 8.00 per cent by July 2011. It is expected that inflation should come down towards the later part of this year.

Why has inflation been so high and persisted for so long? This is the theme of my talk today. In my presentation, I propose to address the following questions: Is India an outlier among major countries in terms of recent inflation performance? Has the inflation process changed? What are the causal factors—global and domestic as well as supply and demand? I will conclude with some thoughts on managing the inflation dynamics on the way forward.

Is India an Outlier in the Inflation Performance Among Major Countries?

It is important to appreciate the global backdrop in which we are experiencing a resurgence of inflation now. In the last decade, inflation was low, both in advanced countries and in emerging and developing economies till the global financial crisis unfolded. Consequently, global economy got into a recession and global output declined by 0.5 per cent in 2009. However, global output growth rebounded to 5.0 per cent in 2010.

As the global economy recovered from the worst effect of the global financial crisis, inflation picked up in emerging and developing economies. This was because the global recovery was largely driven by emerging market economies (EMEs) what was termed as a two-speed recovery—a faster growth in EMEs accompanied by a slower growth in advanced economies. As output gaps closed, there was increasing inflationary pressure in EMEs, particularly in Asia. According to the International Monetary Fund (IMF), consumer price inflation in developing Asia almost doubled from 3.1 per cent in 2009 to 6.0 per cent in 2010 and is projected to be around the same level in 2011. Latest data suggest that inflation in rapidly growing BRICS[1] remains elevated (Table 9.1).

Global Factors

With recovery, global commodity prices rebounded given the higher level of commodity intensity of growth in EMEs. There was also an element of financialisation of commodities given the global excess liquidity.[2] Crop loss due to adverse weather conditions in many parts in the world coupled with increased diversion of foodgrains towards biofuel exerted added pressure on global food prices. Thus, global commodity prices including food prices rose sharply. For example, the IMF Commodities Index rose by 24 per cent in 2010 on top of an increase of 43 per cent in 2009. It further rose by 20 per cent in

Table 9.1: Inflation* in BRICS Countries

Country	2010 (Average)	2011 (Latest)@
Brazil	5.0	6.9
Russia	6.9	9.0
India	9.6	9.4
China	3.3	6.5
South Africa	4.3	5.0

* WPI for India and CPI for other countries.

@ June/July (year-on-year)

December 2010-April 2011, before moderating by about 2 per cent during June-July 2011. Notwithstanding some softening in the last few months, it is important to recognize that the current level of commodity prices is almost double of that two and half years ago (Table 9.2).

Table 9.2: Global Commodity Prices
(IMF Primary Commodity Index: 2005 = 100)

	Dec-08	Dec-09	Dec-10	Apr-11	Jul-11
All Commodities	98.4	140.9	174.7	209.9	198.9
Food	119.6	139.5	176.4	190.9	180.3
Beverage	132.5	176.7	192.6	216.6	210.0
Agricultural Raw Materials	87.6	111.2	146.9	171.6	161.5
Metals	107.5	176.8	233.6	250.1	242.2
Energy	91.6	137.9	167.1	212.6	200.7

The increase in commodity prices has affected different countries differently depending on whether they are net importers or exporters of commodities. India being a net importer of commodities, the adverse impact on domestic inflation has been stronger. Inflation increased in developing and emerging economies with a combination of closing of output gaps and sharp increase in commodity prices. In this regard, India is not an exception. But the level of inflation in India has been high compared to those in many EMEs. This suggests that apart from global factors, domestic factors have had a significant influence on the inflation trajectory in India.

Has the Inflation Process Changed?

In India, we have multiple price indices—six consumer price indices and a wholesale price index (WPI). While the Reserve

Bank examines all the price indices both at aggregate and disaggregated levels, changes in the WPI is taken as the headline inflation for policy articulation. Within the WPI, non-food manufactured products inflation is considered the core inflation.[3]

Going by any measure of inflation, India comes out as a moderate inflation country, though occasionally inflation crossed the double digit mark. The historical average long-term inflation rate was around 7.5 per cent. But significantly, there was substantial moderation in inflation in the 2000s. The annual average inflation rate was around 5.5 per cent irrespective of the inflation indices taken, whether WPI or CPI. This raises the question: did the inflation dynamics change in the 2000s? Monthly WPI inflation data suggest that there was a structural break[4] around the mid-2000s with the inflation rate during the latter half being higher (Fig. 9.1).

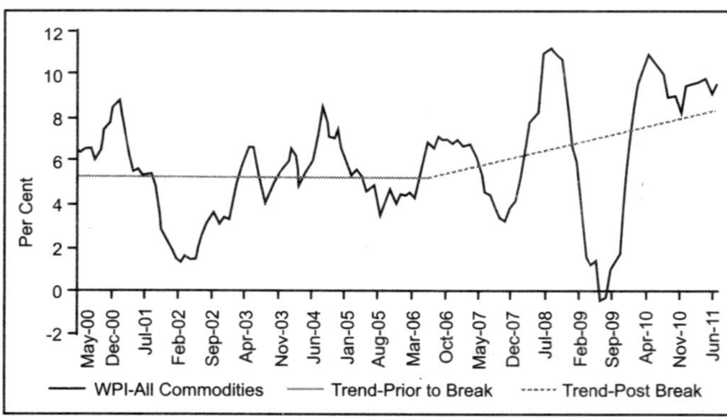

Fig. 9.1: WPI Inflation Shows Structural Break

Average WPI inflation increased from 5.2 per cent in the first half of 2000s to 5.5 per cent in the second half. This was largely contributed by primary food inflation. In fact, the core non-food manufactured products inflation moderated from 4.2 per cent to 3.9 per cent. What did cause the structural break in the mid-2000s? A disaggregated assessment suggests that protein items largely contributed to this change in trend (Table 9.3).

Table 9.3: Average WPI Inflation

(in Per Cent)

Group/Sub-Group	2001-10	2001-05	2006-10	2010-11	Q1:2011-12
WPI	5.4	5.2	5.5	9.6	9.4
Primary Food Articles (14.3)	5.8	2.4	9.2	15.8	9.1
Protein (6.4)	6.3	3.5	9.0	20.5	5.9
Milk (3.2)	6.3	4.5	7.9	20.6	7.3
Egg, Meat & Fish (2.4)	5.6	2.3	8.8	26.6	9.0
Industrial Raw Materials (16.2)	7.9	8.4	7.4	17.2	16.5
Non-Food Manufactured Products (55.0)	4.0	4.2	3.9	6.1	7.2

Figures in bracket indicate weights in WPI.

Not only did the average food prices rise during the second half of 2000s but they were more volatile (Table 9.4).

Table 9.4: Average and Volatility in WPI-Inflation

Groups/Sub-groups	Mean		Standard Deviation		Coefficient of variation	
	Prior to break	Post break	Prior to break	Post break	Prior to break	Post break
Primary Food Articles	3.5	10.6	0.4	3.8	11.6	35.9
Protein	3.8	9.9	1.3	4.8	33.6	48.3
Milk	4.3	10.3	1.5	5.0	35.4	48.4
Egg, Meat & Fish	2.6	12.0	1.2	6.4	45.5	53.5

Structural Food Inflation

Food prices being subject to supply shocks tend to be volatile. For example, the performance of monsoon has a significant bearing on the trend of domestic foodgrain prices. Spikes in food prices normally subside as they are transitory. However, empirical analysis suggests that inflation in protein items has become persistent.[5] This suggests that protein inflation has assumed a structural character and is partly driven by demand factors. Within the protein group, persistence was lower for pulses as well as 'egg, meat and fish', but it was markedly higher for milk. Thus, the persistence of protein inflation has changed the inflation dynamics in the latter half of the 2000s. Increase in demand for protein appears to be an inevitable consequence of rising affluence (Gokarn, 2010).[6] This process was further accentuated by renewed global food price shock during

2010-11. Among the processed food items, the persistence of inflation for edible oils was high (Table 9.5).

Table 9.5: Persistence of Inflation

Commodity/Subgroup	Sum of AR Coefficients
Food	
Protein Items	0.58
Milk	0.81
Edible Oils	0.56
Non-Food	
Non Food Manufactured Products	0.69
Industrial Raw Materials	0.55
Non-Food Articles	0.56

International Price Pass-through

While the persistence of inflation on protein items has increased, it still has a relatively smaller share in overall WPI inflation. What matters more for the overall inflation trajectory is the non-food manufactured products inflation which has a higher weight of 55.0 per cent in the WPI. It averaged 4.0 per cent in the 2000s with a moderation in the second half (Table 9.3). Subsequently, there has been a sharp increase in 2010-11 and 2011-12 so far. The non-food manufactured products inflation shows a major structural break towards the middle of 2009-10 around the time the global commodity prices rebounded (Fig. 9.2). This has also raised the question: Is the non-food manufactured products inflation an imported inflation?

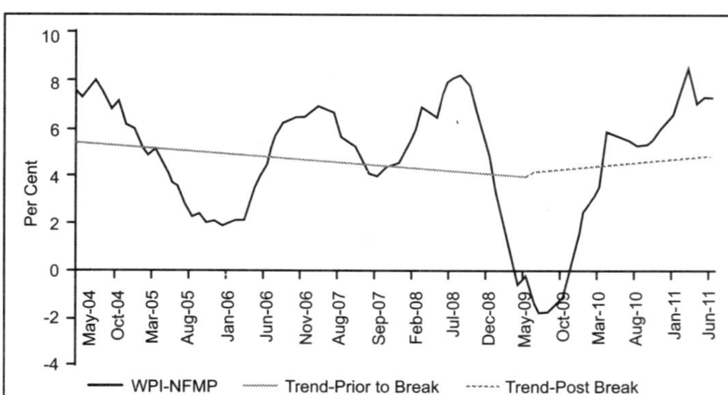

Fig. 9.2: Non-food Manufactured Production Inflation Trends Shifts UP

Further, analysis suggests that industrial raw material[7] prices also showed a structural break in early 2009 and the average price increase has been high and volatile (Fig. 9.3). Moreover, the pass-through from non-food international commodity prices to domestic raw material prices has increased particularly in the recent years reflecting growing interconnectedness of domestic and global commodity markets (Fig. 9.4).

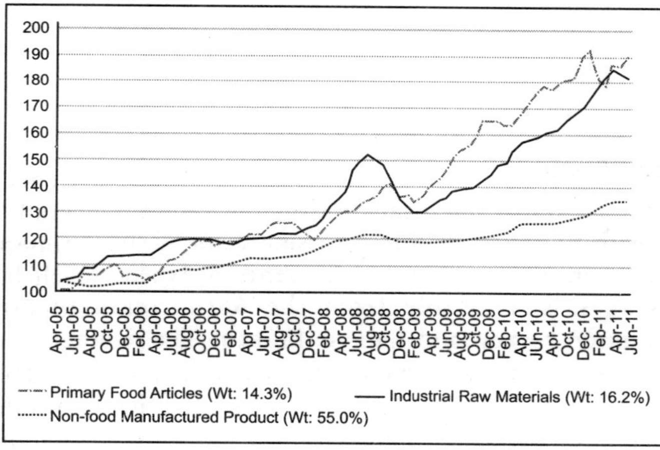

Fig. 9.3: Price Levels Surge from Early 2009

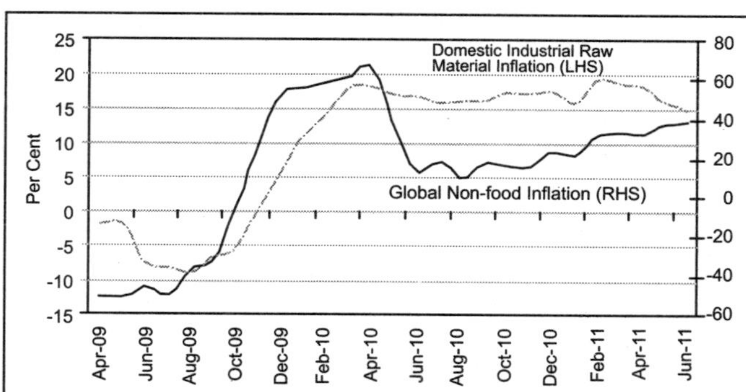

Fig. 9.4: Pass-through from Global Prices Rises

This trend is also corroborated by corporate finance data which show that the share of raw material costs as a percentage of both expenditure and sales has been rising (Fig. 9.5).

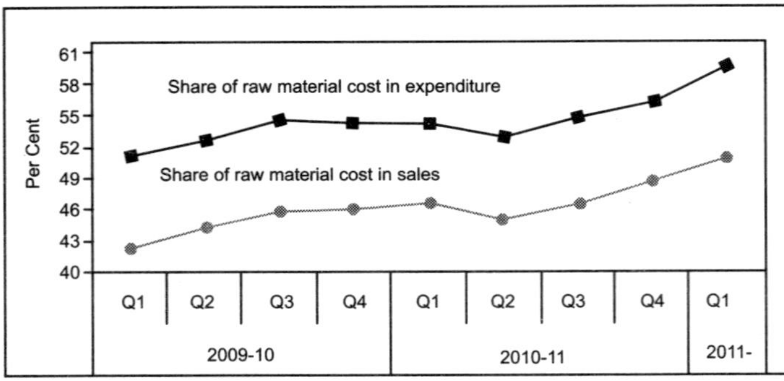

Fig. 9.5: Raw Material Costs Rise for Corporates

Demand Factors

Price pressures can emanate from the supply side but it will be difficult to sustain it without rising demand. In this context, important information on recent trend in expenditure pattern and wages is available from the 66th round of NSSO consumption survey and Labour Bureau. The average annual monthly per capita expenditure has increased at a faster pace in the second half of 2000s as compared with the first half, both in nominal and real terms (Table 9.6).

Table 9.6: Monthly Per Capita Expenditure
(Average Annual Growth)

(Mixed Reference Period Basis)

	2000-05	2005-10
Nominal Growth		
Rural	3.6	10.5
Urban	5.3	10.9
Real Growth*		
Rural	0.2	1.2
Urban	1.3	2.0

*Real growth for Rural and Urban population are worked out using CPI-AL and CPI-UNME respectively, with base 1999-00.

While the share of per capita expenditure in food has gone down, as could be expected from rise in income levels, both in rural and urban centers, the dietary pattern has shifted in favour of protein items whose share has gone up markedly in the second half of 2000s (Fig. 9.6).

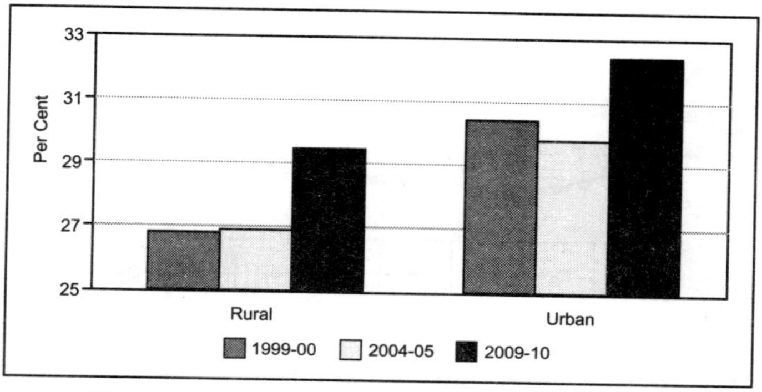

Fig. 9.6: Share of Protein in Food Consumption Rises

The sharp increase in rural consumption of protein seems to have been sustained by increase in wage rates of the unskilled rural labourers both in nominal and real terms (Fig. 9.7).

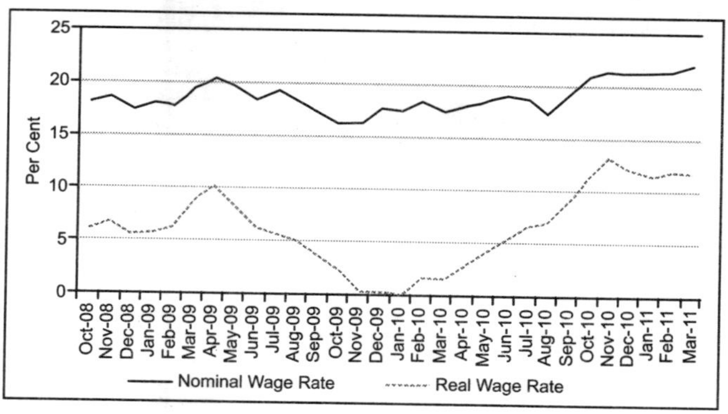

Fig. 9.7: Wage Rates of Unskilled Rural Labourers Rises

In the formal sector, company finance data suggest that the wage bill has risen at a faster rate since the middle of 2009-10 (Fig. 9.8).

As per the NSSO surveys (61st round and 66th round), nominal wage rates of skilled workers in both rural and urban areas increased much faster in the second half of the 2000s than in the first half. While the real wage rates declined in the first half, it increased significantly in the second half of 2000s (Figs. 9.9 and 9.10).

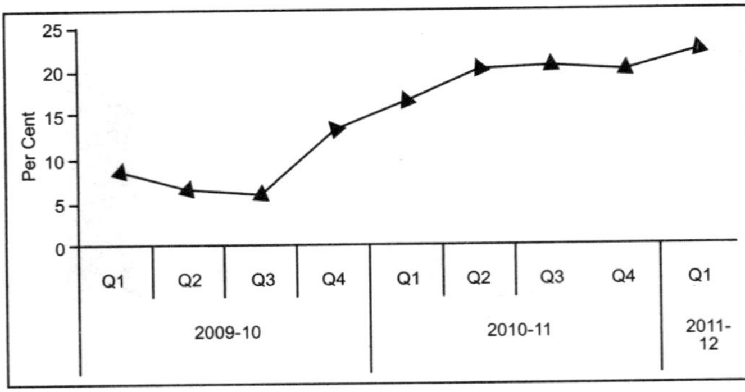

Fig. 9.8: Corporate Wage Bill Rises

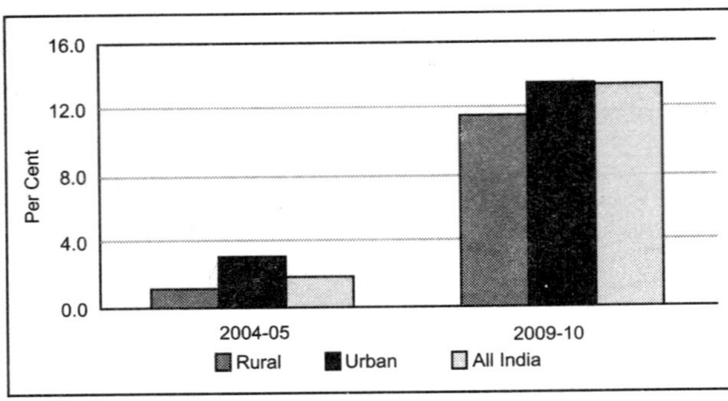

Fig. 9.9: Nominal Wages Increase

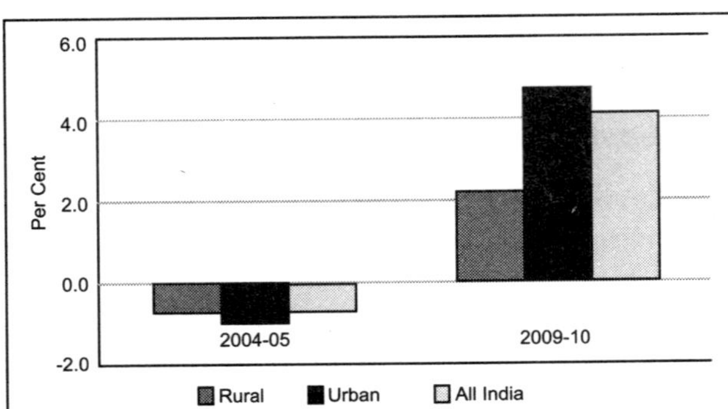

Fig. 9.10: Real Wages also Rise Further

There has also been added stimulus from the crisis driven fiscal expansion as the fiscal consolidation process was reversed in 2008-09 and continued through 2009-10 (Fig. 9.11).

These evidences taken together suggest that sustained rise in real wages both in the formal and informal sectors in the recent years contributed to increase in demand.

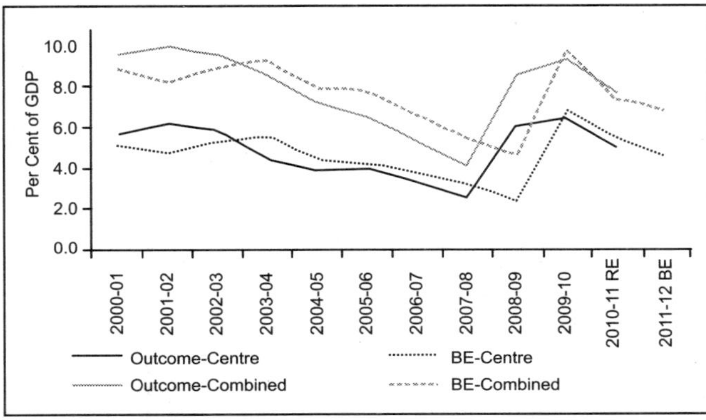

Fig. 9.11: Rise in Fiscal Deflict Adds to Demand Pressure

Conclusions

The recent surge in inflation has become more generalised. Food inflation, prone to supply shocks, is also assuming a structural character given the change in the dietary habits and high demand, in absence of adequate supply response. Sharp increase in non-food manufactured product inflation suggests that producers are able to pass on the cost increases, given higher demand. While the persistence in non-food manufactured products inflation is high, the persistence of food inflation has increased making the overall inflation rate sticky. The current inflation process, therefore, is an amalgam of both supply constraints and demand pressures.

Prolonged high inflation even if originating from supply side would give rise to increased inflation expectations and cause general prices to rise. Poorly anchored inflation expectations make long-term financial planning more complex with potential adverse effects on investment and growth. Moreover, high inflation is the most regressive form of taxation, particularly on the poor. It is, therefore, important to contain inflation and keep inflation expectations anchored so that consumers do not mark up their long-run inflation expectations by reacting to a short period of higher-than-expected inflation.

Keeping in view the costs of inflation and the fact that high inflation is inimical to sustained growth, the medium-term objective of the Reserve Bank is to bring down inflation to 3.0 per cent consistent with India's broader integration with the global economy. In this direction, monetary policy aims to contain perceptions of inflation in the range of 4.0-4.5 per cent with a particular focus on the behaviour of the non-food manufacturing component, which is considered as core inflation given its high degree of persistence. Going forward, both global and domestic factors will shape the inflation outlook. With increasing global integration, global commodity prices are having an increasingly significant influence on domestic prices. It is expected that global commodity prices will peak in 2011 which should provide some relief to domestic inflation scenario.

The Reserve Bank signaled the reversal from its crisis driven expansionary monetary policy stance in October 2009. Since then, the cash reserve ratio (CRR) has been raised by 100 basis points. The policy repo rate has been raised by a cumulative 325 basis points. As the liquidity in the system transited from surplus to deficit, the effective tightening has been of the order of 475 basis points. Thus, the cumulative monetary policy action would have the desired impact on inflation.

While inflation is expected to moderate towards the later part of the year reflecting monetary tightening and likely softening of global commodity prices, fiscal policy needs to be supportive in containing aggregate demand. In addition, there is an urgent need to address the issue of structural supply constraints, particularly in agriculture, so that these do not become binding constraints in the long-run hampering the task of inflation management.

Notes

1. Brazil, Russia, India China and South Africa.
2. While there is disagreement over the role of financial investment in commodity markets, financial flows to commodity funds typically increase with higher commodity prices further accentuating price pressures.
3. Core inflation is generally estimated by excluding volatile food and fuel components from the headline inflation, though there

are various statistical methods of estimation of core inflation. Analytically, core inflation is considered as an indicator of demand conditions.

4. Estimated by Bai-Perron test.
5. Persistence is estimated as the sum of autoregressive coefficients of the inflation series of the relevant items; a coefficient of over 0.5 is considered to be an indication of persistence.
6. "The Price of Protein", Inaugural Address at the Special Conference in honour of Dr. Kirit Parikh at IGIDR, Mumbai, October 26, 2010.
7. Includes non-food articles, metallic minerals, other minerals, coal, aviation turbine fuel, high speed diesel oil, naphtha, bitumen, furnace oil, lubricant, electricity for industry, cotton yarn and paper pulp with a weight of 16.2 in WPI.

(Speech by Deepak Mohanty, Executive Director, Reserve Bank of India, delivered at the Motilal Nehru National Institute of Technology (MNNIT), Allahabad on 13th August 2011)
• *Courtesy*: www.rbi.org.in

10

Sustainability of Economic Growth and Controlling Inflation: The Way Forward

Subir Gokarn, Deputy Governor, RBI

05 Apr. 2011

...As many observers have been highlighting, after a relatively long phase of benign, growth-friendly macroeconomic conditions, things have begun to look somewhat hostile on the macroeconomic front. The most significant manifestation of this is the acceleration of inflation, a trend that was visible even before the impact of the financial crisis was felt in late 2008, but which very quickly and strongly re-emerged as the economy began to recover in the second half of 2009-10. Despite significant actions on both policy rates and liquidity by the Reserve Bank, inflation remains high, giving rise to some very fundamental questions: Is this high rate of inflation, previously believed to be unacceptable, now the new normal? Is it an unavoidable price to pay for sustaining the current growth trend? Or, will it actually work to undermine the sustainability of the current trend?

Before arriving at a firm policy position on this issue, we must examine all the risks associated with persistently high rates of inflation over relatively long periods of time. In this address, I propose to do three things:

1. Examine the growth-inflation dynamics in the Indian economy over the past couple of decades to see if any patterns can be discerned;
2. Examine the drivers of the recent trends in inflation and relate them to underlying growth drivers;

3. Present some key issues and concerns that I believe should influence our policy thinking.

The Growth-Inflation Relationship in India: The Post-1991 Experience

Figure 10.1 displays the trajectories of growth and two indicators of inflation over the past two decades—the Wholesale Price Index (WPI), reflecting headline inflation and the Non-Food Manufacturing component of it. In our policy framework, we see the latter as a measure of 'core' inflation—that which is driven by demand side pressures. A number of patterns emerge that might provide a useful backdrop to the discussion of what lies ahead.

First, we do see a striking contrast between the two episodes of high growth that the economy experienced after 1991. During

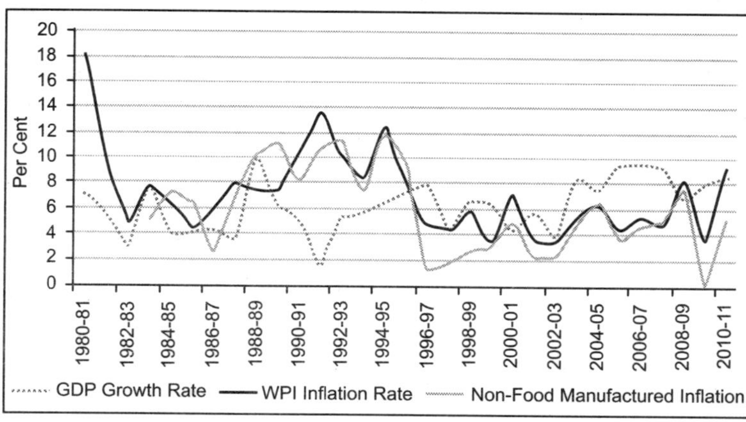

Fig. 10.1: Growth-Inflation Dynamics

the first episode, from 1994-95 to 1996-97, both measures of inflation ran relatively high. In fact, the growth began to accelerate in the midst of an already uncomfortable inflationary environment, reflected by both the headline and core measures. The proximity between the two suggested that demand pressures were predominant. In this scenario, the only way that inflation would come down would be through demand compression and that is indeed what happened. An anti-inflationary monetary stance combined with a shock to exports in the wake of the

East Asian crisis and a bad monsoon achieved this. Over the next few years, both growth and inflation rates were relatively low.

The second high-growth episode began in 2003-04 and, with the exception of the slowdown during the crisis period, is still continuing. However, from the inflation perspective, this episode itself has two distinct segments. In the first few years, high growth was accompanied by low inflation, both headline and core. On the eve of the crisis period, both indicators increased significantly, suggesting the emergence of demand-side pressures. During the brief slowdown, both inflation indicators dropped sharply, but core fell far more than headline, indicating that supply-side pressures were now visible. The resurgence of inflation over the past year is the result of both demand and supply forces, as can be seen from sharp climb in both inflation indicators and the persistent gap between them.

One impression from the contrast between these two episodes is that growth in a low-inflation environment can be more robust and enduring. This is partly because monetary policy can afford to accommodate growth by keeping interest rates low. However, as we saw, even in the more recent episode, demand pressures were driving inflation up, which saw the monetary policy stance, which I shall discuss in somewhat more detail later, reverse course during that period. A second observation, relating to recent developments, is that, while supply-side pressures have clearly impacted headline inflation, the relatively brief and shallow slowdown did not fully eliminate demand-side pressures from the system and these too have contributed to the recent behaviour of inflation.

For comparison purposes, I will briefly discuss the Chinese growth-inflation dynamics before coming back to a more detailed discussion of recent Indian patterns. Figure 10.2 depicts the growth rates achieved by the Chinese economy since its own liberalization of the late 1970s and the behaviour of its Consumer Price Index over the period. Two episodes—one in the late 1980s and one in the mid-1990s—stand out. In both, a sharp rise in the inflation rate was followed by a decline in the growth rate. This was quite pronounced in the first episode and somewhat

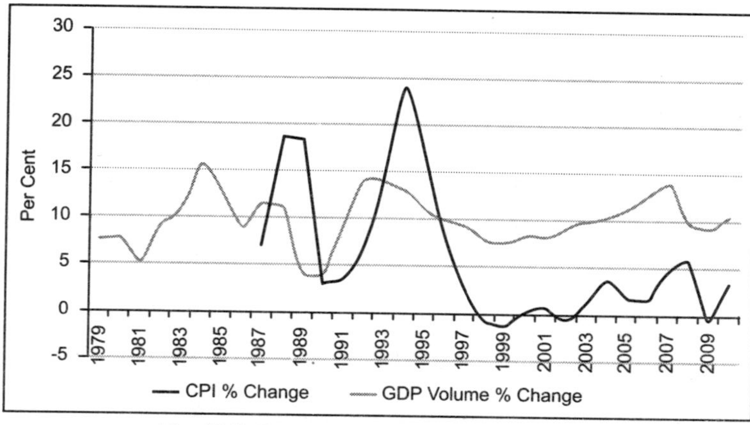

Fig. 10.2: Growth-Inflation Dynamics in China

moderate, though unmistakable in the second. After that, growth has sustained at a relatively fast pace accompanied by relatively low inflation. Immediately before the crisis period, both growth and inflation accelerated sharply, suggesting the build-up of demand-side pressures. However, the overall impression, over a somewhat longer period than for India is that sustained high growth is concomitant with relatively low inflation.

A final issue that I want to look at in this long-term perspective is the behaviour of crude oil prices. Figure 10.3 displays the trend of nominal prices as well as real prices, derived by deflating by the US Producer Price Index. During the period that we have been talking about, both moved in tandem. The 1990s were a benign period, with oil not exerting significant global inflationary pressure. In contrast, oil prices have risen persistently over the past decade, aggravating demand-driven inflationary pressures in the period before the crisis and continuing to do that after a brief respite.

Recent Inflation Dynamics

To provide a backdrop, let me first talk about some important characteristics of the recent episode of fast growth. Figure 10.4 displays the annual contribution to growth made by each of the components of aggregate demand. Private Consumption, the largest single component makes a steady

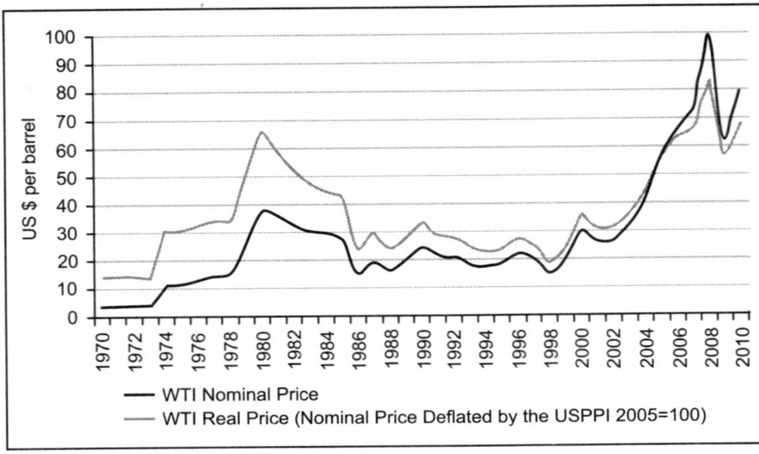

Fig. 10.3: Real Oil Prices

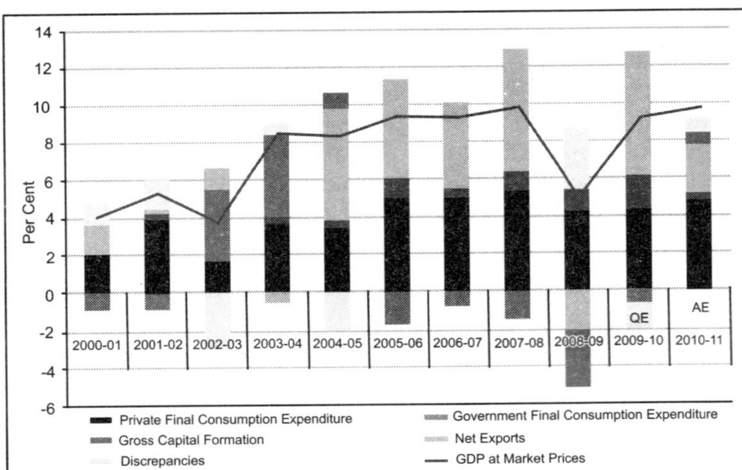

Fig. 10.4: Drivers of Demand Growth

contribution throughout the period, a factor influenced by its sheer size. But the most significant feature of the period is the relatively large and sustained contribution of capital formation, or investment. The acceleration in growth seen since 2003-04 was preceded by a surge in investment spending, which then remained a very significant contributor to growth over the entire episode. It slumped during the crisis period, reflecting its high sensitivity to macroeconomic conditions, but recovered noticeably in the following year.

When we bring the inflation trajectory back into the picture, we might infer that the combination of fast growth and low inflation is actually very conducive to high investment spending. With reference to today's theme, this is obviously a relationship of great significance. Investment has the twin virtues of creating demand for goods and services in the present while simultaneously expanding the capacity to produce them in the future. It follows that a growth process that is more conducive to investment spending is more likely to be sustainable than one that is less conducive. The recent episode of fast growth in India suggests that low inflation is one factor that encourages investment spending. From this perspective, the reduction of the contribution of investment to growth in 2010-11 raises some concerns.

Let me now provide some perspectives on recent inflation dynamics in India. Figure 10.5 displays the relative contributions of different components of the WPI to aggregate inflation over the past decade. There are a number of significant patterns in the graph. First, food inflation may have grabbed the headlines in recent months, but the fact is that it has been steadily

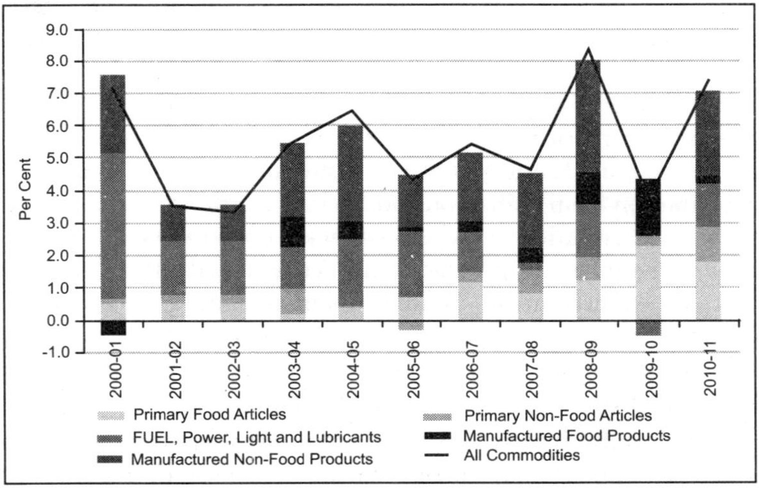

Fig. 10.5: Drivers of Inflation

increasing its contribution to overall inflation for some time now. A combination of factors may have aggravated the situation in the recent past, but the impact of sustained high growth on food consumption patterns cannot be wished away. In the absence of a strong supply response, increasing demand will inevitably lead to higher prices, a trend that may be reinforced by a monsoon failure or other shocks. This is what we are seeing on the food front today.

Second, even though crude oil prices were increasing steadily over this period, the contribution of energy prices to inflation was variable. This was the result of a combination of differential rates of annual increases and restrictions on pass-through to domestic consumers. In fact, during the three-year period 2005-08, while aggregate inflation remained relatively steady, the relative contributions of food and energy swapped positions. In a sense, incipient food inflation was being offset by the moderating contribution from oil.

Third, non-food manufacturing inflation, which, as I indicated earlier, we interpret as reflecting demand-side pressures, while contributing to inflation throughout the period, was fairly steady. However, in 2007-08, as overall inflation accelerated, so did this component. One explanation for this is that, with capacities being stretched, producers had significant pricing power. Consequently, the intensification of supply-side drivers, which is clearly visible in the graph that year, spilled over into a more generalized inflationary process. Of course, the picture changed dramatically during the crisis period, but it is striking that in 2010-11, the pattern is quite similar, with the added contribution from rising non-food primary articles. We do appear to be in a situation in which capacity constraints are helping convert supply-side pressures into generalized inflation. If, in fact, the contribution of investment spending to growth is declining, the constraints can only become more binding, further aggravating inflationary pressures if the growth momentum is kept going by other components of demand.

I will end this section with a brief discussion on the monetary and fiscal policy trajectories during this period. Figure 10.6 displays the movement of monetary policy instruments before, during and after the crisis period. In the first phase depicted on the graph, there was a steady reduction in policy rates, motivated by a moderating inflation scenario. This was presumably supportive of investment activity, which, as we saw earlier, was relatively buoyant during this period. In 2005-06, the cycle turned and there were steady increases in policy rates and the cash reserve ratio (CRR) in response to the acceleration in inflation that was displayed in the previous graph. It is important to point out that investment activity apparently did not change course even as interest rates were being increased. This suggests that it is not just the immediate interest rate scenario that influences investment decisions. Actions taken to control inflation also help by providing reassurances about macroeconomic stability.

As the impact of the crisis was felt, there as a sharp reversal in all policy instruments, a movement consistent with the inflationary pattern during the year, as seen by the complete disappearance of non-food manufacturing inflation. As the economy recovered, bringing with it a rather quick resurgence of inflationary pressures, the monetary stance has responded. The pace of action has been influenced by a number of domestic and global factors; the primary motivation being to keep the

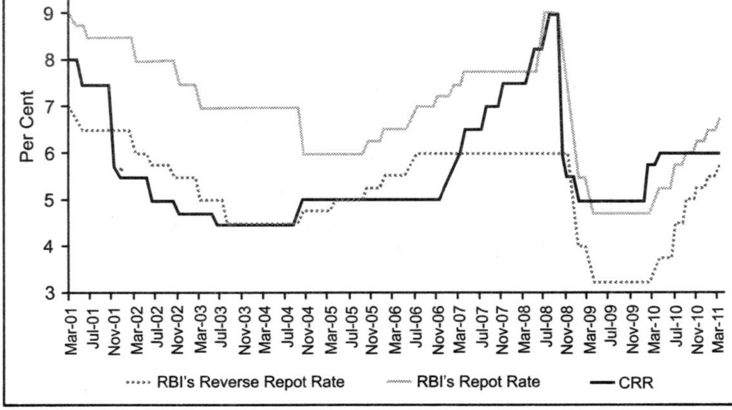

Fig. 10.6: Monetary Policy Trajectory

recovery going, while preventing the spill-over of supply-side pressures into a more generalized inflationary process.

Figure 10.7 displays trends in the fiscal position, showing the combined revenue and fiscal deficits for centre and states. The main point that I would like to make from this picture is with reference to the fast growth episode of 2003-08. On the fiscal front, this period was characterized by a steady decline in the combined fiscal deficit, but, most importantly, a very sharp decline in the revenue deficit. What this meant was that not only was the government claiming relatively fewer resources, it was devoting a greater proportion of its spending to creating capital assets. In terms of the virtuous combination of high growth, low inflation and high investment that I have already characterized the episode by, these fiscal characteristics add another dimension to the understanding of conditions conducive to sustaining growth.

The Way Forward: Issues and Concerns

I would like to highlight three key messages from the preceding discussion as we look ahead at the challenges of sustaining growth while controlling inflation. First, from our own experience, low inflation and fiscal moderation, particularly on the revenue deficit, seem to be conducive to high investment

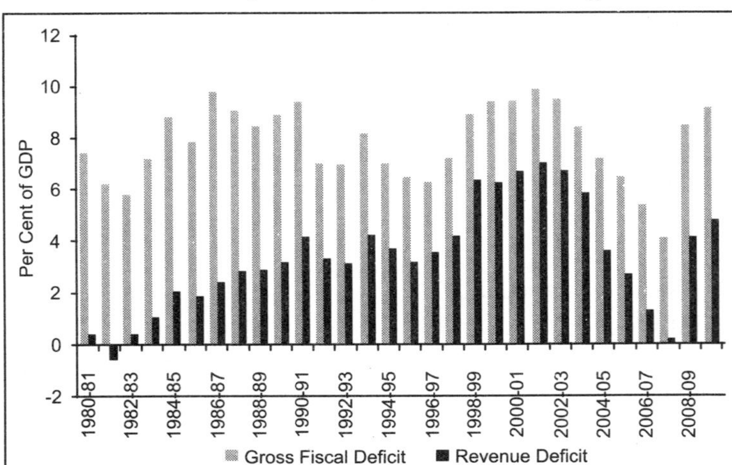

Fig. 10.7: Combined Deficits of Central and State Governments

rates and, consequently, to high and sustainable growth rates. Second, when growth is relatively rapid, supply-side inflationary pressures do spill-over into more generalized inflation, presumably reflecting high pricing power of all producers, including workers. The implications of this for monetary policy are quite clear and direct: if there are signs of spill-over from supply-side to core, then a monetary response is warranted to prevent the process from spiralling out of control. Third, looking back at the previous high-growth episode, slower growth over a period of time will result in lower inflation, but we must recognize that both high inflation and slow growth have significant welfare costs. In essence, the challenge is to keep growth as high as possible without the risk of inflation spiralling out of control.

In this context, there are two bodies of evidence that have a bearing on policies intending to sustain growth while controlling inflation. First, analysis of a large sample of countries over long periods of time does not suggest that more rapid growth phases were accompanied by higher rates of inflation. There have, of course, been periods when inflation rates have been high, but these have typically been followed by a slowdown in growth rates, presumably as a result of monetary actions but, more fundamentally, because the prospect of macroeconomic instability may lead to lower rates of investment. In general, the evidence across a large set of countries bears out what we observed in India over the high growth episode in India immediately before the crisis period and also in China over the past decade. Faster growth seems to persist in an environment of low inflation.

Second, recent analytical work on the Phillips Curve, which represents the trade-off between growth (unemployment) and inflation suggests a break in the relationship between growth and inflation at some threshold rate of inflation (Akerlof et al., 2000[1] and Palley, 2003,[2] 2008[3]). If inflation is below that rate, the analysis suggests that there is a trade-off between growth and inflation; growth can be accelerated (unemployment can be reduced) with some concomitant increase in inflation. However, above that threshold, the relationship is reversed; higher rates of inflation are accompanied by slower growth (higher unemployment). The main reason for the existence of such a threshold rate of inflation is the speed and magnitude with which the inflation rate feeds into inflationary expectations. Below the threshold, workers and producers do not raise their wage and price demands very often because the impact of inflation is not too visible. By contrast, they respond very quickly above the threshold because they are worried that high inflation will rapidly erode their living standards or profitability. In short, when inflation is high, the behaviour of workers and producers increases the likelihood that it will increase further.

Putting the two together, one could argue that keeping inflation below the threshold at all times serves both the short-term objective of macroeconomic stability, or minimizing the deviation of the growth rate from its sustainable trend, and the long-term objective of raising the trend by encouraging investment activity. Do we know what the threshold is for the Indian economy? The Report on Currency and Finance, an annual research publication of the Reserve Bank of India, examined this question in its 2000-01 issue and came to the conclusion that the "growth-maximizing rate of inflation" for the Indian economy was 5 per cent.[4] Of course, in a rapidly evolving environment, this number could well be different now; the average rate of inflation during the pre-crisis period high growth episode was slightly below this number. But, even if it is different, it is unlikely to be significantly higher. The current rate of inflation does raise concerns about the risks of spiralling, as high inflation becomes increasingly entrenched into the wage and price setting behaviour of workers and producers. In turn, if this were to adversely impact investment activity, the growth momentum would inevitably slow down. In essence, the trade-off is more between inflation now and growth in the future.

Before I conclude, I would like to briefly address the very fundamental issue of food inflation. Figure 10.8 displays the relative contributions made by different food groups to overall food inflation. For much of the past several months, the dominant contributors to it have been pulses, milk, eggs, fish and meat and fruits. Cereals have made virtually no contribution, while

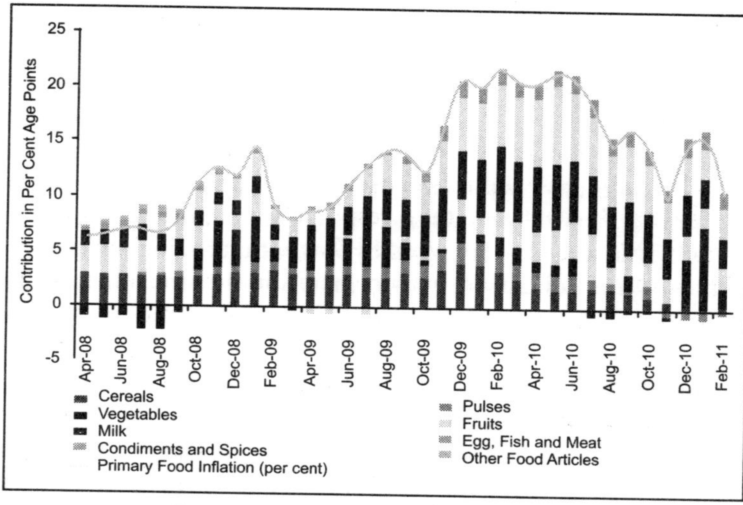

Fig. 10.8: Recent Drivers of Food Inflation

vegetables, with the exception of the onion spike (other vegetables also contributed) in late 2010, were not very significant contributors. To reiterate a point we have been making in both our policy statements and other communications: this pattern is the outcome of consumption baskets being diversified by an increasing number of households as they cross some income threshold. The increase in prices indicates that supply is just not keeping pace with demand. The only way to keep food prices in check is to produce more of what people want to consume. There are several initiatives in the Union Budget for 2011-12, which are based on this recognition. Now, the emphasis must be on implementing the schemes for quick increases in productivity and output of the items in question.

Concluding Remarks

I began by raising three questions: Is this high rate of inflation, previously believed to be unacceptable, now the new normal? Is it an unavoidable price to pay for sustaining the current growth trend? Or, will it actually work to undermine the sustainability of the current trend?

Based on the preceding discussion, let me attempt a combined answer. Acceptance of a higher rate of inflation as the new normal—an inevitable consequence of rapid growth—will raise risks of accelerating inflation. In turn, this is likely to weaken incentives for investment, which will threaten the sustainability of growth. This is a vicious circle of high inflation, low investment and slowing growth.

The alternative is the kind of virtuous circle that the economy has already experienced during the five years preceding the crisis period. This was characterized by low inflation, high investment and fiscal consolidation, particularly on the revenue account, accompanying high growth as well as resilience during the crisis period. That is the configuration that we need to re-create to sustain growth.

Both monetary and fiscal policies have a role in achieving this configuration. The challenge for monetary policy is to prevent supply-side inflationary pressures from spilling over into more generalized inflation, both by managing expectations and by reining in demand. This needs to be done with minimal disruption to growth, particularly investment activity. The challenge for fiscal policy is to bring down the fiscal deficit, particularly on the revenue account. This needs to be done while ensuring both resource allocation and effective implementation of programmes dealing with critical supply constraints in food and elsewhere. Significantly, both sets of challenges have to be met amidst an uncertain global environment, both generally and with respect to oil prices.

I shall end with reference to the topic of today's address. The issue is not so much one of higher inflation for faster growth in the present. It is about the risks that higher inflation now poses for faster growth in the future. In other words, sustainability of growth over the long term does require controlling inflation.

Notes

1. G.A. Akerlof, W.T. Dickens, and G.L. Perry (2000), "The Near-Rational Wage and Price Setting and the Long Run Phillips Curve", *Brookings Paper of Economic Activity*, 1: 1-60.
2. T.I. Palley (2003), "The Backward Bending Phillips Curve and the Minimum Unemployment Rate of Inflation (MURI): Wage

Adjustment with Opportunistic Firms", *The Manchester School of Economic and Social Studies*, 71(1): 35-50.

3. T.I. Palley (2008), "The Backward Bending Phillips Curves: A Simple Model", Working Paper No. 168, Political Economy Research Institute, University of Massachusetts, Amerhest.
4. Reserve Bank of India (2002), "Growth, Inflation and the Conduct of Monetary Policy", Report on Currency and Finance 2000-01.

(Address by Dr. Subir Gokarn, Deputy Governor, Reserve Bank of India at FICCI's National Executive Committee Meeting at Mumbai, April 5, 2011) • *Courtesy*: www.rbi.org.in

11

Managing the Growth-Inflation Balance in India: Current Considerations and Long-term Perspectives

Subir Gokarn, Deputy Governor, RBI

05 Oct. 2010

Introduction

...Sustaining the current growth momentum over a long period of time will clearly depend heavily on the ability of new business ideas to first, find start-up funding and then, grow to scales at which traditional funding sources can be accessed. Historically, this role was played in the Indian economy by the Development Finance Institutions. In the current and future scenario, the function has shifted to companies like the ones represented at this forum, whose business model depends on successful navigation of the start-up to listing phase of the businesses that they finance. In turn, the likelihood of success depends on a stable and predictable macroeconomic environment.

The long-term growth prospects of the Indian economy provide an enormously attractive investment environment for a range of businesses and, consequently, for the people who would finance them. However, as attractive as the opportunity may seem, the assessment would not be complete without a full understanding of the risks. In my address, I will focus on the risk of macroeconomic instability, with particular emphasis on the issue of inflation: what drives it and whether it threatens to get out of control. An unavoidable consequence of runaway inflation, however we define it, is that drastic action by the central bank and also by the government is needed to rein it in, which is bound to disrupt the growth process. The challenge, therefore, is to keep inflation in check over long periods of time, allowing the economy to grow at its potential rate with minimal disruptions and deviations. This is the best way in which the macroeconomic environment can contribute to a positive business climate.

I will begin by discussing the current inflationary scenario in India, which, as we have been saying in our recent assessments, is not very reassuring. I will then place this scenario in a broad historical context, with the intention of demonstrating that India has a good record of reining inflation in, regardless of what has driven it. The structure of the domestic economy and the financial system may have changed and the global context may be different, but the effectiveness of inflation control over the decades has not diminished.

The Current Scenario

As you well know, the predominant policy concern in the Indian economy as recently as one year ago was the significant slowdown in growth in the wake of the financial crisis in the advanced economies. As Fig. 11.1 shows, the inflation rate, which was briefly negative in the middle of 2009, began to accelerate rapidly later in the year. This upward momentum continued into the first half of 2010, with double-digit inflation persisting for a few months. The rapidity of the transition was surprising, given the fact that the recovery in growth was just getting under way and, importantly, the global situation was still very uncertain. However, as Figures 11.2 and 11.3 indicate, the reason for the sharp increase was that all the possible drivers of inflation were simultaneously contributing. Each one by itself may not have resulted in the outcome that we saw, but all three working together resulted in a rather sharp acceleration. Figure 11.2 displays the pattern of supply-side pressures, as manifested in the food and fuel components of the Wholesale Price Index. Food prices rose sharply because the monsoon of 2009 was deficient in most parts of the country, impacting agricultural production. However, there are, I believe, longer

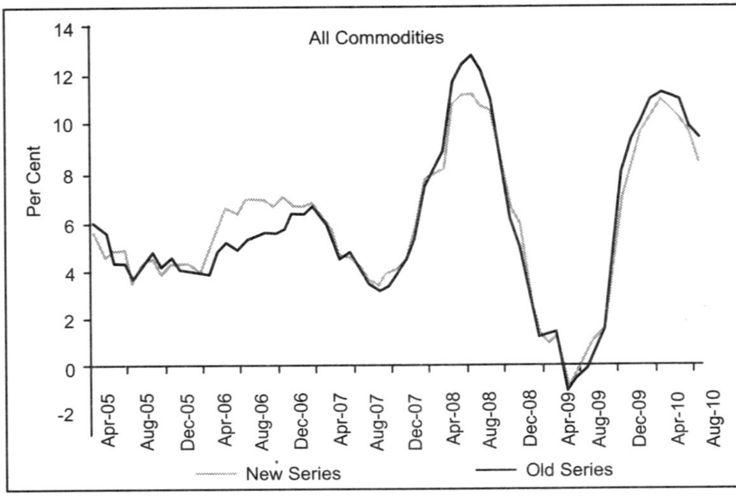

Fig. 11.1: Recent Inflation Dynamics

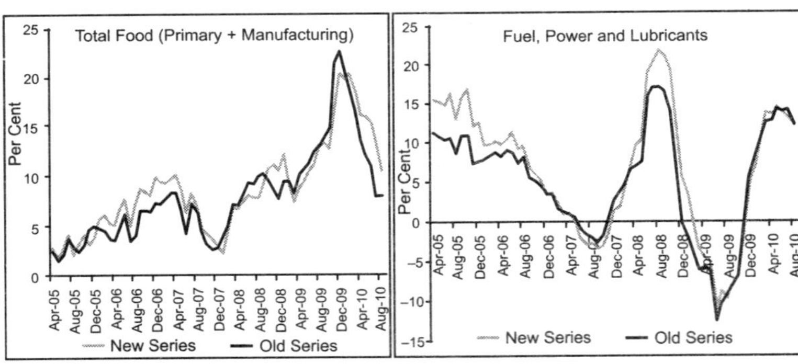

Fig. 11.2: Supply-side Pressures

term forces at work on food prices, which are a matter of concern. I shall address these later on in the speech. Fuel prices also rose as the prospects of a global recovery improved and, particularly, the Emerging Market Economies actually saw a sharp acceleration in growth.

However, what was most significant from the monetary policy perspective was the growing visibility of demand-side pressures. Figure 11.3 tracks the price dynamics of the manufacturing sector—overall and without the food processing

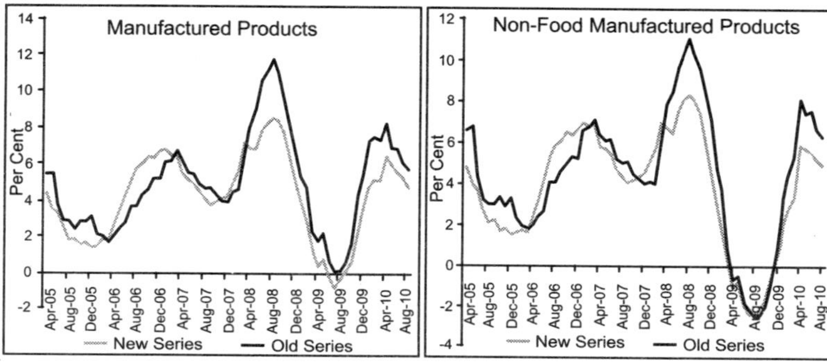

Fig. 11.3: Demand-side Pressures

component. The latter has been used by many analysts as a reasonable proxy of demand-side inflation, which is the phenomenon that monetary policy can and should influence. Both graphs in the figure and, particularly the one displaying non-food manufacturing inflation, show a tremendous acceleration from a significantly negative rate of inflation during 2009 to reach rather worrisome levels by the middle of 2010.

Figure 11.4 compares the relative contributions of the supply and demand drivers. The graph shows quite clearly that food and fuel prices, reflecting supply-side forces and the prices of manufactured goods, reflecting demand-side ones, all contributed significantly to the recent rise in inflation. If we look back a little at the inflationary surge immediately preceding the crisis, we can see that the pattern is quite similar. This leads me to a broader point about the drivers of inflation in India. Whenever we see worryingly high levels of inflation, both supply and demand pressures seem to be at work.

The final point in the discussion on the current scenario is with reference to monetary policy responses. Figure 11.5 shows displays the movement of the overnight call money rate, which reflects the combined actions taken by the Reserve Bank on policy rates and liquidity. To place the recent policy actions in perspective, we must remember that the response to the crisis involved an enormous reduction in both policy rates and the cash reserve ratio in late 2008 and early 2009. Along with this, a number of ad hoc measures were also taken. As the crisis

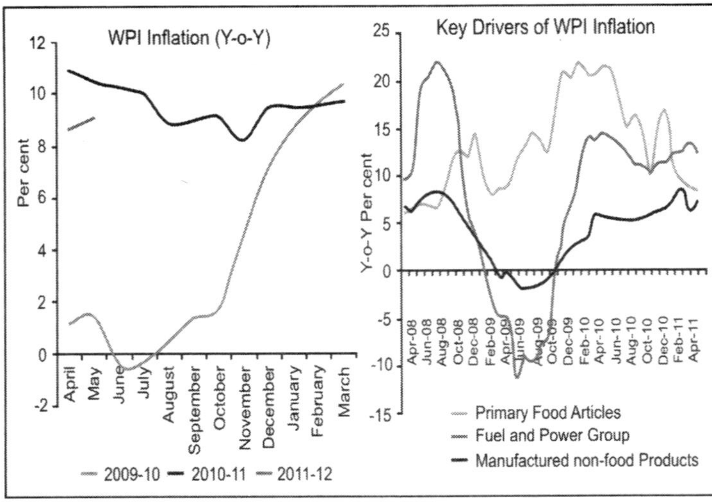

Fig. 11.4: Drivers of Recent Inflation

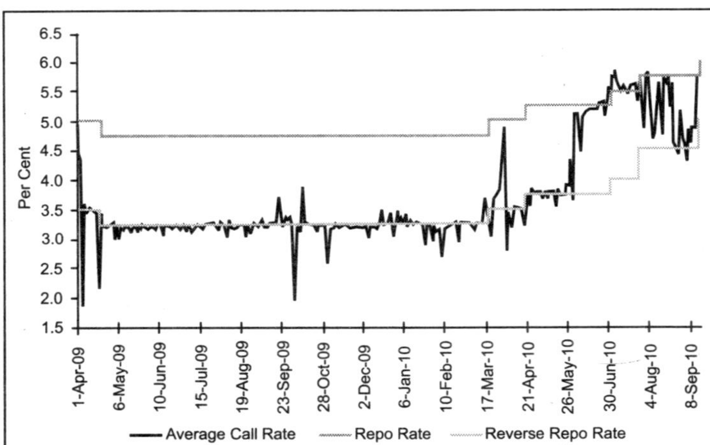

Fig. 11.5: Monetary Policy Response

abated, even if inflationary pressures had not manifested as they did, the need to exit from the crisis management stance would have motivated some actions on rates and liquidity—of course, at a pace that would not derail the still incipient recovery.

This process began in October 2009, with the withdrawal of most of the ad hoc measures, but gained momentum in January

2010, with an increase in the cash reserve ratio and, further, in March 2010 with the first of a series of rate hikes. The pace and sequencing of actions was, as we articulated in our various assessments, determined by the need to balance a number of potentially conflicting factors. First, we needed to address the rapidly mounting demand-side inflationary pressures while ensuring that the recovery was not cut short by a surge in interest rates. Second, while the domestic economy was doing well, the global environment remained uncertain, with a number of new stress points emerging periodically.

Third, apart from everything else, it was imperative that we normalize the monetary policy stance from where it had moved during the crisis management phase. Not doing so would have put us in the situation of being unable to respond to another negative shock, were it to materialize. In sum, our policy actions over the past several months were motivated by the twin objectives of sustaining the recovery while reining in inflation and normalizing the policy stance as quickly as possible. In our mid-quarter assessment, we indicated that the normalization process is now close to being complete and that further actions on rates and liquidity will be driven more significantly by what the growth and inflation numbers tell us, both domestically and globally.

Of course, the proof of the pudding is in the eating. Do we believe that our actions are having the desired effect? On the growth front, while there is a certain amount of volatility visible in industrial production, by and large, there is no significant indication of the recovery stalling. On the inflation front, as was visible in the figures that I showed earlier, there are distinct signs of a deceleration of inflation over the past couple of months. The turnaround coincides with our expectation that inflation begins to respond to monetary actions after a six month lag. To examine this more closely, we look at the Seasonally Adjusted Month-on-Month rates of inflation, which give a sense of the momentum of inflation. Figure 11.6 displays the pattern of this indicator. It clearly suggests that the momentum is currently negative. While the turning point on the overall index is early in 2010, the sharp deceleration in recent months may reflect the

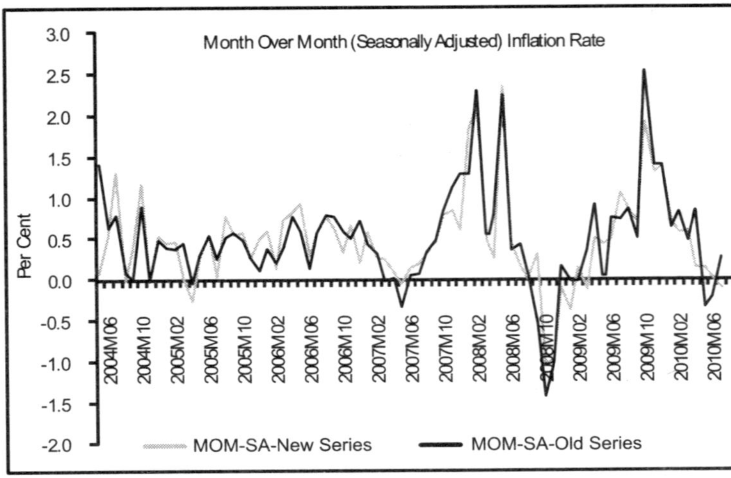

Fig. 11.6: Inflation Momentum

impact of monetary actions and gives us confidence that the inflation rate will moderate significantly by the end of the fiscal year 2010-11.

I would like to conclude this discussion by emphasizing the point that the current episode of inflation posed a significant challenge to policymakers by virtue of its timing. Monetary policy responses had to be calibrated to the needs of dealing with inflation while sustaining a growth recovery in a still uncertain global environment. The choices on the magnitude, sequencing and timing of actions were driven by the need to find a balance between these factors.

Long-term Perspectives

Let me now take a longer term view of the growth-inflation balance in the Indian economy. To begin with, we do have a fairly explicit statement of what we see as a desirable rate of inflation, consistent with the economy growing at its potential rate on a sustained basis. Our policy reviews say that we would like inflation to be in the 4-4.5 per cent range in the medium-term, while aspiring for a 3 per cent rate in the long-term. This might sound a little unrealistic in the current scenario, but in order to both justify the aspiration itself and assess its realism we need to look at the historical record of inflation management in the Indian economy.

Figure 11.7 provides a very revealing picture of how the growth-inflation balance has shifted in the Indian economy. The first graph, relating decadal averages of growth and inflation over the past several decades clearly indicates that a steady upward movement in the growth rate has been accompanied by a steady downward movement in the inflation rate. The contrast is even more striking when we remove the agricultural sector, which is the slowest growing among the three—Agriculture, Industry and Services—over long periods of time, from the growth calculations. These patterns clearly suggest that there is no long-term trade-off between growth and inflation; if anything, accelerating growth is accompanied by decelerating inflation.

This may appear to be an obvious conclusion. The textbook treatment of the growth—inflation trade-off sees it as an essentially short-run phenomenon, with the quantum of resources and capacity in the economy being fixed. However, the reason I specifically mention this point is that in the wake of recent assessments that the Indian economy is poised to significantly increase its growth rate many people have asked me whether this will be accompanied by an inflationary surge. My answer to this is precisely with reference to the distinction between the short-run and the long-run relationship between growth and inflation. In the short-run, with capacities fixed, a surge in growth can cause the economy to overheat, thus stoking inflationary pressures. This is the bread-and-butter issue of monetary policy,

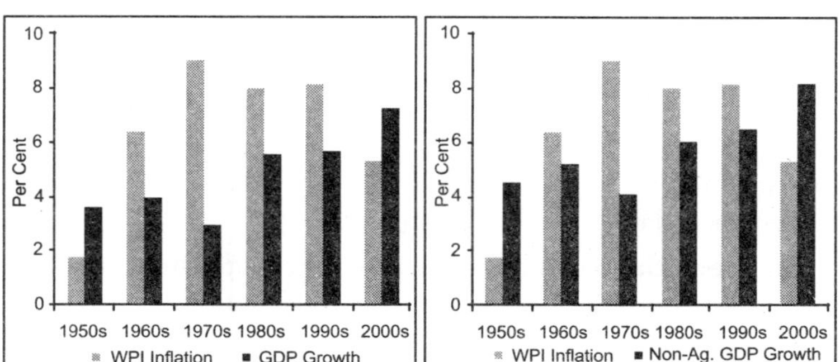

Fig. 11.7: Growth-Inflation Balance

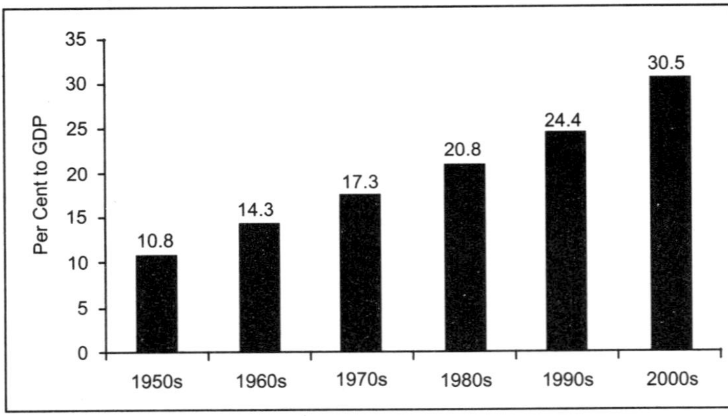

Fig. 11.8: Investment Rate

the effectiveness of which must be judged by its ability to keep the economy growing at a rate just short of overheating, thereby keeping inflation in check.

In the long run, capacities are not fixed. Acceleration in growth over long periods of time occurs in part because investment activity, which itself contributes to growth, leads to an increase in capacity. This pushes up the potential growth rate of the economy, i.e. the rate at which it can grow without causing overheating. Looking back over the growth performance of the Indian economy, it is quite evident that the acceleration of growth from the 5-6 per cent range to the 8-9 per cent range was accomplished by a massive increase in investment. As Fig. 11.8 indicates, the Investment-GDP ratio rose quite sharply over the decades. Even the relatively high number of 30.5 per cent during the last decade masks the sharp surge in this ratio towards the middle of the decade, which saw it rise above 35 per cent. At that rate of investment, the capacity of the economy to increase output is growing quite rapidly and its ability to meet the requirements of a growing and increasingly affluent population is clearly expanding.

In short, the secret to accelerating growth while still being able to keep inflation in check over long periods of time is in the speed and efficiency of the supply response. As long as the growth in supply keeps pace or even exceeds the growth in demand, inflationary pressures do not sustain. Supply can be

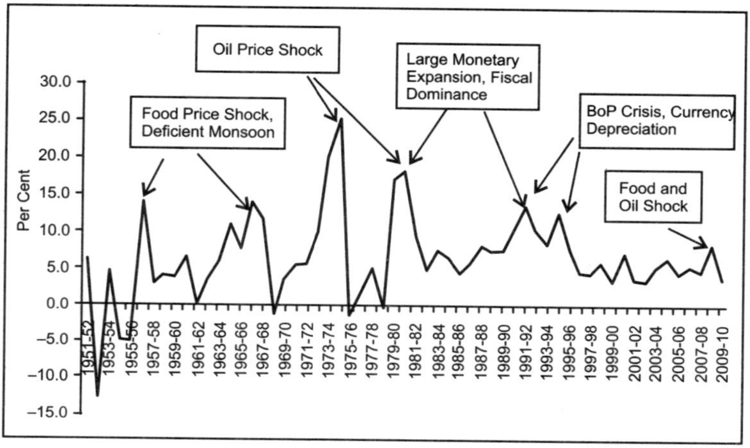

Fig. 11.9: Major Sources of High Inflation

expanded by enhancing domestic capacity, which the Indian economy has clearly done, or by tapping into global sources, which the significant liberalization in trade policy, particularly since the early 1990s, also enabled.

However, while this combination of domestic and global supply responses has helped to steadily bring the inflation rate down, the Indian economy has always been vulnerable to inflation shocks, which have caused uncomfortable spurts in prices across the board. Figure 11.9 identifies some major shocks to the system, all of which required strong policy responses. As is evident from the graph, the vulnerability of the Indian economy to supply shocks on the food and energy fronts is persistent. There have also been periods in which a significant fiscal expansion accompanied by an accommodating monetary stance—i.e. demand-side pressures—raised the inflation rate significantly. Sharp depreciation of the rupee in the midst of an oil shock has also played a role on one occasion. While the demand driven inflation shocks can be avoided by prudent monetary and fiscal policies, the vulnerability to supply shocks in the form of a failed monsoon or a surge in oil prices will obviously remain.

Figures 11.10-11.12 display some of the characteristics

of the transformation of the inflation scenario in India. On Fig. 11.10, we see how the relative contributions to inflation have changed over the decades. Food has been a steady source of inflation over the entire period. Energy became a significant factor during the 1970s, following the first oil shock of 1973. It has persisted in its contribution since then. Adding up the two provides the overall contribution of supply-side factors, which,

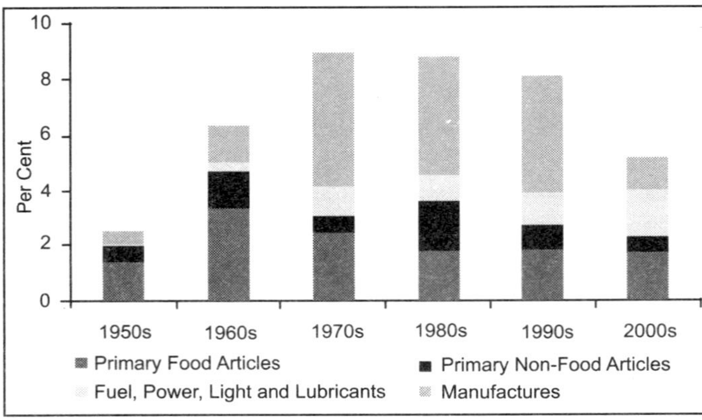

Fig. 11.10: Sources of Inflation

as the graph suggests, have persisted in one form or another through the entire period. Looking ahead, it would be reasonable to argue that these pressures are likely to persist, as a result of both global and domestic imbalances between demand and supply.

On the energy front, one of the fundamental drivers of high oil prices is increasing demand in Emerging Market Economies, whose rising affluence is resulting in very rapid growth of energy-intensive activities. As relatively low-cost reserves of fossil fuels are exhausted, rising global demand is being met by exploiting higher cost sources. The cost differential between petroleum and alternative sources makes such sources viable even at their relatively high costs. Steadily rising costs of production, in turn, exert inflationary pressures on the global economy, which hits those economies hardest whose energy intensity is increasing most rapidly. In recent years, the prices of petroleum, as well as other commodities, are perceived to have been further impacted by their emergence as an attractive asset class. However, as significant as the contribution of this factor may have been to price increases, the underlying fundamentals are what will continue to drive prices in the coming years.

As regards food, the pressures in the Indian economy are predominantly domestic. Our Green Revolution in the 1960s raised the production of cereals dramatically, which increased availability and stabilized prices. However, what we are seeing today is the impact of increasing affluence on the demand for a variety of food items that go far beyond cereals. As people become more affluent, their diets diversify. Just as the growing Indian consuming class has stimulated a boom in the demand for consumer durables, vehicles and mobile phones, to give but a few examples, it has also manifested an enormous increase in the demand for various food items beyond cereals. Demand for protein sources—pulses, milk, meat, fish and eggs—has surged as has the appetite for sugar, fruits and vegetables.

In the case of consumer durables, vehicles and mobile phones, the expansion in capacity was enormous and rapid, resulting in the demand being met without prices increasing. In fact, economies of scale and technological advancements actually helped to bring down the prices of many products even as volumes were increasing. The globalization of the supply chain also contributed significantly, as global capacities were brought into play to meet the rising demand. This combination of forces has certainly not been in play in meeting the rising domestic demand for the food items mentioned above. Supply is predominantly domestic and, for the most part, is unable to respond effectively to the expansion in demand. The inevitable consequence of this is an increase in prices. This is a significant structural driver of inflation in the Indian economy. A good monsoon may provide some relief, while a bad one will aggravate the pressures, but the enduring solution to this problem lies in a rapid and sustained increase in the supply of these items.

Figure 11.10 also displays the positive impacts of effective supply response. The contribution of manufactured goods to inflationary pressures has declined significantly over the decades. This decline can be attributed to increasing effectiveness of policy reforms in increasing domestic capacities and competition and integrating domestic markets with the global supply chain.

In Fig. 11.11, we look at inflation dynamics from the macroeconomic policy perspective, i.e. monetary and fiscal actions that may have contributed to the rise and fall of the inflation rate. During the 1970s and 1980s, the monetization of the fiscal deficit, as reflected in the height of the bar showing the growth in net RBI Credit to Government, was clearly a contributor to inflationary pressures in the economy. Government spending boosts demand and if the government faces no effective financial constraints, it can increase spending without limit and, certainly beyond the capacity of a relatively closed economy to meet the demand.

The emergence of an effective constraint on monetization of the fiscal deficit during the 1990s helped to rein this source of inflationary pressure in. Now, if the government wants to increase its spending, it has to raise resources from the market, bringing in some realistic cost-benefit calculations, including the fact that the cost of funds for the private sector will also increase. Against this backdrop, the government's commitment to fiscal prudence in the form of fiscal responsibility legislation is an important contribution to maintain the growth-inflation balance.

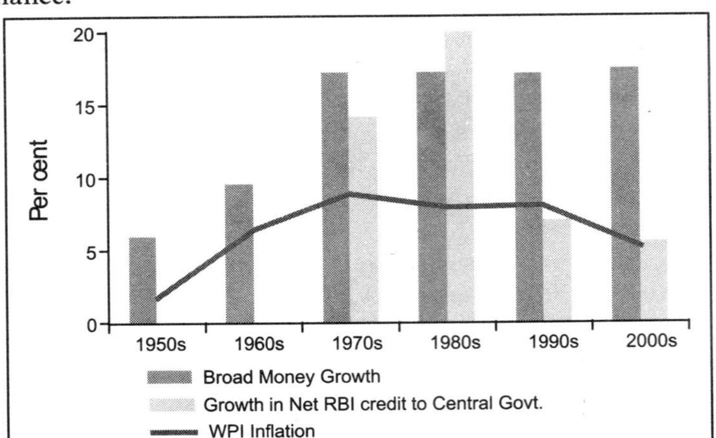

Fig. 11.11: Monetary and Fiscal Drivers

It is also striking in Fig. 11.11 that, contrary to popular notions about the link between the growth in money and the inflation rate, the rate of growth of money remained constant even as inflation declined. The reason for this was that the expansion in money was absorbed by the growing volume of transactions that involved money exchange. This absorption mitigated the potentially inflationary impact of money growth.

One important consideration in inflation management is the stability of the inflation rate. Forward-looking transactions build in some expectations about inflation rates over the tenure of the contract. Significant deviations of actual outcomes from expected ones can cause huge losses to one of the transacting parties, thereby acting as a deterrent to what may be growth-enhancing transactions. The more stable the inflation rate, the less these deviations will be. There appears to be an almost universal correlation between the level of the inflation rate and its stability. As Fig. 11.12 shows, this relationship is quite evident in the Indian context. The reduction in the average inflation rate over the years has been accompanied by a sharp reduction in the volatility of that rate. The aspiration of a "low and stable" inflation rate is a realistic one.

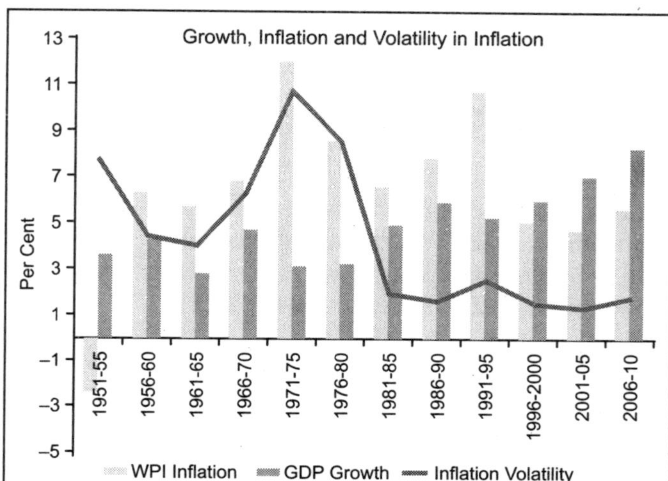

Fig. 11.12: Inflation Volatility

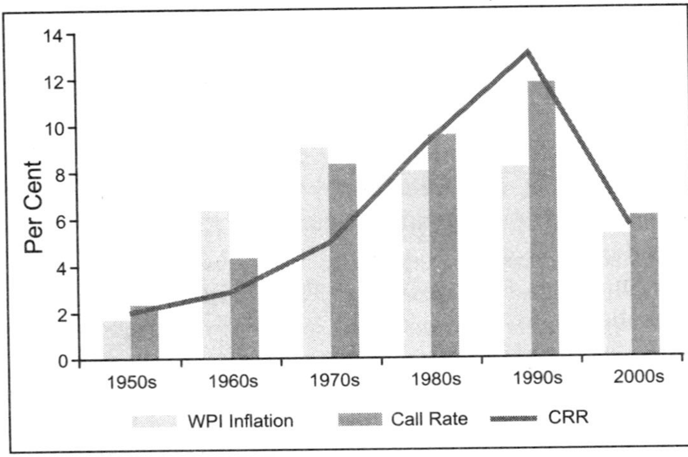

Fig. 11.13: Monetary Policy Trajectory

Finally, let me make a few comments on the role of monetary policy in this transition from a relatively high-inflation economy to a relatively low-inflation one. Conventional monetary policy began to apply only during the 1990s, with the freeing up of restrictions and mandatory allocations of credit to various sectors. Genuine markets for both products and credit emerged after the reforms of the early 1990s. As Fig. 11.13 shows, the persistent inflationary conditions during the 1990s were responded to by significant monetary actions in terms of both rates and liquidity management. As the inflation rate trended lower, a process to which the monetary policy actions of the period contributed, the policy stance in turn changed to accommodate the new circumstances. In other words, monetary policy has been aimed at keeping inflation under control, which involves tightening when inflation exceeds the comfort level and loosening when it falls below.

Concluding Remarks

The current inflation scenario is a cause of concern, as the inflation rate persists well above the upper bound of the comfort zone. The fact that these inflationary pressures emerged rather quickly in a situation in which the economy was just beginning to recover from the significant slowdown of 2008-09 made the policy challenge more complicated. The monetary policy response to these pressures has been a calibrated one, seeking a balance between sustaining the recovery and reining in inflation, while being mindful of the risks that still remain in the global environment. Recent data suggest that the approach is working, with the economy set to grow at a reasonably healthy rate during the current year and the inflation rate beginning to decline, including, significantly, in the manufacturing sector, where inflation is seen as being most responsive to monetary actions.

This approach must be viewed in the context of a long-standing policy commitment to maintain a balance between growth and inflation in the short run, while fostering faster growth with lower inflation over long periods of time. The growth pattern of the Indian economy over the past six decades clearly shows that accelerating growth has been accompanied by declining inflation. This is primarily because growth has been driven by expanding capacities across the board as well as, in recent years, by increasing global linkages. Both these factors have helped to achieve a strong supply response to growing demand, thus keeping inflation in check.

This is not to say that the Indian economy is now invulnerable to inflation shocks. Food and energy price shocks have been a regular part of the economic landscape and may continue to be so in the future. Food prices, in particular, are now being driven by some structural imbalances between demand and supply, as increasingly affluent consumers diversify their dietary patterns away from cereals and towards protein sources. This calls for an effort to quickly increase the availability of these items, on which is contingent the longer term outlook for food price inflation.

However, over the years, both fiscal and monetary policy approaches have clearly assimilated the lessons of the past and have moved in a direction which helps contain inflationary pressures even as growth remains robust. Making inflation low and stable was the outcome of a combination of long-term and short-term policies over the past decades. Keeping it there remains the objective, while an appropriate combination of long-term and short-term policies will provide the instrument to achieve it.

(Keynote Address by Dr. Subir Gokarn, Deputy Governor, Reserve Bank of India on October 5, 2010 at The Private Equity International India Forum) • *Courtesy*: www.rbi.org.in

12

Price Behaviour in Indian Food Grains Market

Suresh P. Singh and *Vijayvir Singh*

Abstract

Despite impressive growth in per capita income and consistent increase in the production of food grains over the last four decades—food grains production doubled—India is nowhere near the status of being a food secured country. Millions of people still suffer from poverty, hunger, and malnutrition. It appears that impressive economic growth has remained concentrated and has not percolated to benefit the poor. Rapid increase in per capita income on the one hand, and inadequate increase in production of food grains is putting pressure on the food market, making food prices move in only one direction. Increasing food price is affecting poor adversely. India is not the only country; many other developing and least developed countries are suffering from this menace. The paper analyses the current state of food price situation in India and its determinants by converting wholesale price indices (average of weeks) of forty years (1970-71 to 2009-10) spanning more than one base year into a single base year (1993-94) to assess and view overall changes in price levels over a period of four decades. It also makes suggestions on India's short-term and long-term responses to its food problem. The paper argues that India can go a long way in addressing the concerns relating to its food security by developing localized infrastructure and plugging of leakage in the public distribution system.

I. Introduction

Accessibility to food by the poor is becoming a serious issue in India for more than one reason. While there are issues such as inadequate increase in production leading to a sort of decline in per capita availability and inefficient supply chain, consistent increase in food prices can be cited as the most serious reason that is making food accessibility to the poor more and more difficult. It appears that impressive economic growth has remained concentrated and has not percolated to benefit the poor. Rapid increase in per capita income on the one hand, and inadequate increase in production of food grains is putting pressure on the food market, making food prices move in only one direction. Increasing food price is impacting poor adversely.

The food price increase in India has recently become a contentious issue for obvious reasons of its adverse impacts on people below or near the poverty line. Current food price scenario, existing for quite some time now, is badly hurting the economy in general, and people in the low income category in particular. This upward price trend is on the back of a very impressive GDP growth and significant increase in per capita income over the last few years. The economy is growing at about 8 per cent and per capita income has doubled in the last five years. On the other hand, production of food grains has failed to keep pace with these two. Going by the growth in per capita income and increasing population, the food market size in monetary terms has more than doubled in the last five years. It is now increasingly argued that one of major factors for food price increase is sustained economic growth over the last one decade. This sustained growth is, however, critical for an emerging economy such as India which has a large size of its population below the poverty line.

Annual inflation in food articles, which touched 22.9 per cent in June 2010, created a sort of panic among the consumers, policymakers, researchers and also the media. The rise was in fact unexpected and unbearable. It was, however, argued by the policymakers that the increase was due to seasonality factors and it will come down in three to six months period. It also led to some action in the form of government interventions (through its monetary policy and other tools). The seriousness of the problem can be understood by the fact that in the period of March 2010 to July 2011, the Reserve Bank of India spiked its key rates a record 11 times. During the period, the central bank has pushed up the short-term lending (repo) and reverse repo or borrowing rates by a massive 275 basis points. One year later in June 2011, the food inflation stood at 9.13 per cent, marginally lower than March figure of 9.47 per cent. This, however, cannot be a stage of complacency as even this relatively low figure is dangerous, if one consider the fact that in the last two years (June 2009 to June 2011), food prices have increased by over 32 per cent.

The inflationary pressure on food and its adverse impacts have put the policymakers in a dilemma with two possible but contradictory choices. Option one, to continue with the present growth strategy with aim to achieve higher growth, and let the growth take care of inflation through increasing per capita income leading to reduction in poverty (through percolation effect). Option two, to focus on reducing inflation by resorting to monetary and other policy tools and allow economic growth to moderate. The available options have landed policymakers in a conflicting state of mind. On the one hand, the country needs growth to facilitate development while on the other hand measures to facilitate growth are resulting in creating inflationary tendency in the market including food market. Choosing either of two options seems to be a difficult task for the policymakers. This creates scope for a third option which can be a combination of both the above options with policy responses giving due weightage to facilitating growth on the one hand and reducing inflation on the other.

The critics including researchers, media, civil society organisations, and others are at a consensus that policymakers in India need to protect people who are vulnerable to price volatility impacts. It is also argued that failure to address the issue might turn the situation from bad to worse and can derail the economy from its growth trajectory. It can also neutralise recent gains made in poverty reduction which is said to be about 5 per cent.

The present paper seeks to analyse the current state of food price situation in India, and what should be India's short-term and long-term responses to its food problem. The paper is divided into five sections. Section 2 describes impact of continuous rise in food prices on poor in India and the world. Section 3 deals with the issue of volatility and price rise with a focus on analysing whether current food price scenario in India has elements of volatility in it. Section 4 analyses the factors that are contributing to the upward movement in food prices. Section 5 seeks to identify possible options for India to secure lives of people living below the poverty line and concludes.

II. Cost of Food Price Rise to the Poor in India and the World

The food price situation is getting serious in India and households are paying a heavy price for this. According to a recent report by Crisil, the rise in inflation to 8 per cent per year during 2008-09 to 2010-11, from 5 per cent in the preceding three years, eroded the purchasing power of money and inflated the consumption expenditure bill of Indian households by ₹ 5.8 trillion (Crisil, 2011). This is a huge cost by all standards. In addition, the expectation that food inflation is going to stay in the future will further aggravate the problem. An Asian Development Bank study estimates that India will be badly affected by high food prices as a 10 per cent increase could push close to 30 million Indians below the poverty line (ADB, 2011).

India is not the only country; there are several other countries, which are expected to move towards a crisis like situation in near future, if immediate steps are not taken to address the issue. The report by the ADB projects an alarming scenario for Asia. A sustained 10 per cent increase in domestic food prices could push an additional 64 million people, nearly 2 per cent of Asia's 3.3 billion people, below the poverty line. According to an Oxfam report, the 2008 food prices spike pushed around 100 million additional people into poverty in the world, while the current spike has pushed 44 million more into poverty so far in this year (Oxfam, 2011). It may be recalled that in 2009 the number of hungry people in the world reached a record one billion, which is one-sixth of the world's population. This figure has a probability to increase further if current price situation continues.

Another report by the United Nations and Organisation for Economic Cooperation and Development (OECD) predicts that food price explosion will devastate the world's poor. Any further increase in global food prices, which have already risen by 40 per cent over the past year, will have a devastating impact on the world's poor and is likely to lead to political unrest, famine and starvation. People are going to be forced either to eat less or find other sources of income (Neate, 2011). The prediction has a good probability to occur as the report also indicates that food prices are likely to soar by as much as 30 per cent over the next 10 years. In short, the world is moving towards a very serious food crisis.

III. Volatility versus Price Rise

Volatility is an economic term and in economic theory, volatility connotes two principal concepts: variability and uncertainty. While the former describes overall movement, the latter refers to movement that is unpredictable (FAO). Volatility is described as the pace (which is relatively faster than the normal market condition) at which price of a product or service move. This movement can be both higher and lower, and therefore, it can adversely impact both demand and supply, and also the whole supply chain. By this definition, when the movement is on lower side, it is indicative of decline in demand as a result of some issues relating to products' acceptability. This may happen due to changing consumer dynamics, change in consumer tastes and preferences, increasing supply with constant demand, etc. A higher movement in price, on the other hand, is due to increase in products' demand—arising out of increased income level, change in consumption pattern—decline in production, and some other related factors. One can, therefore, describe volatility as a situation where both demand side and supply side factors work in tandem, with each trying to outpace the other, and, therefore, volatility has risk element for both—demand side (consumers) and supply side (producers and other actors in the supply chain).

Are Food Prices in India Volatile?

A review of Wholesale Price Index (WPI) data during the last four decades shows that there is significant increase in price levels across all food and non-food items. This is duly reflected by movement of WPI over the period. However, since base year is changed at regular intervals, WPI does not reflect movement of price over a longer period from the point of view of consumers. The present paper seeks to highlight increase in food prices from the consumers' point of view for a longer term by converting wholesale price indices (average of weeks) of forty years (1970-71 to 2009-10) spanning more than one base year into a single base year (1993-94). This is to assess and view overall changes in price levels over a period of four decades.

The results of the converted WPI data reveal some interesting facts. In the last four decades, while WPI for all commodities has increased by nearly 17 times (from a WPI of 14.3 in 1970-71 to 242.7 in 2009-10), the price increase in case of primary articles is over 18 times (from a WPI of 15.1 in 1970-71 to 276.6 in 2009-10). The increase in food prices have been the highest and it has multiplied by 18.3 times (from a WPI of 15 in 1970-71 to 274.9 in 2009-10). The data reflects a continuous rise in price levels over this period, on year-to-year basis. A new peak has been attained almost every year. The only major variation during the period has been the difference in rate of

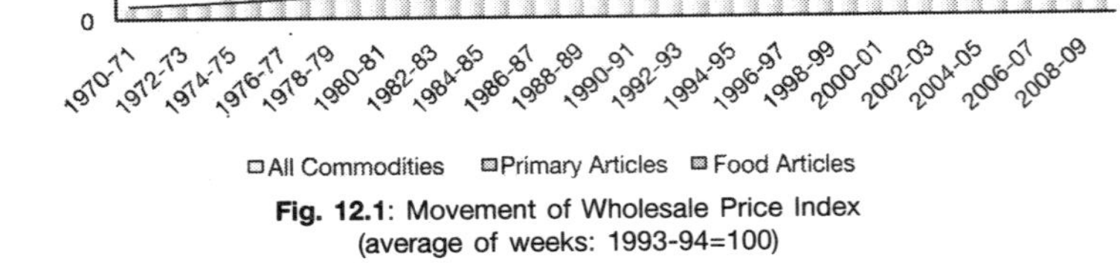

Fig. 12.1: Movement of Wholesale Price Index (average of weeks: 1993-94=100)

Source: Office of the Economic Adviser, Ministry of Commerce and Industry, Government of India. Price data with base year of 1970-71 and 1981-82 converted into Base Year 1993-94

increase. While for some years the rate was lower, in others it was unexpectedly high (Fig. 12.1).

There are some distinct features of movement of price before 1991 and after this. While during the period preceding 1991 wholesale price indices of all commodities for most of the years were found to be above food articles indices, whereas in the later years, this has changed. For most of the years after 1991, which is incidentally the year of introduction of economic reforms in India, data reveals that the value of food articles indices are greater than the value of wholesale price indices (all commodities) (Table 12.1). This can be argued to be due to unbalanced growth in demand for food not duly supported by increase in supply. This also reflects that food prices in the post reform years influenced WPI more than the non-food prices. This seems to have generated pressure on food prices. In both the periods (before and after 1991), however, prices show continuous increasing trend.

Table 12.1: Movement in WPI v/s Food Price Indices

Period	WPI exceeding Food Articles Indices	Food Articles Indices exceeding WPI
1970-71 to 1990-91	14	6
1990-91 to 2009-10	4	16
1970-71 to 2009-10	18	22

Source: Based on converted data as shown in Fig. 12.1.

The variations in trend of movement of the WPI and food price indices do not alter the fact that food prices have continuously increased in the last four decades. The only issue, as indicated above, is rate of increase. The data indicates that food price movement in India is not a case of volatility but rather a case of continuous rise, and therefore it need not be confused with food price volatility.

The trend is further reinforced by the data on Consumer Price Index (CPI) for agricultural labourers and industrial workers. In both the cases, food price index for the period 2000-01 to 2009-10 shows faster increase than general index. For agricultural labourers, the Food Price Index has increased by nearly 89 per cent, more than the increase in General Price

Index (84 per cent) during the period. Similarly for industrial workers, the food price index increased by 113 per cent, more than the increase in General Price Index (109 per cent) (Figs. 12.2 and 12.3).

Going by the price data as reflected by the movement of WPI and CPI, one can say that much talked food price volatility does not seem to be of Indian origin; it might be a relevant issue

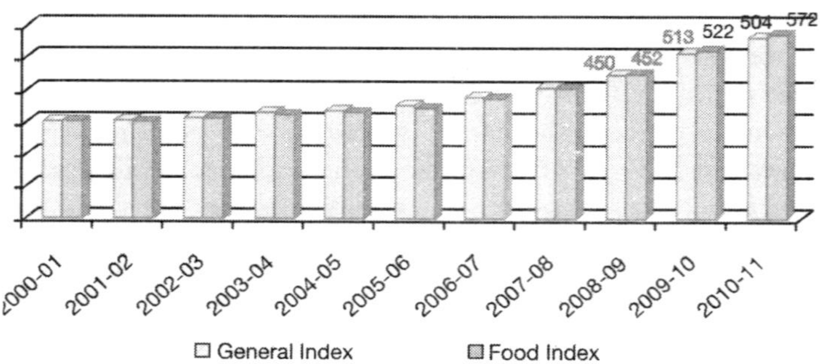

Fig. 12.2: Food Price Index for Agricultural Labourers and Industrial Workers Increasing Faster than General Index

Source: Economic Survey 2010-11 (For industrial workers, figures from 2000-01 to 2004-05 converted to Base Year 2001=100)

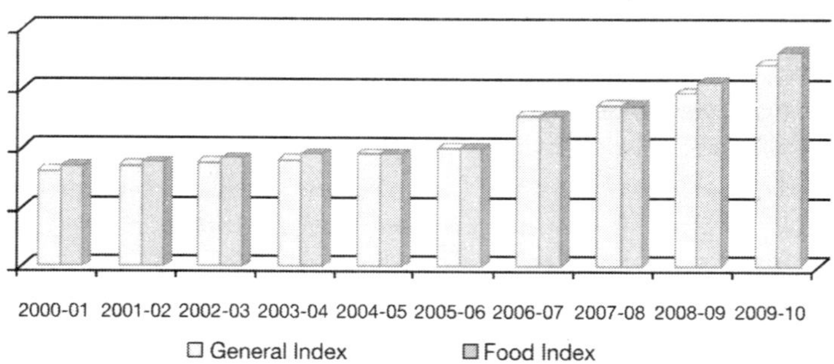

Fig. 12.3: Food Price Index for Industrial Workers Increasing Faster than General Index

Source: Economic Survey 2010-11 (For industrial workers, figures from 2000-01 to 2004-05 converted to Base Year 2001=100)

in the world food market. A comparison between India and global price movements in the 2000 to 2009 periods can probably help in clarify the argument.

Food prices have increased in India and also in the global market. In case of India, comparing the trend (2000 to 2009) with earlier period does not show many variations. Even during this period, food prices have increased regularly and prices have attained one high peak after other. Within the year, however, there are fluctuations that arise because of seasonality and interventions by the government from time to time. One important feature of this price movement during this period is that while there is no significant change in the price levels between 2000 and 2005 as shown in Figs. 12.4 and 12.5, an increase of about 50 per cent was realised in 2009 (December) over 2005 (December).[1] Movement of the WPI (food grains) for all the months (except December when the index was at the same level as in November) shows a continuous rise.

In comparison to food price experience of India, one observes a different pattern in world food market. Fluctuations (both upward and downward) in price levels are more pronounced. For all the three selected years a new price level was attained, even though these were significant fluctuations within the year, especially in 2005 and 2009. It is also observed that monthly food prices in the later years are always higher than the preceding year monthly price levels. Another important feature common to both India and the global food market is that the price levels

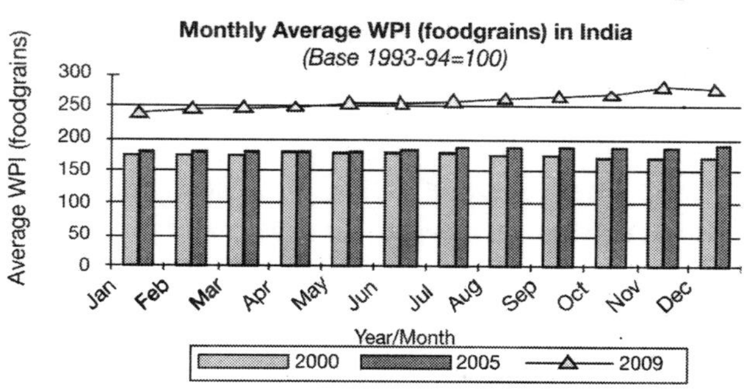

Fig. 12.4: Food Price Trend in Indian and Global Market

Source: IndiaStat

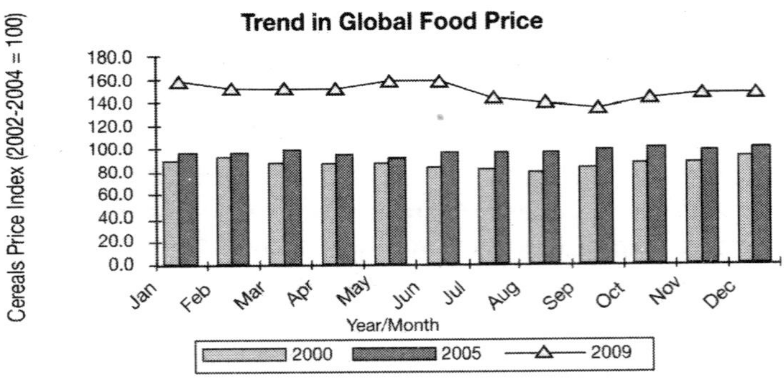

Fig. 12.5: Food Price Trend in Global Market

Source: Food and Agricultural Organisation

show no tendency to go back to the previous year's levels in any case.

Going by the price data for all the three selected years over a span of nine years (2000 to 2009), it becomes clear while food prices in India show a definitive sign of continuous increase; it shows significant fluctuation—say volatility—in the world market. One can also say that there is not much sign of volatility in the Indian food grains market. On the other hand, world food market show element of volatility. Additionally, it can also be said that this volatility in the world market is a short-term phenomenon, as prices get stabilised only at a higher level in later periods.

IV. Understanding Continuous Rise in Food Prices

It is pertinent to assess as to how India has reached the present position of high food prices. India has realised significant gains in a large number of economic and social indicators during the four decades period, especially during the post-economic reform years. These include increase in gross domestic product leading to increase in per capita income; increase in population; and some other indicators such as increased literacy rate and increased life expectancy. These are the factors which are now exerting pressure on food prices. Changes in some of these factors over the four decade period vis-à-vis price dynamics are demonstrated by Fig. 12.6.

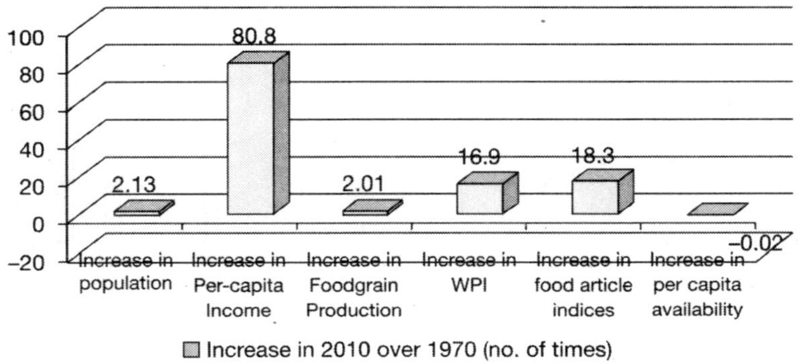

Fig. 12.6: India's Growth Dynamics

Source: Various, including Economic Survey of India, 2010-11

Figure 12.6 can be segmented into two parts. One set—increase in population, increase in per capita income and increase in food grains production—can be termed as influencer; and the other segment consisting of increase in WPI (including increase in food price indices) and increase in per capita availability as influenced. Taking into account increase in population (2.13 times over 1970) and increase in per capita income (nearly 81 times over 1970), one can say that the effective demand for food has significantly increased over the period of four decades. Since production of food grains has not kept pace (as it only doubled during this period), it has resulted in decline in food availability in 2010 compared to 1970. There is, in fact, no surprise element in this. This unbalanced growth in demand has led price level to go up. The influencer show significant impact on the influenced. Besides these, there are other major factors which are influencing food prices in India. Some of these are dealt with in following sub-sections.

Where is the Pressure on Food Prices Coming From?

Data on food consumption expenditure indicates that there is a definitive shift towards consumption of protein based food. Data for both rural and urban areas shows that per capita expenditure has more than doubled during the period 1993-94 to 2007-08. In urban area, the increase is slightly more.

For all the food items except cereals and cereal products, per capita expenditure has more than doubled in 2007-08 as

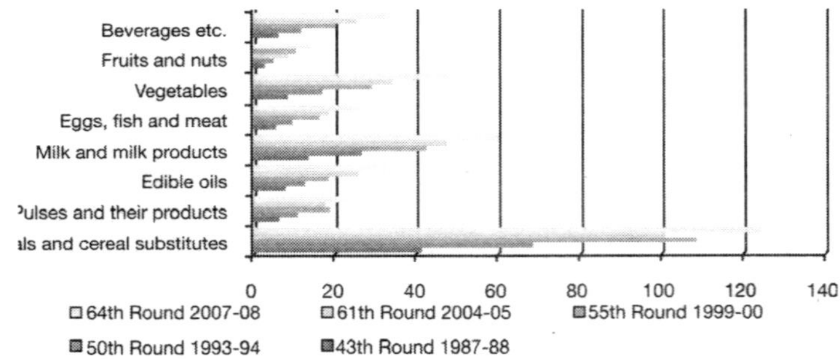

Fig. 12.7: Trend in Per Capita Food Expenditure (Rural)

Source: Report No. 530: Household Consumer Expenditure in India, 2007-08, National Sample Survey

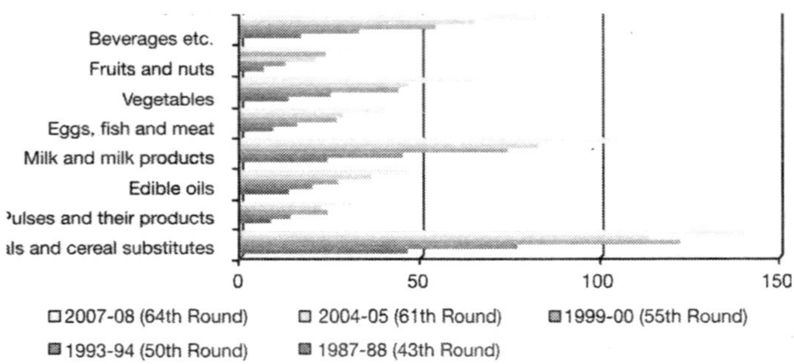

Fig. 12.8: Trend in Per Capita Food Expenditure (Urban)

Source: Report No. 530: Household Consumer Expenditure in India, 2007-08, National Sample Survey

compared to 1993-94. However, if we look at item wise expenditure, there is a different trend. Out of the total increase in per capita expenditure on food, while vegetables has the highest share in rural areas, milk and milk-based products account for largest pie in the urban areas. Cereals and cereal-based products are ranked third in terms of its share in the increased per capita expenditure on food in both rural and urban areas (Fig. 12.7). Hence, it is evident that the pressure on food prices is coming from both rural and urban India.

There are also other factors influencing food prices (Box 12.1). Each of these factors generates tremendous pressure on food market and appears to have its share in final food pricing.

Food Production not Keeping Pace with Increasing Consumption

Trends in food consumption and production of major food items show mixed performance over last five decades period. It is observed that while growth in production outpaced consumption in some decades; in others consumption prevailed over production. These two distinct features are, however, confined to two phases: one preceding economic reform programmes; and other in the post-reform periods. Examples of wheat and rice production and consumption would probably

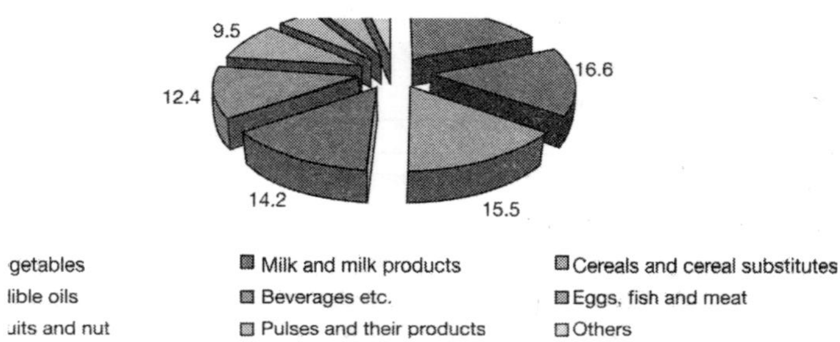

Fig. 12.9: How is Increased Per Capita Expenditure on Food is Distributed (Rural India) (in % based on increase in 2007-08 over 1999-00)

Source: Report No. 530: Household Consumer Expenditure in India, 2007-08, National Sample Survey; adapted from Food Inflation in India: Encourage Competition for a Long-term Solution, Briefing Paper, 3/2011, CUTS International

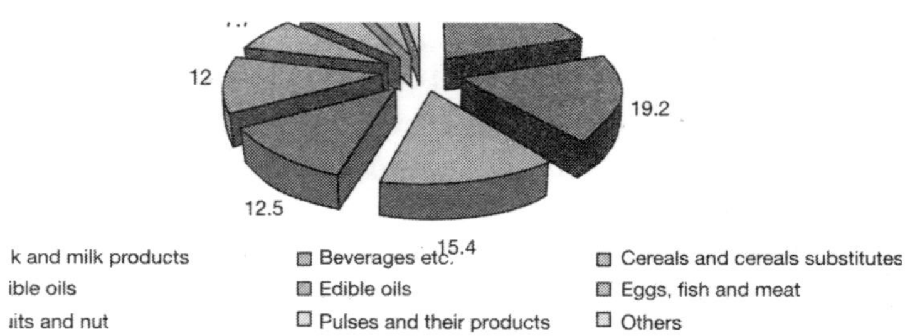

Fig. 12.10: How is Increased Per Capita Expenditure on Food is Distributed (Rural India) (in % based on increase in 2007-08 over 1999-00)

Source: Report No. 530: Household Consumer Expenditure in India, 2007-08, National Sample Survey; adapted from Food Inflation in India: Encourage Competition for a Long-term Solution, Briefing Paper, 3/2011, CUTS International

Box 12.1

Increase in per capita income (doubled in the last five years and increased by 81 times since 1970)	**Speculation in the food market** (huge money has flowed in the Indian and global food market. Earning through speculation is the primary motive of most of the speculators)	**Increase in population** (growing at the rate of about 1.7 per cent during the last decade and has doubled since 1970)
Leakages in the food supply chain (especially in PDS with leakage estimated at 43 per cent)	**Food price increase** (over 18 times since 1970 and about 50 per cent in last five years) ***Where is the pressure coming from?***	**Inadequate storage facilities** (over 30% of produce —food grains, vegetables and fruits— rotting due to lack of proper storage facilities)
One way integration of Indian food market with the global market (while supply shocks in global food market lead to increase in food prices in India, the reverse rarely happen)	**Shift in consumption pattern** (with increase in per capita income, people are shifting for more protein based food such as pulses, generating pressure on until now unaffordable food items)	**Increasing cost of production** (mainly due to increase in price of fertilizers, pesticides, irrigation, etc.)

Source: Singh, Suresh P., Food Inflation in India: Encourage Competition for a Long-term Solution, Briefing Paper, 3/2011, CUTS International

reflect the position. In the case of wheat it is observed that while growth in production was greater than consumption in the three decades (1960s to 1980s), growth in consumption outpaced production in the latter two decades (1990s and 2000s). For rice, almost a similar trend is observed, except that production outpaced consumption growth in 1990s. This might be because of existing economic and social dynamics in the respective decade. The relative higher growth in consumption is due to increasing affordability of consumers, especially in the post-1990s period.

The slow growth in production along with a rising population is adversely impacting per capita availability of food grains (cereals and pulses). Analysis of data for two decades of post-reform periods reflects significant variations. And in the year 2009, it has, in fact, come down for both cereals and pulses—per capita availability of both cereals and pulses has declined. This implies that the country has not made any significant progress as far as increasing the production of food grains is concerned. This is in sharp contrast to increased affordability and accessibility (due to increase in per capita income) (Figs. 12.7 and 12.8).

Box 12.2

Typology of Supply Chain for Wheat

An example of how complex is the food supply chain in India

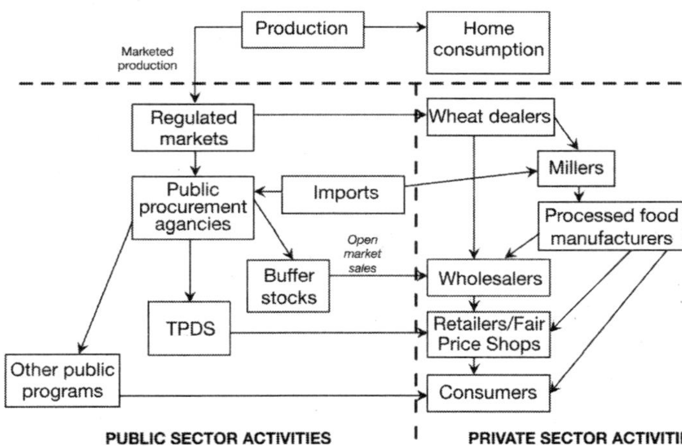

Source: World Bank (1999)

Table 12.2: Growth Trend in Production and Consumption of Wheat and Rice in India (in %)

Decade	Wheat		Rice	
	Production	Consumption	Production	Consumption
1960s	8.2	5.0	9.3	5.5
1970s	7.1	5.4	4.8	4.7
1980s	4.7	4.4	**4.6**	**5.4**
1990s	**2.9**	**3.0**	2.6	1.4
2000s	**1.2**	**1.6**	**1.6**	**2.8**

Source: Reserve Bank of India

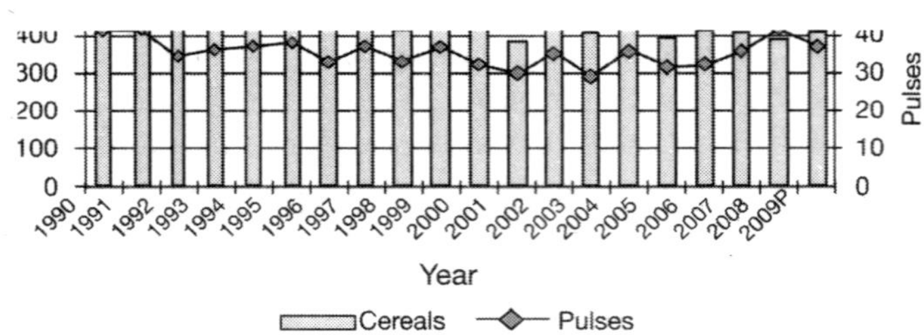

Fig. 12.11: Trend in Per Capita Availability of Cereals and Pulses (gram/day)

Source: Economic Survey 2010-11

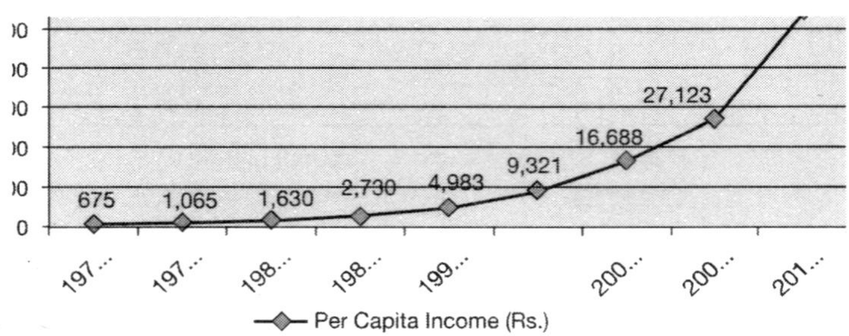

Fig. 12.12: Increase in Per Capita Income

Source: Economic Survey 2010-11

Food Supply Chain and the PDS in India

In India, there are two different types of food supply chains—a government controlled supply chain for those who are below poverty line, and the other being market controlled supply chain for people not covered by the above chain. In other words, food supply chain in India has involvement of both public and private sectors (Box 12.2: Wheat Supply Chain). The box makes abundantly clear that in both the cases (food distribution by the government to poor as well as open market), wheat changes hands five times before it reaches the ultimate consumers. Both the chains converge at the stage of retailers or fair price shops.

There is nothing wrong with the structure, and this is, in fact, required for a country like India with a large number of people below the poverty line. However, the structure does not appear to guarantee effectiveness. The problem encountered by the system has been revealed by various studies on food supply chain—both in public distribution system (PDS) and in open market sales. On the public distribution side, issues of procurement prices, lack of food storage capacity, and leakage in the PDS have been reported, there are issues of hoardings and manipulation of market forces in open market sales. Studies also show that food grains meant for poor is channelled to the open market. According to the World Bank (2011), though India's social sector spending is higher than many other developing countries, one of its flagship welfare programs—the PDS—is fraught with leakages. The PDS scheme, which consumes around one per cent of the country's gross domestic product (GDP) and covers upto 25 per cent of the poor households, has had limited success, as only 41 per cent of the food grains released by the government reach their target, according to the report.

Box 12.3

How serious is the leakage in the Indian PDS?

Under the Public Distribution System, there is a common tendency among owners of fair price shops/distributors in some parts of the country to distribute the government's subsidised food at an interval, often every alternate month. This implies, only half of the subsidised food is distributed amongst the poor, and the other half indirectly going to the open market. By this description, and considering that total food distribution through the PDS was 42.3 million tonnes, more than 21 million tonnes of food grains did not reach the intended beneficiaries. This is also reflected through a study by Khera (2011), which demonstrates that leakage constituted about 44 per cent of the total food allocated to the PDS in 2007-08. While this creates inaccessibility to food amongst the BPL households, these people, in turn, are forced to approach market for buying the same foods which was siphoned off. An unnecessary pressure is built on food market as a result of this. The intended beneficiaries of subsidised PDS food thus have almost equal dependence on PDS on the one hand and open market on the other. The issue needs immediate government attention.

Speculation, a Potent Force that Influences Food Inflation

Commodities futures, including agricultural commodities, are now increasingly treated as an asset class that is capable of delivering equity—like returns while at the same time reducing overall portfolio risk. Speculation in food market has increased significantly over the last two decades. Reports indicate that billions of dollars are being made globally by investors in a speculative food bubble that has created record food prices. And this is leading to starving millions and destabilising countries (Leahy, 2011). According to a FAO report, the world markets since 2007 have seen a series of dramatic swings in commodity prices. Food prices reached their highest levels of 30 years during the summer of 2008, collapsing the following winter, before rapidly rising again in the months that followed. Food prices are expected to remain volatile due to rapidly evolving global economic order. Reports also indicate that in the last five years (2005-10), speculators have bought more commodities futures contracts. Money is poured into commodities futures to diversify portfolios, and to hedge against inflation or bet against the dollar. This has created bubbles, which has no relation with food market mechanisms. Further, as markets are increasingly integrated in the world economy, shocks in the international arena are now expected to transpire and propagate to domestic markets much quicker than before (FAO, 2010). In such conditions, efforts of many countries to use food reserves to buffer volatility proved unmanageable, costly and ineffective.

In India also, speculative activities are believed to be a major source of increase in agricultural commodity prices. Since introduction of economic reforms, Indian economy has become more integrated with the world economy and therefore has become more exposed to the global food market and price volatility increasingly driven by speculative financial activity in commodity futures. This exposure and market inefficiency has added two new features to Indian food market. While an increase in global food prices always lead to increase in food prices in India, but the market does not respond to situations when price of food decline in the global market as it happened during the second half of 2008. This implies that the recent increases in food prices in India is more home grown. It reflects the ineffectiveness of domestic food management. This can be argued to be the reason why temporary shortages translate into major price spikes. Controlling these activities through regulations could help to bring more stability to the commodity market. It also suggested the Central Government should co-ordinate with state governments while taking measures against hoarding and black-marketing.

V. Possible Way Out and Conclusion

A multi-pronged attack on food inflation is required through policy response—for both short- and long-term. Addressing standalone issues, as identified above, can be the objective of short-term responses. The short-term responses should include:

- Plugging holes in the public food distribution system and making the system more efficient could help in reducing the pressure on local food market. In quantitative terms, it can save over 21 million tonnes of food grains, and could substantially reduce dependence of poor households on market.
- Creating and strengthening localised infrastructure for storage of food, especially non-cereal perishable food items such as vegetables, fruits, meat, fish, etc. could help in reducing wastage and transportation cost, and thus final cost of food items. It is understood that transportation cost accounts for 30 per cent of the price of fruits and vegetables, whereas wastages accounts for another 45 per cent (Gupta, 2011).
- Inventorisation and popularisation of production enhancing local innovations. Government should also take steps to facilitate adoption of such technologies at the local levels.

The other set of issues, especially interrelated issues of speculation in the food market and integration of Indian food market with the world market, need to be addressed through long-term policy response. There is a need for better coherence and coordination in policy responses. These must have the elements of both greater assurance of unimpeded access to global supplies, and improved confidence and transparency in market functioning. It is often observed that while in the case of global supply shocks, Indian food market responds with increase in food prices, the reverse rarely happen. This gives an indication of one-way integration. This integration needs to be transformed into a two-way process.

Note

1. It may be recalled that during this period per capita income has almost doubled, reflecting the fact that increase in per capita income has direct influence on food prices.

References

Asian Development Bank (2011), Global Food Price Inflation and Developing Asia, http://www.adb.org/documents/reports/global-food-price-inflation/

Assocham (2011), Assocham statement to the government, http://business-standard.com/india/news/assocham-demands-govt-to-curb-speculation-in-agri-futures/142851/on

Crisil (2011), Inflation Hurts. http://www.crisil.com/pdf/economy/eco-insight-inflation_jun11.pdf

FAO (2011), http://www.fao.org/economic/es-policybriefs/briefs-detail/en/?no_cache=1&uid=48900

FAO (2010), Price Volatility in Agricultural Markets, Evidence, Impact on Food Security and Policy Responses, http://www.fao.org/economic/es-policybriefs/briefs-detail/en/?no_cache=1&uid=48900

Gupta, Shyamal (2011), Wastage, transport cost make vegetable farming unviable, http://articles.economictimes.indiatimes.com/2011-05-20/news/29564819_1_vegetable-prices-food-prices-farmers

Leahy, Stephen (2011), International Environmental Journalist, http://stephenleahy.net/2011/02/28/rampant-speculation-inflated-food-price-bubble-wall-stgrain-traders-pushing-price-rises/

Neate, Rupert (2011), Food price explosion 'will devastate the world's poor', http://www.guardian.co.uk/environment/2011/jun/17/global-food-prices-increase-united-nations

Oxfam (2011), Growing a Better Future: Food Justice in a Resource Constrained World, http://www.oxfam.org/sites/www.oxfam.org/files/cr-growing-better-future-170611-en.pdf

Singh, Suresh P., Food Inflation in India: Encourage Competition for a Long-term Solution, Briefing Paper, 3/2011, CUTS International.

Times of India (2011), In UP, 30% food produce rots due to lack of storage facilities, http://articles.timesofindia.indiatimes.com/2010-07-22/lucknow/28286700_1_storage-capacity-pack-house-rot

World Bank (2011), Social Protection for a Changing India, http://www-wds.worldbank.org/external/default/WDSContentServer/WDSP/IB/2011/04/20/000333037_20110420235516/Rendered/PDF/612750v10ESW0P1rt0Volume0I01PUBLIC1.pdf